AMERICA'S OTHER YOUTH
growing up poor

ALL ROYALTIES
WILL BE CONTRIBUTED TO
THE RENAISSANCE FUND OF
THE PENNSYLVANIA STATE UNIVERSITY

This fund provides aid to those youth who,
without financial assistance, would not
have the opportunity to enroll at a
college or university.

AMERICA'S OTHER YOUTH

growing up poor

Edited by

DAVID GOTTLIEB
The Pennsylvania State University

ANNE LIENHARD HEINSOHN
The Pennsylvania State University

PRENTICE-HALL, INC.
Englewood Cliffs, New Jersey

P–13–032524–4

C–13–032532–5

Library of Congress Catalog Card Number: 72–145700

LS /795/4 80/4/19/71

Printed in the United States of America

Current Printing (Last digit):

10 9 8 7 6 5 4 3 2 1

PRENTICE-HALL INTERNATIONAL, INC., London
PRENTICE-HALL OF AUSTRALIA, PTY. INC., Sydney
PRENTICE-HALL OF CANADA, LTD., Toronto
PRENTICE-HALL OF INDIA PRIVATE LIMITED, New Delhi
PRENTICE-HALL OF JAPAN, INC., Tokyo

PREFACE

This reader is distinct in several ways. First, the materials included seek to portray the status and conditions of poor youth as described by those who have been part of "the culture of poverty." While a number of the authors possess the "credentials" of professional social scientists, they reflect insights rarely expressed in the writings of behavioral scientists. More specifically, this represents the observations, interpretations, and feelings of those who have grown up among the poor; those who have lived with the poor; and those whose concern with poor youth goes beyond a primary desire for basic empirical investigation. Each author "tells it like it is" among the millions who are this nation's "other" youth. The emphasis is not on demographic data: How many are living below the established poverty level? How many of which race have not completed high school? Rather, the concern here is with the day-to-day feelings and attitudes of certain groups of young people.

Second, the authors seek something beyond the publication of their experiences and observations. They want to see some action taken so that fewer and fewer children will have to experience the dehumanizing indignities and injustices that are in fact an integral part of growing up poor. They are, for the most part, individuals who believe that the time has come for a shift from emphasizing the study of poverty, to the implementation of programs and policies directed toward the elimination of poverty.

Finally, the reader is unique in that its very publication and sale will enable some poor youth the chance to break away from poverty and live as productive, responsible, dignified citizens. The editors of this reader will contribute all royalties from the sale of this reader to THE RENAISSANCE FUND, a program established at the Pennsylvania State University. Its major purpose is to provide aid to those youth who, without financial assistance, would not have the opportunity to enroll at a college or university.

In my role as Chairman of the 1970–1971 White House Conference on Children and Youth, I have been exposed to and obviously concerned with the problems of children and youth in our society. The problems are many and go beyond any single economic regional, or racial group. It is my own conviction that these problems are resolvable. The need is to understand that we cannot survive unless we absorb and integrate all of our children into the workings of our social system. The need is to commit and to involve our resources—human and physical. The need is to understand that we do have the ability to bring about a society in which every child can develop his potential.

STEVEN HESS
Director, 1970 White House Conference on Children and Youth

INTRODUCTION

Early in 1961, President Kennedy called for a major effort in space exploration. The ultimate goal was to land an American on the moon by the year 1970.

In 1966, Sargent Shriver, then Director of the Office of Economic Opportunity, noted that this nation could commemorate its two-hundredth year of independence by a successful completion of the war on poverty. The magic year was to be 1976.

The Kennedy prophecy was fulfilled. The Shriver goal, taken seriously by few in 1966, was in reality abandoned by President Johnson and the Congress in 1967.

Numerous explanations can be offered to account for the contrasts between these two efforts. Generally, however, it would seem safe to say that success in one and failure in the other reflects an essential societal characteristic. As a nation we have always invested most heavily in technological rather than social change; hardware and not software; physical as opposed to human resources. The Department of Defense is able to make long range plans regarding our "military needs" to the year 2000 and beyond, yet The Department of Health, Education, and Welfare is unable to note with any degree of accuracy or certainty our needs for education and welfare even during the next few years.

Long before middle-class youth showed signs of alienation and discontent there were, and still are, the White, Black, Chicano, Puerto Rican, Indian, rural, urban, and poor youth who were angry, cold, sick, and hungry. Long before marijuana came to the suburbs, heroin was killing youth in the ghetto, yet we— those in power, those with the resources—gave these poor youth only passing consideration.

One result was that, when the opportunity arose to bring about some change in the status of poor youth, we were far from prepared.

Our research focus and institutional emphasis had been on the in-school, middle-class adolescent. We knew too little about the youth who were out of school, poor, and/or non-white.

As a result, our curriculums, teacher training programs, and guidance programs were directed toward the middle-class white adolescents. We were not prepared to meet the needs of the other youth with the appropriate teaching materials, teachers, or counselors.

Because we knew so little about the status of poor youth, we could not anticipate just how physically sick many of these youth were.

Since so few of these young people had been exposed to the service and research instruments of psychiatrists, psychologists, and social workers, we knew little of their mood, their fears, their alienation, their anger, or their feelings of self-worth.

The research emphasis on poor youth was limited mostly to studies of "deviant behavior." We knew little of the aspirations, expectations, attitudes, and values of the majority of poor youth who are neither drug addicts nor delinquents.

With the declaration of a war on poverty came numerous programs directed at the re-socialization of poor youth. Federal funds (meager at best, said many social scientists) for research were available. In a short time countless reports, books, and articles dealing with the poor were produced.

For the most part, this plethora of poverty research was either too abstract, too narrow, or too confusing to be of any immediate value to those responsible for policy and program development. Empirical research presented in tabular form can hardly portray the mood, sense, feeling, and day-to-day frustration of growing up in poverty. Reports illuminating methodological techniques but not dealing with the consequences and implications of these findings were of little help to the practitioneers.

A major stimulus for this collection of works was the desire to bring together materials that would provide the reader with a more direct understanding of poor youth.

Our preference was for literature that deals with the socialization and life styles of different groups of poor youth. The materials presented in this reader represent the work of a heterogenous group. The authors differ in training, ethnic background, and in political, and social attitudes. Our goal was to bring together the work of authors who had been involved with those they wrote about. Secondly, but certainly as importantly, we searched for comprehensible materials that were relatively free of professional jargon.

We are appreciative of the dedication and talents of Carol Goss, Christopher Bellavita, Stephan Haimowitz, and James Guillaumez, students who assisted us in the selection and evaluation of materials. As indicated in the preface, all editor royalties earned from the sale of this collection will be contributed to the Renaissance Fund at Pennsylvania State University. The Renaissance Fund has been established in order to provide financial assistance to poor youth. Needless to say, we are grateful for the cooperation and understanding of those publishing companies and authors who waived normal reprinting fees as their contribution to this effort.

Finally, our sincerest thanks to Mr. Arthur Rittenberg, Vice President of Prentice-Hall for his support, enthusiasm, and understanding.

DAVID GOTTLIEB
ANNE L. HEINSOHN
University Park, Pennsylvania

CONTENTS

BLACK YOUTH   155

SUGGESTED READINGS   203

PUERTO RICAN
YOUTH

Excerpts from

TWO BLOCKS APART:
JUAN GONZALES AND
PETER QUINN

Charlotte Leon Mayerson, Editor

JUAN GONZALES

Man, I hate where I live, the projects. I've been living in a project for the past few years and I can't stand it. First of all, no pets. I've been offered so many times dogs and cats and I can't have them because of the Housing. Then there's a watch out for the walls. Don't staple anything to the walls because then you have to pay for it. Don't hang a picture. There's a fine. And they come and they check to make sure.

Don't make too much noise. The people upstairs and the people downstairs and the people on the side of you can hear every word and they've got to get some sleep. In the project grounds you can't play ball. In the project grounds you can't stay out late. About ten o'clock they tell you to go in or to get out. Then . . . there's

trouble because they don't want you to hang around in the lobby. They're right about that one thing, because like in good houses, the lobby should be sort of like a show place, I think. You know, then you could have something special.

The elevators smell and they always break and you see even very old people tracking up and down the stairs. That's when the worst thing comes. People are grabbed on the stairs and held up or raped. There was this girl on the seventh floor who was raped and there was a girl on the fourth who was raped and robbed. There was an old man who was hit over the head—about fifty years old—he was hit over the head on the stairs and beat up bad. I don't know, maybe it's not always the people who live there. Maybe there's a party going on in the nextdoor and there are strangers in the party. You know how it is, not everybody is a relative. And those people come out and they start fights and arguments. Or they go around banging on the doors when they are drunk.

Before, when things happened in the halls, nobody would come out for nothing. When there were muggings, nobody wanted to come out in the halls and maybe have to face a guy with a knife or a gun. Lately, though, it's a little bit more friendly. Like my mother might have somebody come into our house to learn how to make rice and beans and then I tell my mother to go with them and learn how to make some American foods for a change. So now people are beginning to see on our floor that it's better to have someone help you if you are in trouble than to be alone and face the guy.

I guess in some ways the projects are better. Like when we used to live here before the projects, there were rats and holes and the building was falling apart. It was condemned so many times and so many times the landlords fought and won. The building wasn't torn down until finally it was the last building standing. And you know what that is, the last building . . . there's no place for those rats to go, or those bugs, or no place for the bums to sleep at night except in the one building still standing. It was terrible. The junkies and the drunks would all sleep in the halls at night and my mother was real scared. That was the same time she was out of work and it didn't look to us like anything was ever going to get better.

Then they were going to tear the house down. When I was about eleven or so we moved to another neighborhood. Down there I met one of the leaders of a gang called the Athletes, and the funny thing is that even though this boy was the leader, he didn't really want to belong to a gang. He only went into it because he was alone and everybody else was belonging. What could he do? Then I got associated with him and he quit his gang and we walked along together. Finally we had a whole group of us that were on our own. We still know each other. Even now sometimes I go over there or sometimes he comes here. When I was living there, sometimes he'd go away to Puerto Rico and I was always waiting for him to come back. You know, I missed him and he missed me.

My friend kept me from that fighting gang even though he was the leader. And he lived there with us, so we didn't have any trouble on the block because other gangs were afraid to come. We all lived together—Negroes, Puerto Ricans, and Italian kids—and we got along happy before I moved.

But my mother was afraid because the gang wars near the block made the other streets dangerous. You'd have all kinds of war. The Athletes would fight the Hairies. Then the newspaper had it the Hairies were fighting somebody else. My mother wanted to transfer back here, to the old neighborhood we'd lived in before the projects came.

Well, we did. But you know, every time you move you feel like it's not right because you're leaving part of yourself back there. I used to go back down there every weekend because, when we moved back here, everything was different. The projects were up, no more small houses, all twenty-one floors. There were new kids, a new school.

That time, before I knew anyone here on the block, I would have to fight a person to get introduced, and then finally either he'd beat me or I'd beat him. That way we'd get to know each other. I was new, you know. It was my building and my neighborhood, but I was new.

I would fight one guy in front of

about twenty kids and I was afraid they were going to jump me. One time I said, "Look out, one guy and all of you gonna jump me. Is that a way to fight?" The guy I was fighting said they wouldn't jump me, and we fought that day and I went home bleeding. And then the next day I didn't get anybody to help me, but I went back and we fought again, and he beat me again. Then one day, I beat him. I proved him that I had courage and that I could succeed, and then, when the other boys came, this boy I had beaten up told them to lay off me.

Like back then, when I first came back to the neighborhood, my mother didn't want me to go out with all those kids on the street. I'd say to her, "Man, what am I going to do? I don't have any friends here. All I can do is just go out and look at people. You could go crazy." There were like groups of boys around and they stuck together. There were coloreds, Puerto Ricans, and Italian boys all together. But they were all friends with each other and they didn't want anybody crashing in on them. But after those fights we shook, and that was it. From then on, I was in.

In that gang the kids felt like they had protection, but now I think that it's better fighting for yourself. Otherwise you need the gang like an addict who needs the drug. You never see one of those boys fight anybody alone. Like in the school I used to go to, the junior high. They used to have lots of gangs there and it was rough in the nighttime or even in the daytime. But whenever you'd meet one of those boys alone, you'd have no trouble with him. So what happens when they have nobody, when all their friends are in jail or when everybody else is killed, or something? What do they do?

They were chicken when they were alone and they couldn't think for themself. I wasn't used to that. With me, from the time I was eight, nine, ten, I was always on my own. Always running outside, figuring things out. I think I developed too young. I really did. My mind developed too quick, I think. I was thinking like an adult before I knew what was going on. I don't even think I liked being developed so young.

Of course, you get things in there if you do join a gang. First of all, you won't be bothered by this gang that you're joining. That's one. Second of all, you have protection. And three, you belong. You know that always comes up. You belong. You know, maybe your mother and father don't care, but one of these boys, if you plan to run away or something, they'll give you money or they'll keep you in their house for a while. You develop a friendship like brothers. Then, if you both think evil, that's what you do. You either run away together or do something that's against the law together or if you get caught, you get caught together. No one's going to run away from his buddy and leave him there with the cops. He'll either come back and hit the cop over the head, or he'll surrender.

But I got tired of it. You see, a while before they threw me out of the block, out of the club, all the little kids were smoking pot. Little guys, eight and nine years old. Well, that got me, and then, one day, I saw that there were boys sitting out there by the baker passing things back and forth. Little kids would come and pay them money and they would get pot. I didn't want that. I never took pot. I didn't want my little brother to do it or those little kids there either.

Like when I go to my school there

are a lot of boys who do it, a lot of boys from my neighborhood who are in the school. I figure out that maybe those boys in my school who lived on my block were buying from the boys in the school and selling it home. Of course, I couldn't prove anything, but all I knew was that all of a sudden the little kids on the block were having it. So I figured out for myself that there's a time to tell and a time to keep quiet, and I figured that my time to tell had come. Or else I'd see my own little brother walking around with pot. So I told the policeman, but I told him not to tell my name. They got those boys and some of them they sent away and some of them they didn't.

Well, for a couple of days I didn't see anybody around the block and I decided not to hang around any more because I knew that I was going to get into trouble. But one day, I stayed in the movies too late, and I didn't get home until nine or nine thirty. It was very dark and there was nobody on the street, and as I walked along I saw them, all ganged up, about twenty-five of them, waiting. It was just like one of those things you see in the movies.

I figured they were going to kill me. I mean that's the first thing that comes into your mind. So I tried to bluff my way out. I didn't act scared. There they were, all lined up there on the stoop and I told them, "All right, I don't want any part of you." Right then and there I told them I didn't want anything to do with them and that there was going to be trouble for them because whatever I found out bad about them I was going to tell. I still know them, but I don't speak to them. Ever since that night they tried to jump me I consider them invisible. And some-

body I consider invisible, I don't speak to, I say to myself, "They're not there." And I walk by.

Now, I've got my own one or two friends or I walk alone. I'm older, I don't care.

Things have cooled down in my neighborhood a lot. Old ladies, baby kids, all that kind walking around, playing. There's not much to do, so what we sometimes do is we look for a place. We look for something you can do that's exciting, that's fun. We go out to have fun, some excitement in there. It doesn't have to be exactly fighting, but lots of times there's a fight on Friday nights around my block. At the playground, or in the park. You find out about it like you know when there's going to be dances, or when there's going to be a little club meeting. The same way, I know usually when there's going to be a fight.

Maybe I see somebody and he says, "Hey, man, come to the playground or come up to the park and we're going to have a fight at seven thirty. Bring a knife, you know, or a club or something." And you go up and twenty or thirty guys go up there and fight for half an hour or an hour. Usually they have two or three young ones looking out for the police.

Lots of times the young kids in the group, just starting out, they get the worst of the beating. Because that kind of kid, he's stupid. I mean, everybody else is way over his age, but he wants to prove he's a big man. So he gets beat up two or three times, or else he's the one that might kill a guy because he can't fight him with fists, so he has to fight him with a knife or something.

Usually everybody is carrying a knife, but nobody much uses it. Only if three or four guys are jumping on one boy, and there's only that one way out. Everybody tries to start with a fist fight, though.

But there's one thing I don't ever do. I don't ever fight with my friends, even if they're on the other side. It's better to hit somebody you don't know than hit one of your own friends.

Usually the police get in the way. We've been caught a couple of times, but we make believe we're just sitting and watching, and you say, "Well, I had nothing to do with this, officer," and most of the time you get away with it.

Around my block, there aren't too many of these fights, only once every two or three weeks. But where my friend lives, over in Jersey, it happens every Friday. Over there, they seem to fight more often. Over there the police are worse; different, way different. They insult the people, they have a curfew. Every policeman has a J.D. card on everybody in the neighborhood, everybody that's walking on the street. And the police there have no kind of decency. They stop girls and take them home and assault them themselves. And the girls can't say anything about them because it's their word against his. And the boys get beat up for no reason, like Jack, my friend, and his friends are always being beat up like that.

Sometimes you go to the fight for the excitement, or because you don't want to be called chicken, or just to see what's going on around the block. But usually you have to get into it because, you know, they say, "What are you looking at?"

Once a boy got caught up on the barbed-wire fence. He was cut up, stuck up there with his chest caught and everything. And there was only one thing to do—run. The police were right behind us, and anyway we couldn't do anything for that boy. What were we going to do? Take him to the hospital? And then the police would ask what happened to him? So when the police were coming, we all ran. When they got that boy down off the fence, he was pretty close to dying. His chest was all cut up and he'll always have a lot of scars from that. Well, his parents had him put away in a home. I guess that's better than letting him stay around here and get himself killed.

But that kid, he was crazy. I mean, only a little boy, fourteen or fifteen, and he started fighting with those big guys.

It's funny. I can't really explain what a real tough guy is. My little brother says that a guy that never talks, and walks alone, is a tough guy. But then, there's the other tough guy who has a gang that's strong. Or a Puerto Rican kid, who's maybe built up his physique. He's tough, I guess, but not the Paddy boy who took a few boxing lessons. He's not tough. Those kids in Jersey are supposed to be real tough, there's so many gangs there. But once I went there with my friend and we were walking down the street. There were three boys ahead of us and they were about the same age and the same size as we are. And two of them were Puerto Ricans and one was colored. They started laughing at one of us, I don't know which. Since I figured it was me, I stepped right on that guy's foot, and I kept my foot there, and I walked right across him. Well, we were walking ahead now, and I wondered what was going to happen. But they were all quiet and still. I turned right around to my friend and I said, "These are your big gangster friends? They just chicken out."

Friday night is supposed to be the night everybody in town fights down there, but we couldn't find anything. I was looking for a fight because this was supposed to be a tough neighborhood, and it gets me mad because they have this big reputation and they were all hanging around big and tough, but you insult them, you step on them, and they won't do anything.

Around here, if I can't find a fight on my own block, I go to the East Side. Once, we ran into a gang there and by luck I happened to say where I was from. They had a treaty with my neighborhood and it was all right, but if you make a simple mistake, like on a train, and you land up in Brooklyn, it's a big difference. You say you're from my neighborhood—well, they might kill you. If I got off the subway, and let's say I was trying to round up boys for a fight of ours, Brooklyn wouldn't be the place to go.

It's kind of impossible to have a treaty with one of the gangs over there. The War Lords don't know each other and they don't know the same enemies. The only time you could really have a treaty where all four or five boroughs get together would be if the adults were going to attack us, you know, and everybody would have to get together. It would have to be something really big like that. Usually, Brooklyn doesn't want any New York boys coming over there and asking for help and he doesn't want New York boys coming over there and walking on their territory.

It works out simple. Let's say that I am the leader of one of the gangs and three or four guys come over to me and start beating me up and I know they're not from this neighborhood. This doesn't go. I mean, I can't go over there and start fighting those guys myself. So what I do is, I contact all the boys all over the place that I know, or that we have treaties with. And I get them all out. You have to have a lot to go over to the East Side. I tell them to go in small groups, here and there, and to meet on the East Side in a special place.

All of us go over there and I go to the leaders on the other side and I say that four boys jumped me last week and I want to see his gang and to have them stand up so I can find out if any of those were in their gang. And the leader goes and does it or else we have an all-out war.

But there is not too much fighting now. Down further on the street they were really a fighting gang. They used to run around in cars with all their equipment—knives, guns, grenades—in the back. Then they just got tired of cutting all those little guys, so they moved. They got old and decided to settle down to a peaceful life, raising up their hoodlum children.

I suppose the little kids are still doing all that, but, anyhow, gangs change their name every day because they don't want the police chasing them and it's hard to keep track. If you're a Persian Angel, man, and somebody in your group kills somebody, you change your name real quick.

Another thing is, white kids don't belong to gangs much. They're usually cowards. Only maybe sometimes, if one white, he lived around a colored neighborhood for a long time, and he proved he's not scared, then they take him in. Me, I'm not afraid of tough kids. It's bad when you're afraid of them. Like a Paddy boy will chicken out if he was alone. Really scared to death, you know. But not me. Oh, I was smeared a lot of times—smeared is you don't have a chance. I was jumped in the park a couple of times. I was jumped down there once by a group of guys I didn't even know. Those guys jumped on me and started beating the heck out of me, kicking, cursing, using their cigarettes. That time I went to the hospital and they patched me up and took me home. But the thing is I wasn't afraid of them. Why they did so good, what happened, was they just caught me by surprise. I mean I would have caught a couple of them and they wouldn't have been able to hurt me that badly, but the trouble was they caught me by surprise and I didn't have a chance. If I knew them I would kill them afterwards. Do you think I would come home bandaged up, and you think I'm not going to do anything about it? I get riled sometimes when a guy looks at me the wrong way. You think I'm not going to get those that got me? I'll get them one at a time if I'm alone, or all at once if I have a group with me. I'm not scared to walk down the street ever. I can handle myself and I might take on a guy, he's alone, because I've seen him act big when he's with his men and now I want to test him, like alone. But taking on a whole gang, that's another thing.

Going home from school once, there was big trouble like that. On the subway, right on the train when it was moving, some guys grabbed a couple of white school girls . . . and they raped them. I couldn't stand it, right there on the subway and they did it without interference. That's something in my life I'm not proud of.

Man, you believe me? I ran all over that train trying to find a cop. And I wouldn't have minded jumping in and stopping it, no matter what, if there was a way. I got very upset but, see, I go in there, without a knife, alone, I'm going to get my brains knocked

out. Even that, I wouldn't mind so bad, if I knew the girls were going to come out all right. But I knew they were still going to be played around with.

And there was nobody else who wanted to come with me. I don't think the guys I was with, they cared at all. Nobody would help me, not old people or kids. On that whole train, nobody, nobody. I was alone.

I feel lousy about it. I mean, even now, sometimes I look at a girl and I think, "Suppose that happened again? What would I do *this* time?" And I promise myself I'll go in, no matter what. But I couldn't do anything about it that time. I'm not afraid to fight, I've been fighting all my life. But nobody would help me start a little riot and get them off those girls.

There are some times, though, when everybody in the neighborhood does get together, agrees on one thing. Like the time there was one policeman who used to tease and bother everybody around the block. It got so bad that we had to fix that policeman. So everybody got together. Nobody was on the street that day except one boy, up on a stoop. The policeman said, "Get off. Get off that stoop. You don't belong here." Well, the boy stepped quickly back and the cop came up on the stoop. Up above there on the roof, they had a garbage can and they sent it right on his head. He was in the hospital for about three or four months, something wrong with his head. And the next policeman they sent wasn't so bad; he was just bad like a regular policeman.

The police are the most crooked, the most evil. I've never seen a policeman that was fair or that was even good. All the policemen I've ever known are hanging around in the liquor store or taking money from Jim on the corner, or in the store on the avenue. They're just out to make a buck no matter how they can do it. O.K., maybe if you gave them more money they wouldn't be so crooked, but what do you need to qualify for a policeman? I mean, if you have an ounce of brain and you have sturdy shoulders and you're about six feet one, you can be a policeman. That's all.

I mean, you've got to fight them all the time. A policeman is supposed to be somebody that protects people. You're supposed to be able to count on them. You are supposed to look up to policemen and know that if anything goes wrong, if any boys jumped me, I can just yell and the policeman will come running and save me. Around my block, you get jumped, the police will say, "Well, that's just too bad." He just sits there.

Even the sergeants are crooked. It's the whole police force is rotten. There was a man, I don't know who he was, way out in Brooklyn somewhere. He broke down a whole police station, a whole police force, the detectives, the policemen, the rookies. Everybody that was on that police force was crooked. Everybody in the precinct was crooked. He had to tell them all to go home.

Like take the Negro cop. The police towards discrimination are the same as anybody else. You have colored policemen, Italian policemen, every kind. But, you know, a Negro policeman will tend to beat up another Negro more than he would beat up anybody else, because he says to himself, "I'm a cop, and this guy is going to expect special privileges. I've got to show the other people it doesn't mean anything to me, that I'm really not going to treat them different." I think the Puerto Ricans would be just the same as the Negroes. He would tend to beat up Puerto Rican people more than he would a Negro or anybody else. Maybe you think he'd feel the Puerto Ricans were somebody he should help and he should try to solve some of their problems. But that's not the way it works.

And like I said, you think they protect you? When I lived downtown, it was a terrible neighborhood. There were so many killings, and people were being raped and murdered and all. Guys, you could see them, guys you could see jumping out of windows, running away from a robber, using a needle or something. I worked in a grocery there and I was afraid to go to work, but I guess I was lucky anyhow. I mean, I never got in any kind of real cop trouble or anything. They'd pick me up only in sort of like routine. They picked up everybody once in a while to make sure, you know, that nobody is carrying weapons and there is not going to be a fight that day. Of course, as soon as the police left, everything was the same all over again, anyhow.

That time they picked me up, I was halfway home from the grocery store where I worked and—well—I'll tell you how I felt like. I felt like the policeman was the rottenest person in the world. What would happen, see, is that I was always tall, and being tall, they think that I'm older. Then, no matter what you tell them, they believe that you're older. They were looking for a draft card and I didn't have one. I was too young and I told them I didn't have a draft card. Man, I was only twelve, thirteen or so, you know. Then they'd take me on the side and hit me a couple of times and I'd go home black and blue.

You wouldn't get picked up alone,

even now. A person alone they never bother with, unless he's looking at cars or something. Whenever I get picked up, it's with a group. Like if I'm walking along and there's a group here and at the same time I'm walking, even though I don't know them, a policeman comes. They take all of us. Once I got picked up when there was a poker game going on or a crap game. They picked us up and they wanted to find out who had the money, who had the dice. They hit everybody. I think I even got hit the worst because I was a little taller than the rest of them. It happens right out on the street.

They tell you to get up against the wall of a building, and then they start searching you. And you can't talk to the policeman. Never say a word when they have you against the wall. Say anything and he thinks that you are making a false move and then he has the right to shoot you. So I would stand there and he asked my name, and I'd tell. And then he'd ask for my age and when I'd tell him twelve, thirteen, fourteen, he wouldn't believe me. They didn't think a Puerto Rican kid could be so young, so tall. Then they'd take me over the side and hit me a couple of times.

I'd be scared. Half the time I was petrified from being hit and because I was thinking of what my mother would say, you know, if I was taken down to the station. That I didn't do anything didn't make any difference to the police because I was still picked up. But I guess I was lucky because every time I was picked up I got sent home. There were a couple of boys that time that were Spanish and they didn't understand the language too well. When they tried to tell the policeman something, they got black and blue marks

all over. Well, they didn't like it too much and they started trying to run away and talking back and pushing around, you know. The policeman just grabbed them, got them in the car and took them away. But me, I never went to the station house.

It's happened twice over here, too. See, when I was still hanging around the block, when we first came here, I used to go up the street. But twice I got picked up there. Once, this boy asked me for a light up there on the corner. He was with some friends, so I gave it to him. I didn't want to start any trouble. Just then the police came.

First of all, they didn't like smoking. They took the cigarettes and tore them up. Second, they didn't like the way the boys were hanging around the corner. They thought they were insulting the people walking by. You know, when a person is walking by and there's a bunch of boys, they maybe start looking at people as if they were trash, or start calling names, or if they see a girl walking by, they call her a name or grab something up. So, me, I agreed with the policeman that time, but he sure didn't agree with me.

Well, that time the cops started searching. Now I don't like being searched and as I get older I'm—I'm sort of ready to strike out. Well, they searched us and one of the boys had a knife. It was John, and he was about seventeen then. By the way, his father was the one who was killed in that bar —he was working in a bar and a man shot him? Well, anyway, John had a knife that he used just for fooling around with a piece of wood or for fishing sometime. John isn't the kind of guy that would ever use a knife. The policeman took it and asked him what he was going to do with it and John told him that it was his fishing knife. The policeman said, "You're not fishing now." The cop hit him and he hit me. He hit me because I was taller than he was and he'd asked again for the draft card. Now, I get very mad when they ask me for that. And John was crying and I was on the verge of tears, you know, because the night stick really hurts. But they let us go after that. There was a whole crowd there and I felt very embarrassed, you know. People watching you and girls, and old people that know your family and they see you being picked up.

Then there was another time. I wasn't even there, but there were a bunch of boys and a couple of girls all standing out in the hall that sort of extends into the stoop. They were playing cards, poker for pennies and nickels—nothing more. Well, an old lady came walking by, and she couldn't get past in the hall, and they were bothering her, sort of. She went up and called the police and just as the police car was coming down the block, I was walking down the street. At the same time that I hit that stoop, walking by that stoop, they came out of the car and grabbed all of us. They took us and they lined us up. They took the other kids' money, but I was broke that day, so I felt good. At least, you know, they didn't get anything from me that time.

The way it goes, other times, if you're playing cards, the police say that the money you've got in your pockets is from playing and they take all of it. That time they lined us up and asked our age and boy, I was the oldest one. I told them that I was just walking by, and they said, "Oh, yeah. We know." And I got the worst of it. They took down my name and they gave me a

J.D. card. A juvenile delinquent! That's a good one for you. Me, after all this, I'm suddenly a juvenile. Then, if that wasn't bad enough, they wanted to take me home. Can you imagine being driven home? And then they leave you right in front of the door and you get out of a police car where you live. That's the worst thing. That police car right in front of the building with my mother living there and all.

I don't think, if I have to live in this neighborhood when I get older, I would let my son go to P.S. 305 * or 96 ** or any of the other schools that I went to. I would do something like the middle class does. I would get a tutor, one of the best, and let him teach my son or daughter everything he has to know.

My school is bad. I really think it was the only thing my parents could do to send me there and it has no problems for me, but it's bad all right.

You know, kids walk down the halls, just walking down. They bump into somebody, they slug somebody, a kid always feels like he is being pushed. The kids, especially in the Adjustment classes, the kids are rough. You know what Adjustment classes are? Oh, boy! The teacher, he sees you doing something wrong, he doesn't ask you, out you go to the office.

I didn't do anything to get there. I just transferred from P.S. 305 to the seventh grade in 96 and I had to go into an Adjustment class and *wham!* I was in that class and I knew I had to get out. I couldn't stand it. I asked for a transfer and they wouldn't give it to me, so what I did was that I studied real hard and my marks went up to

* Elementary School.
** Junior High School.

90–95. Study! All the time I studied to get out of there. My marks went up to 90–95 and the teacher said, "Well, this kid doesn't belong here. He sits in that little corner over there. He keeps quiet. He doesn't forget his work; he comes nicely prepared. How can you keep a boy here like that?"

So they took me out and put me in honor class. From then on I have been in an honor class. But, even so, what I'm saying is that I wouldn't let my kids go to a school like that.

Now you see, you take your boy and you bring him up not to curse, not to say bad words, not to do anything wrong, not to smoke pot, or drink, or anything. And then he goes to school and there are five hundred to a thousand boys there and they are opposite him. All they *do* is curse. All they *do* is have bad manners. All they *do* is fight and make trouble for the boys. How are you going to keep your boy from turning out the same way? Like taking pot?

One thing, I never took pot. I wouldn't be standing here if I did. I'd turn myself in.

There used to be a lot of kids who took dope in school. They'd be passing it under the tables at the lunchroom and in the classroom. And then they would have it outside at three o'clock, or in the morning they would be out there, saying, "Seventy-five cents. You want one? Go on and try one." Lately, those types have been cooling down around us big guys in the school. The big guys, especially now, they don't come near us. They know it's bad, but they don't use it mostly because those who took it, they've dropped out now. The ones that are left, they don't want to take a chance. Nobody wants to be kicked out after all these years, just be-cause they're carrying a stick, or tasting powder, or using it in a handkerchief.

The younger boys still do it because they don't know what they're up against. See, somebody tells them not to worry about getting the habit and they want to try the kicks out of it.

Like Silva, a friend of mine, real close. He used to take it when he was in his first year here. I was with him even then, and I asked him why he did it. He tells me and he tells me, and what he says is, "Well, I feel good, I feel good inside. After all the crap I feel good, I get away from it all with this stick. I feel strong, important. Sometimes I just feel—*myself*."

Me, I want to forget all about that now. Silva is off it now, too. We took each other in hand and he doesn't go around with that gang that smokes pot any more.

In my school there are mostly Puerto Ricans and Negroes, but in my honor classes, there are almost all whites. They're all trying for careers that you have to have a very good average for. They all want to go to college, so they have to have a good average. They get into the honor class very easily.

But there is no favoritism in our school. That's one thing I like about it. Everybody has to do their own work to get what they want. And there's really no trouble with the whites as long as they stay on their own side. You know, it's sort of like, "You leave me alone, I'll leave you alone."

There was only one tough guy in all the whites and I took him on. He was pushing everybody in the honor class around, picking on his own race, and then picking up on everybody else. I was second tallest, like now, and I wasn't afraid of that big mouth at all.

I punched him in the face and I told him to sit down and to keep his mouth shut and not to bother anybody in the class. The teacher was right there when it happened, but he didn't say anything. There was nothing he could do about it and he was glad that I got that guy into line. I mean, everybody's sixteen, seventeen years old. The teacher's not going to come and stop one boy, because then he might have the whole class on him. So he lets us do what we want, but he writes it down. That time he didn't write anything down about me punching that kid because he was looking for somebody to take care of him, anyhow.

There isn't too much trouble these days in my classes. By the time you get to the junior or senior year, you can't afford to do anything you might get thrown out for. Before now, most kids were just staying in school because the law says they have to. They didn't think that it would matter later on, so they would insult the teacher and ask for a fight.

There once was a big fight in my math class in junior high. We were all playing around just waiting for the bell to ring but, like always, pretty soon it turned into a big fight, with four or five fights going on right there in the room. The teacher came and he tried to break them up; but some kid jumped him, too, and they beat him up bad.

He quit the school, teaching, everything. Funny thing, I saw him one day on the bus and he's a nice, young, clean-cut fellow, you know. And when I saw him that time, after he left, he looked so—you know—so nice, I was really sorry it happened.

But he could never handle the class. They were always throwing paper airplanes, cursing at him, and asking for fights all the time. So it was lucky for him to get out. Anyway he did better, got a better job.

With teachers, it all depends on how they handle themselves. They ought to make sure the kids don't think they are playing favoritism. They've got to be fair with all the boys so that it's all free. And if you have like a Negro little kid, and maybe a big white kid who is bothering him, the teacher's got to stop that. They can't tolerate that because they know that any little thing could start a racial riot.

But like I said, we don't have much race trouble in my school. We stay on our own sides. Like I never see the kids in the honor classes after school. After school, everybody leads their own lives. I don't go to their place and they don't come to mine. But with the Spanish boys, I know a lot of them and I go to their houses. We have a good time even though maybe they come from a different neighborhood, too. The Spanish boys go with the Spanish boys, the white boys go with the white.

But it doesn't really make a difference in the colors when you go to school. The trouble is, how could I go to a colored's house when he didn't want to be ashamed because he lived in a bad place, or he didn't want to bring me there because he lived in an all-colored neighborhood and I could get in trouble on his block?

And it works out. You know, in the lunchroom with all of those Spanish kids in one section, maybe sometimes a couple of colored boys we know are with us, or some of our Spanish boys might go over to their section. There are no racial riots between the Puerto Ricans and the Negroes there anytime I have been in the school. The only time there was any trouble was when a white person bothered a colored, a Puerto Rican.

I guess it looks kind of funny there in the lunchroom. This section, Puerto Rican. Up here, Negroes. And in the middle, whites. Negroes might come down here. Puerto Ricans might go up there. But the white stay by themselves and they do it different.

An example: they bring their own lunch. They never eat the food from the school cafeteria and we always eat from the school cafeteria, or if we can, sometimes we sneak out for lunch. My mother made my lunch a couple of times. I liked it all right, but I couldn't trust myself to take it all the way to school. I don't know why the others bring their own stuff. I guess it's cheaper, but a couple of lunches were stolen once or twice and I decided that it would be better to buy it there.

Another boy used to play it real smart about that. He wanted to catch the crook that was stealing his food? So he put rat poison in it. He caught the guy all right. The guy was real sick. Had to go to the doctor. Oh, he got even, I mean.

You know, I like to get even just like everybody else. To get even. They stole my sneakers from out of my locker once and I went out and I stole five pair of sneakers. Five sneakers came out.

I don't know who took mine or whose I took. Look, they didn't even fit. But what I know is, I broke five lockers and stole five sneakers and I'm even. It didn't matter any more.

Another play like that worked good once. I had this crummy pair of coveralls. So I played a sob story with the teacher. You know, he said, when the laundry came back, he couldn't find my coveralls anywhere; couldn't under-

stand it. Ha! So I told him that was the only pair I had and I couldn't afford any more money because . . .

And he says, "All right. We'll look for a pair for you." And then he gave me a brand-new pair of one of the teachers. And I was the only boy in that class with a teacher's uniform. I still have it.

The worst thing a teacher can do is to make a boy feel like he is losing his pride, something like that. They've done that to me lots of time. And there is nothing like it. I tell you, if I didn't have more self-control, I would probably beat up the teacher or knife him.

They can kill your pride. They make you feel like dirt and it's nothing nice to feel like. O.K., so you don't know something, you don't know it. But if you *do* know something, they give you an argument so good on it that they make you feel wrong even about what you *know*.

Let's take an example. Let's say, here I am talking about a car, about something wrong with the engine. And I know what's wrong with the engine because I have taken it apart and put it right, right in front of you. I tell you, "This is what is wrong with it. You can fix this part and the car will run." And he'll answer that the car will run without this part, or with it. If I tell him then that he's crazy, then it comes: "Don't tell me I'm crazy. I know what's going to happen. You're just a student, I'm a teacher, I'm better than you are."

The teachers can really hurt you if they want to. Like we had a teacher who would write up on the board before we even came in. All the boards would be filled with writing. And he wouldn't explain a thing to us. Every day the same thing—writing but no explanation for the things he wrote. And when the tests came, everybody failed.

And then he would criticize us, give us zeros, demerits and all these kinds of crazy things, and there was no way of getting to him. So we all got in a little group and went down to the principal's office. He didn't believe us. So what we did is, we stopped work. We never worked in that class and the teacher called the principal. We told him, "We won't work because he won't explain the things he writes up on the board and we can't learn unless he explains."

Finally they threw out that teacher and they brought in another one. That new one, all he ever did was explain. He never wrote anything on the board.

I mean, you get aggravated. All of these teachers are just too much for the boys. So there was only one way out. You play hooky, you cut out of that class, you sleep, you get even on him, you hate it. You live through it to get out of school.

Then you'd think a Negro teacher would be better, but one Negro teacher I had, she despised the Negroes and the Puerto Ricans more than anybody else. I guess some don't though. I had another Negro who liked us and was very kind and nice. Maybe it was just their own personalities.

My best teachers were mostly for English. They seemed to really want you to learn, they really strive for you to learn. Whereas most of the other teachers just don't care. They'll pass you either with a 65 or fail you with a 55. Good teachers are the ones that want you to get a high mark, and to join an honor class, like I was in. They really stress it; they really want you to go to it.

And with the kids, it's this way. Half of them want to learn and half

of them don't. Half want to play around, whereas the other half, although maybe they do the same things, they *know* it's important. And on the sneak, away from the other boys, they study.

They don't want to let them know that they are *smart*. Well, you want to be somebody odd? I mean, everybody else is dumb. You have to be with the group.

Then there's another trouble. It's not really the language—most people know English. But you see like even I do, it's the slang. You know, like instead of saying "officer," I say "cop." It's sort of something that gets into your head.

Like, if you are used to saying, "I ain't gonna do that," you know, and you go out into the street and that's all you hear from the people, "I ain't gonna do that, I ain't gonna sit over there."

Well, you go to school and the teacher says you aren't supposed to do that and the boys think she is crazy. I'm not going to go out in the street and talk like that. They won't believe me.

You know, in school you learn words and you read Shakespeare and you can't talk like that. There's some kid, he might know all of Shakespeare by heart, but when he gets out into the street, he can't talk to his friends like that; he can't talk to *anybody*. You have to use words that other people understand. Well, take a boy that can recite all of Shakespeare and all his plays—that kind of boy, one that can understand words that he hears in political speeches. He knows the words, the language, inside out. He'll soon get tired of the neighborhood where they only talk in slang or they only talk bad language. He won't have anyone to talk to. He will have to go and look for another kind of job, and he'll try to live in another kind of neighborhood where everybody talks in the fashion that he can understand; where, for once, he can just show what his real feelings are.

It's rough. How's a boy going to ever find out anything he has to know? The teacher says, "Does anybody not understand?" Well, he doesn't want to raise his hand and feel like an idiot, so he keeps his hand down and forty boys out of that class keep their hands down and forty boys at the end of the year won't graduate, or if they do, they won't know anything anyhow.

Like a new boy that was in our class. He, sort of like, he showed that he was afraid at first, that he was little, that he had money. I remember the first day he came in here, they stole his watch. They stole his shoes and he walked around barefooted then. And me, I didn't feel sorry for him at all.

You know, with these kids, you learn how to handle them. You know what to do. If a boy comes in from a rich neighborhood, and he doesn't know how to handle himself, instead of asking for help, he goes right in there and really messes up the works. So he's bound to get beat up. He should stay to himself. If he stays to himself, he makes friends with one of the boys that he knows is good, he has it all right. But if he walks in there and he starts—you know—pulling out his money like this boy did, showing off his watch and answering—you know—answering all the questions in the class, oh, he was dead. I could tell. I didn't feel sorry for him at all because he was stupid.

The questions he would answer! It's not so wrong to answer some of them, but we would never answer all, tell all the answers because we wanted to leave something for the next day. If you answer all of them, the teacher would give you homework, you know. This boy was killing us, and he was so proud of it.

You know how it works. The teacher says to himself, "Well, you know this, I might as well give you some more." And we would never want more homework. So even if we know, we don't say, so as to have something else for the next day. Something a little left over. If you answer all of them, you're cooked. You get new work the next day and you might not know it and then you are really stuck. Stuck for the weekend.

Like that kid, he proved he had brains for the answers, but he didn't even make friends with anybody first. He was bothering everyone. All he had to do was make one snotty remark to anybody. Man!

He got beat up outside the school; practically every day for months it happened. As far as that goes, he didn't really have to do anything. Just go along minding his own business. Otherwise he'll have a lot of trouble.

And nobody helps. That's one good thing about our school. If they're all fighting one guy, unless you know the person that is getting it, you won't go into the fight. No matter how old, or how many, you let them.

And you know why I let them? Because it's happened to me so many times and if it hadn't happened to me, I would finally have been like maybe the boys in those other houses near me, in my neighborhood, afraid to fight, afraid of being hit, afraid of walking down the street alone at night. Afraid of coming out of their high-class hole in the ground.

Now, today, when I'm almost out of the whole mess, I know I'd rather have been in an academic course. To be able to go to college. Ah—a college degree is much better because I'd have more opportunities open to me. But if I want to go to college now, so late in school, there are bad things that I have to say.

What happened is, when I was in the ninth grade, my guidance counselor told me to be a vocational student. She said that I had the aptitude to be an auto mechanic. I think what must have happened is that some business guy must have called up that day to say that there was getting to be a shortage of garage mechanics—and to train a few jerks so he wouldn't have to pay too high salaries.

Anyhow I got here to a vocational high school, and when my marks were so good they put me in academic classes. You see in a vocational school, when a kid does good, an academic class is like an honor class. Now I'm taking a trade, auto mechanics, so that makes me a vocational student. Then, I'm taking honor classes. So I'm not getting the right training for my vocational course and I'm not getting enough training for my academic course. I'm sort of like in between. So if I want to go to college, I'm going to have to take extra courses at night school. Probably after I'm out of school and working I'd have to take night classes for years before I could even apply to college.

Even if I wanted to become a garage mechanic, I'm going to be in the same spot. I'll have to see if I can gain experience by watching after I'm work-

ing and just hoping that I'll learn. I've only had half a course of that, too. I'm just going to have to make my own way.

My mother, she wants me to go to college. She says the only good jobs are for college students and she tells me she doesn't want me to be a laborer. But she couldn't dish out money for my books, my expenses. She doesn't have to go through what I would. You know how hard it is to stay in college. If I have to be studying during the day time and in the late hours of the night, I can't see working. I'll be killing myself if I started working like something in the middle of the night.

Then, when I figure it all out, I see how much trouble I am going to have. You see, in college you would need a lot of math and I haven't had math since the ninth grade. I can't take it because at night you are only allowed to take one subject if you are still going to day school and I've been taking advanced English there in the night school. So, when I get to college, I guess math will be very hard for me. I was thinking about this last year one time and once, when I delivered some groceries down the street to a woman who lived there, we got to talking and I told her this trouble. So she began teaching me algebra, but it just got to a point where I couldn't take algebra any more.

It wasn't the algebra I guess, it was her house and her. Her house was too beautiful for me. I felt like a creep coming from my house to her house.

You know how those houses are? The patios and everything like that? And everything is carpets on the floor. Those people can afford everything. Whereas in my house it is a little more roomy now than we used to have it, but it's still not the same way as over there.

So when I walk over to her house, I say to myself, "Why can't I have it like this? Why do I have to live over there?"

So then I say to her, "Well, I'll see you," but I know I'm not going back, that's all.

That woman, if I asked her to lend me a book she would tell me, "Well, it costs me thirty-five dollars. You have to come over here and read it and be sure not to damage the pages."

By that time I was ready to break the damn book over her head. You know, I would say she was helping me because she wanted to show her power. She was a good teacher, and maybe she wanted to pass it on, but I couldn't stand that thing about her money. The way she said it, like she was daring me to take her money, you know? More than anything else she talked about that. I'd get mad and kind of disgusted.

I'd say to myself, "Why couldn't my parents have afforded this? Why do I have to work and sweat? For what? For what *they* have."

Maybe, maybe if I work like a dog in school and later, my children will have it good. But I could have had it good if my parents would have done it first.

And then sometimes I envy them because they get to go all over. You know, they get to do everything and I can't, I'm only limited. Oh, in true form I don't show all this, I don't let it out. I hold it in, just like all the other people in Harlem hold it in, until it's too late and before anything happens, I leave.

Oh, not all teachers are like her. I had one very good teacher, in school. He was smart, too. He's young though and maybe he doesn't know as much as the old teachers who have been around for a long time and it shows in one way. He can get very hot-tem-pered, you know? And when he gets hot-tempered he really wants to smash somebody, though he doesn't do anything.

I guess he gets mad that he has been studying all this time to be a teacher and there are kids there, a whole class full, that don't want to learn, and I guess everybody would get mad at that. Like if you study to be a mechanic and nobody wants to bring their car to you, then what's the use? You know?

Like sometimes, him and me, right there in the class we start discussing something back and forth about history or like that. All right, it's good; we're both swinging. But those other kids, back there, in the back of the class? They are playing around. They're throwing papers at each other, or they're cursing, or they are talking about something else, or they're sleeping.

Like in hygiene, half of the kids are asleep. Or maybe even some of them drunk even before they came to school. A kid might sit there in the back of the class and he's a little bit up, you know. He thinks he's well off, but he's not. And he comes to school on a little tightrope. And before he gets to his third class, he's *out*.

All right, so that kid gets transferred, and another kid flunks out, and another kid drops out. A few of us stay and maybe we get to graduate, but it doesn't do much good. Nobody has the right training; most of them, even when they graduate, can't read or write too good. They can't go to college; they haven't got the right training for a trade. Sometimes I think of going into the Navy because there, I'd get more training. I could go into the motor service and maybe learn to be a better mechanic. Anyway, I can study there. I mean, if I can't leave the post, go play pool or go with girls, there is only one thing I can do, I can study. Maybe in the Navy I'll have a chance.

Even if I could, by taking courses at night and get some money help, I think I'd have a big problem with college. I don't know how I would respond to it. College is a whole new thing. Maybe I wouldn't do so good. Suppose I would flunk out after all this time of struggling and working and wishing. I think maybe I better cool down a bit before I go.

UP FROM PUERTO RICO

Elena Padilla

In 1950, Tomas Rios received his terminal leave pay from the United States military base at Arecibo, where he had been steadily employed from 1946 to 1948. In the two years from 1948 to 1950 he moved from job to job, trying small businesses and odd jobs, all of which ended in unemployment for him. His efforts to find steady work were expended in vain, and he managed to earn only enough money to provide the most meager support for his wife, Paz, and his five children, who then ranged in age from four to twelve years. In a flashback of his life story he speaks of the many kinds of jobs he had in Puerto Rico, and says, "I started to work when I was twelve years old. . . . I have worked all my life." He had been out of Puerto Rico before his migration to New York in 1950, traveling as a sailor to South America and also to New York. He had worked and earned substantially in Puerto Rico during the war years in the construction of airports and bases, yet after the jobs created by the war had dwindled away, he could not

Elena Padilla, Up From Puerto Rico (New York: Columbia University Press, 1958), pp. 134–141. Reprinted by permission.

find any job in Puerto Rico that would satisfy the needs of his family. Tomas had a brother in New York, and his wife had two sisters here; he also had nephews and nieces, cousins, coparents, and friends from his home town of Arecibo who had migrated to New York. When he received his terminal pay from the military base—two years after his job there had ended—he decided he would come to New York by himself, get a job, and later send for his family.

He flew to New York, and after his arrival rented a room with a family living near his brother in El Barrio. At the Migration Division office, operated by the Department of Labor of the Government of Puerto Rico in New York, where he had gone in search of a job, he accepted an offer of agricultural work on a New England farm. For three months he was employed as a farm laborer—Tomas's first experience with this type of work. Catching a cold that he "could not get rid of," he left this job and returned to New York. Then, through a private employment agency, he "bought" a job as bus boy in a Bronx restaurant, a job which eventually paid him fifty-five dollars a week, including double pay for overtime. He sent money regularly to his wife and

21

occasionally sent gifts and clothing to her and the children,

A year afterward his wife sold their home in Arecibo, a bungalow they had bought seven years before near the homes of some of her brothers and sisters. Paz used the money she realized on the sale of the house to come to New York with the children. Dalia, her co-mother living in the Bronx, had written her that the whole family could stay in her home until they found an apartment. Paz and the children arrived in 1951, and with Tomas they moved into Dalia's apartment. The Rios family bought their own food and tried to contribute toward the gas and electric bills. This, their host refused. With the help of one of Paz's sisters who had lived in Staten Island for over fifteen years, Tomas found a four-room apartment in Eastville, which had some furniture in it—an old and dilapidated club chair, a love seat, and a bed. They "bought" this apartment from the tenant for $600 cash. Paz's sister lent her $300 to complete payment on the apartment as she and Tomas had but $300 themselves, and the family moved in. The rent was fourteen dollars a month.

Paz says she did not want to come to New York, but she thought her husband might start going out with other women: "On account of my damned jealousy I came. After he left Puerto Rico he never turned his back to look at it," she adds. The children were placed in public schools, and with Tomas's fifty-five dollars a week, the family managed. "We had no debts, we bought with cash in the hand, and I could always save some money," says Paz.

In 1953, Tomas had a work accident. He was hospitalized and released after a few days. Six months afterward a major orthopedic operation—recommended some months previously by his physician—was agreed upon by the New York State Compensation Board and performed. Since Tomas had been bedridden and suffering pain, the family had run out of income. The payments for accident compensation had been discontinued, and they had used up all of their savings. Paz occasionally received small sums of money from her sisters and brothers in Arecibo and from her sisters here. This assistance was used for food and other essentials.

While the family was suffering this economic hardship, Paz became pregnant again. A visiting nurse informed the Rioses that they "should go on welfare" because they could not continue meeting the exigencies of life in this country without a steady income. The children were passing the winter in tropical clothing, and Paz could not step out of the apartment because she lacked a coat. There was no money to pay the rent, nor any for transportation and lunch for the son attending a commercial high school uptown. The visiting nurse convinced them that they should apply for aid, and she herself contacted the Department of Welfare, recommending the Rioses as clients in emergency need.

Paz was listed to receive supplementary aid for herself and the children. By this time Tomas's case had been reopened and the New York State Compensation Board had reinstated an assignment of eighteen dollars a week for him. As required by law the Rios family transferred their life insurance to the Department of Welfare, which became beneficiary in case of death of any of the insured members of the family.

Today, Paz Rios is a forty-year-old woman. Her husband is forty-five. They have been married twenty years. Tomas was always the main provider until his arm was injured in the work accident. Since his surgery he has continued to suffer from illness and has been unemployed. Meanwhile, he has been attending night school, and already has completed grammar school and started junior high. He still receives erratic, though frequent, medical attention, both privately and in clinics, and has continued to appear at hearings before the Compensation Board. Gradually, they have reduced his assignment of funds. Trying to obtain an indemnification settlement for the injuries sustained at work, he frequently consults lawyers and friends. While Tomas has been losing his compensation, the Welfare Department has been increasing their aid to match the funds lost so that the family's income has remained constant. The children, as well as the parents, object to having to receive welfare aid.

The three older boys, aged thirteen, fourteen, and eighteen, have been working Saturdays for the past two years, delivering parcels for shoppers in the local grocery stores and earning from two to five dollars a week, which they give to their mother. Out of this income Paz provides the boys with a small allowance, pays for their haircuts, and manages other miscellaneous small expenses of the family. Paz herself has been supplementing the family income by taking children into her home for day care, and by occasionally cooking Puerto Rican delicacies, which she sells to neighbors who order them in advance. She spends three or four dollars at a time on this project to make a profit of about the same amount.

During this period, also, the family's rent has been doubled, and they have been shopping on credit at a bodega, as they have no cash available until the bimonthly Welfare Department checks are received. The children have been attending school regularly and have obtained special certificates for their good conduct and scholastic performance. They have learned to speak English fluently, while at home they continue to speak Spanish. Paz and Tomas promote the use of "correct" Spanish in the home, at times worrying that their children may "forget their language" and correcting their pronunciation. Tomas has also learned to speak English, and he can use it in conversation with relative ease, though he retains a strong foreign accent. Paz, who spends most of her time in the home, and who in New York for the first time has had to learn to go shopping for clothes and food for the family, understands conversations in English, as well as prices and other related information, but uses only a few scattered words and phrases in this language.

The Rios children now include a preschool-age boy, two children in grammar school, two in junior high, and the oldest son, who simultaneously completed both high school and training as bookkeeper. His special training as a bookkeeper was made possible by rearranging the family budget and through the sudsidiary economic activities of the mother, himself, and two of his younger brothers. Since the completion of his education, he has been employed "obtaining experience" in Hispano-owned enterprises, and expects to find a better-paying job so that the family "can get out of Welfare."

Not allowed to play in the neighborhood streets, the Rios children are growing up "in the home," although the boys are "given permission" to go to the park or to the back alley to play by themselves for a while. The girls are not allowed in the street by themselves, except to go to school or church, but go out visiting or to a home party or community center dance accompanied by their father. The children are active in church work and are members of one of Eastville's store-front churches. Through the church they attend parties, movies, and play groups. The boys are also "given permission" by their father to go to camp during the summer months, also through the church, but a daughter, now aged twelve, is not allowed to go any more. She went until she became *señorita* (menstruated for the first time), when her parents decided that she should not be away from home unless she was chaperoned. Tomas is a member of the same church as his children, and he and his wife insist that the children attend Sunday services. Tomas himself, however, does not go to religious services regularly, and Paz professes that she is an atheist and has never attended any church.

In the Rios family, authority as well as labor is divided among family members. The children are supposed to ask permission of their father and mother before going out of the house. They are expected to comply with parental decisions and disobedience is punished by either Tomas or Paz. Paz and the children acknowledge Tomas as the head of the family and its main authority. On one occasion when he was hospitalized, Paz gathered the children together and warned them to be "good and obedient" with her for their father was sick and "may leave us." Paz, a woman who claims never to have been ill in her life, does most of the household chores and decides which house-

work is necessary to keep the house clean and operating. She does all the cooking, assisted occasionally by her twelve-year-old daughter, who also does the dishes because "she must learn." Her daughter also helps with the small children, sews and repairs clothing, and in her mother's absence, takes over the cooking and assignment of household duties. The boys and Tomas are sent to the stores to do errands. Tomas is also expected to perform such duties as taking the children to the hospital, going to the schools to find out how they are getting along, and doing some of the shopping for the personal needs of his wife and children.

The Rios family receives frequent visitors who drop in to chat day and evening. These include recent migrants from their home town who live in the neighborhood, cousins, nephews, brothers, and sisters of both Paz and Tomas, and non-Hispano friends whom the children have met at school, church groups, and summer camps.

Frequent contact is also maintained with relatives in Puerto Rico. Paz writes her brothers and sisters three times a week. The children have expressed a desire to go to Puerto Rico and speak of their having been able to play more and have more fun there than in New York. Paz says that she would like to return, even if only for a visit, and that when she thinks of the difficulties they have encountered in New York, she would like to return to her family in the island for good. Yet she has not done so because her husband wants to remain in New York, and New York has been good for the children and for their education.

Excerpt from

SPANISH HARLEM

Patricia Cayo Sexton

My days are swifter than a weaver's shuttle,
and are spent without hope. —Job

RENT STRIKE

It was natural that the rent strike, one of the most potent (if controversial and short-lived) direct action devices New York's poor have found, should have begun inside East Harlem.

The Community Council on Housing, led by Jesse Gray, had its offices in East Harlem. One of the first buildings struck was 16 East 117 Street, in East Harlem, owned by a matron living in Teaneck, New Jersey. After the strike began in this building, the landlord tried to dispossess the tenants. The court, inspecting building violations, ordered the rent paid to the court rather than the landlord. Later the city started receivership proceedings, and the rent money was returned to the tenants.

Mrs. Inocencia Flores, Apartment

Patricia Cayo Sexton, Spanish Harlem (New York: Harper and Row, 1965), p. 26. Francis Sugrue, "Diary of a Rent Striker," New York Herald Tribune, February 16, 1964, p. 28. Reprinted by permission.

3W, was among the striking tenants. Born in Puerto Rico, where she attended high school and for a time the University of Puerto Rico, she came to New York in 1944 and began work in the garment district, trimming and making clothes. At the time of the strike, she had four children, was on relief, and separated from her husband.

Her diary, kept while her building was on strike, tells part of her story.*

Wednesday, Feb. 5: I got up at 6:45. The first thing to do was light the oven. The boiler was broke so not getting the heat. All the tenants together bought the oil. We give $7.50 for each tenant. But the boiler old and many things we don't know about the pipes, so one of the men next door who used to be superintendent is trying to fix. I make the breakfast for the three children who go to school. I give them orange juice, oatmeal, scrambled eggs, and Ovaltine. They have lunch in school and some-

*Francis Sugrue, "Diary of a Rent Striker," New York Herald Tribune, February 16, 1964, p. 28.

times they don't like the food and won't eat, so I say you have a good breakfast. Miss Christine Washington stick her head in at 7:30 and say she go to work. I used to live on ground floor and she was all the time trying to get me move to third floor next door to her because this place vacant and the junkies use it and she scared the junkies break the wall to get into her place and steal everything because she live alone and go to work.

I'm glad I come up here to live because the rats so big downstairs. We all say the "rats is big as cats." I had a baseball bat for the rats. It's lucky me and the children never got bit. The children go to school and I clean the house and empty the pan in the bathroom that catches the water dripping from pipe in the big hole in the ceiling. You have to carry umbrella to the bathroom sometimes. I go to the laundry place this afternoon and I wash again on Saturday because I change my kids clothes every day because I don't want them dirty to attract the rats.

At 12:15 I am fixing lunch for myself and the little one, Tom. I make for him two soft boiled eggs and fried potatoes. He likes catsup and he has one slice of spam and a cup of milk. I have some spam for myself and salad because I only drank a cup of coffee at breakfast because I'm getting too fat. I used to work in the shipping department of bathing suits and the boss used to tell me to model for the buyers. I was a model, but now I'm too fat.

After I go out to a rent strike meeting at night, I come home and the women tell me that five policemen came and broke down the door of the vacant apartment of the ground floor where we have meetings for the tenants in our building. They come looking for

something—maybe junkies, but we got nothing in there only paper and some chairs and tables. They knocked them all over. The women heard the policemen laughing. When I come up to my place the children already in bed and I bathe myself and then I go to bed and read the newspaper until 11:30.

Thursday, Feb. 6: I wake up at six o'clock and I went to the kitchen to heat a bottle for my baby. When I put the light on the kitchen I yelled so loud that I don't know if I disturbed the neighbors. There was a big rat coming out from the garbage pail. He looks like a cat. I ran to my room, I called my daughter Carmen to go to the kitchen to see if the coast was clear. She's not scared of the rats. So I could go back to the kitchen to heat the bottle for my baby. Then I left the baby with a friend and went downtown.

Friday, Feb. 7: This morning I woke up a little early. The baby woke up at five o'clock. I went to the kitchen but this time I didn't see the rat.

After the girls left for school I started washing the dishes and cleaning the kitchen. I am thinking about their school. Today they ain't teaching enough. My oldest girl is 5.9 in reading. This is low level in reading. I go to school and English teacher tell me they ain't got enough books to read and that's why my daughter behind. I doesn't care about integration like that. It doesn't bother me. I agree with boycott for some reasons. To get better education and better teachers and better materials in school. I don't like putting them in buses and sending them away. I like to stay here and change the system. Some teachers has to be changed. My girl take Spanish in junior high school, and I said to her, "Tell your teacher I'm going to be in school one day to teach him Spanish because I don't know where he learns to teach Spanish but it ain't Spanish."

I'm pretty good woman. I don't bother anyone. But I got my rights. I fight for them. I don't care about jail. Jail don't scare me. If have to go to jail, I go. I didn't steal. I didn't kill nobody. There's no record for me. But if I have to go, I go.

Saturday, Feb. 8:　A tenant called me and asked me what was new in the building because she works daytimes. She wanted to know about the junkies. Have they been on the top floor where the vacant apartments is? That's why I have leaking from the ceiling. The junkies on the top floor break the pipes and take the fixtures and the sink and sell them and that's where the water comes. . . . I'm not ascared of the junkies. I open the door and I see the junkies I tell them to go or I call the police. Many people scared of them, but they scared of my face. I got a baseball bat for the rats and for the junkies. I sometimes see a junkie in the hallway taking the junk and I give him a broom and say "Sweep the hall." And he does what I tell him and hand me back the broom after he sweep the hall. I'm not scared of no junkies. I know my rights and I know my self-respect. After supper I played cards (casino) for two hours with the girls and later I got dressed and I went to a party for the rent strike. This party was to get funds to the cause. I had a good time. Mr. Gray was there dancing. He was so happy.

Sunday, Feb. 9:　I dressed up in a hurry to go to church. When I go to church I

pray for to have better house and have a decent living. I hope He's hearing. But I don't get discouraged on Him. I have faith. I don't care how cold I am I never lose my faith. When I come out of church I was feeling so good.

Monday, Feb. 10:　At 9:30 a man came to fix the rat holes. He charged me only $3. Then one of the tenants came to tell me that we only had oil for today and every tenant have to give $7.50 to send for more oil. I went to see some tenants to tell them there is no more oil. We all have to cooperate with money for the oil. It's very hard to collect because some are willing to give but others start fussing. I don't know why because is for the benefit of all, especially those with children. We have to be our own landlord and supers. We had to be looking for the building and I tell you we doing better than if there is an owner. Later I went down in the basement with another tenant to see about the boiler, but we found it missing water in the inside and she didn't light it up and anyway there was not too much oil in it. I hope nothing bad happens, because we too had given $5 each tenant to buy some material to repair the boiler. If something happens is going to be pretty hard to make another collection.

Tuesday, Feb. 11:　This morning was too cold in the house that I had to light the oven and heat hot water. We had no steam, the boiler is not running good. I feel miserable. You know when the house is cold you can't do nothing. When the girls left for school I went back to bed. I just got up at 11:30 and this house is so cold. Living in a cold apartment is terrible. I wish I could have one of those kerosene stoves to heat myself.

My living room and my room is Alaska. I'm going to heat some pea soup and make coffee. I sat down in the kitchen by the stove to read some papers and keep warm. This is terrible situation. Living the way I live in this slum house is miserable. I don't wish no body to live the way I live. Inside a house in this condition, no steam, no hot water, ceiling falling on you, running water from the ceiling, to go to the bathroom you have to use an umbrella, rats everywhere. I suggest that landlords having human being living this way instead of sending them to jail they must make them live at least a month in this same conditions, so they know the way they pile up money in a bank.

Wednesday, Feb. 12: I wake up around 5 o'clock and the first thing I did was light the oven and the heater so when the girls wake up is a little warm. I didn't call them to 11 because they didn't have to go to school. It still so cold they trembling. You feel like crying looking your children in this way.

I think if I stay a little longer in this kind of living I'm going to be dead duck. I know that to get a project you have to have somebody prominent to back you up. Many people got to the projects and they don't even need them. I had been feeling [filling] applications I don't know since when. This year I feel another one. My only weapon is my vote. This year I *don't vote* for nobody. May be my vote don't count, but don't forget if you have fourteen cent you need another penny so you take the bus or the subway. At least I clean my house and you could eat on the floor. The rest of the day I didn't do nothing. I was so mad all day long. I cooked a

big pot of soup. I leave it to God to help me. I have faith in Him.

Thursday, Feb. 13: I couldn't get up this morning. The house was so cold that I came out of bed at 7:15. I heated some water. I leave the oven light up all night because the heater gave up. I fixed some oatmeal, eggs and some Ovaltine for the girls. I had some coffee. I clean the house. The baby was sleeping. Later on, the inspector came. They were suppose to come to every apartment and look all violations. They knock at the door and asked if anything had been fixed. I think even the inspectors are afraid of this slum conditions thats why they didn't dare to come inside. I don't blame them. They don't want to take a rat or any bug to their houses, or get dirty in this filthy houses. My little girl come from school with Valentine she made for me. Very pretty. At 8:30 I went downstairs to a meeting we had. We discuss about why there is no heat. We agreed to give $10 to fix the boiler for the oil. A man is coming to fix it. I hope everybody give the $10 so we have some heat soon.

Friday, Feb. 14: I didn't write this about Friday in my book until this Saturday morning, because Friday night I sick and so cold I go to bed and could not write in the book. But this about Friday. I got up at five and light the oven and put some water to heat. At seven I called the two oldest girls for school. I didn't send the little one, because she was coughing too much and with a running nose. I gave some baby aspirin and I put some Vick in her nose and chest and I gave some hot tea. I leaved her in bed.

It was so cold in here that I didn't

want to do nothing in the house. I fixed some soup for lunch and read for a while in the kitchen and after a while I went out and clean the hallway. I didn't mop because there was no hot water, but at least the hallway looked a little clean.

Later on I fixed dinner I was not feeling good. I had a headache and my throat hurt. I hope I do not catch a cold. I hope some day God help me and all this experience I had be restore with a very living and happiness. It is really hard to believe that this happens here in New York and richest city in the world. But such is Harlem and hope. Is this the way to live. I rather go to the Moon in the next trip.

POVERTY ON THE LOWER EAST SIDE: 6 LIVE "HEAVY LIFE" ON $1 A DAY

Paul Montgomery

As the rain splashed in the grimy courtyard outside his apartment yesterday afternoon, Marcello Perez searched for the words that could describe his poverty.

"It's heavy, this life, you know?" he said.

Mr. Perez is 47 years old. For the last two months he has been feeding and clothing himself, his wife and their four young children on $1 a day. In all of 1963 he had $537 to spend on the essentials of life exclusive of rent, gas and electricity.

Mr. Perez is one of the 30 million Americans who live in families with yearly incomes of $2,000. Conservative estimates put the number of poverty-stricken New Yorkers at 815,000.

Both President Johnson and Mayor Wagner have declared their intention

of mounting full offensives against poverty.

Mr. Perez agrees with the President and the Mayor. If he were Mayor he would make poverty his prime concern, he said.

"You have money, I have money, we can make something," he observed yesterday. "But this way is no good. They should let us live."

Mr. Perez lives with his 42-year-old wife and four children ranging in age from 7 to 11 in five small rooms on Rivington Street. He gets the apartment rentfree for acting as janitor of the seven-story building.

He also gets free gas and electricity and $30 a month for his services. Until November he supplemented his income by working as a trucker's helper for a company that manufactures clothing. During good weeks he got 10 hours of work at $1.25 an hour; during bad weeks he got no work at all. He was laid off two month ago.

Mr. Perez would like to collect unemployment insurance, but does not because his former employer told him not to apply. "I don't want the boss to be angry with me and not give me the job back sometime," he explained.

Mr. Perez receives no help from the Welfare Department. He considered applying a few years ago but got impatient with the details and decided against "signing the paper." He wants to make some money and buy a nice home in Puerto Rico and he figures he cannot make much money if he gets on welfare.

His wife, a plump, jolly woman, keeps their apartment neat and clean. Mr. Perez painted it himself—white with blue trim.

The living room, about 10 feet square, contains the only furniture Mr. Perez has bought—blue couch and two orange chairs. He bought them seven years ago from the heirs of a tenant who died. They are covered with clear plastic to protect the upholstery. "The plastic cost $1.10 a yard," Mr. Perez said. "Every week I bought a yard until it was finished."

The three bedrooms are barely big enough to contain their double beds. A metal filing cabinet in one room serves as a chest of drawers. The room shared by the boys—Henry, 8, and Angelo, 7—has no window. They receive compensation, however, by having the only bed with sheets on it.

The girls—Estella, 11, and Betty, 9 —have three changes of clothing between them. The one that is not in use that day is hung neatly on the doorknob of their room. Mr. Perez owns two pairs of pants but one pair is at the cleaners and he has no money to retrieve it.

The kitchen—containing a sink, gas stove, refrigerator and a bare cupboard —is the largest room. The bathroom, off the kitchen, is the size of a large closet and has a bathtub and a toilet.

Mr. Perez thinks the apartment has certain advantages. There is always heat and hot water. The rats come only at night.

For breakfast yesterday the family had bread and milk. For supper there was rice and beans. The children get free lunch at school and Mr. and Mrs. Perez skip the midday meal. "We wait for night," Mr. Perez said.

The total outlay for the day's food was 50 cents for two quarts of milk, 15 cents for a loaf of bread, 25 cents for two pounds of rice and 10 cents for a half-pound of beans.

The last article of clothing Mr. Perez can remember buying was a pair of shoes for Henry "about a year ago." The family has gotten most of its clothing from a Catholic church nearby.

The family gets free medical care from the clinic at Bellevue. The three youngest Perez children were born there, the eldest in Puerto Rico.

For entertainment there is an old television set, given to Mr. Perez by his brother-in-law, that sometimes works, and a radio. There is no money for newspapers or books.

"If I see a paper on the street I pick it up and read it," Mr. Perez said. Movies are out of the question. Once a year the family goes to Coney Island.

Last spring the nearby House of Hospitality of the Catholic Worker movement, having nowhere else to turn, asked Mrs. Perez if she could put up a destitute old woman for a night.

The woman, who had psychopathic tendencies, had been ejected from city and charitable institutions. Mrs. Perez readily agreed, and housed and fed the woman for three months.

MIGRANT WORKERS
YOUTH

THEY HARVEST DESPAIR

Dale Wright

Robert Andrew Robinson unburdened himself of his family's belongings —the bedspread bundle of dirty laundry and the cardboard beer carton—and dumped them into a pile before one of the shanties. He led his wife, Mattie, the sleeping Adolphus in her arms, to a seat on the steps. Virginia Lee tagged along, carrying her rubber doll in one hand and clutching her tattered picture book in the other.

The sun angled obliquely over a corner of the camp clearing. The irrigation pump engine chugged with a mechanical, sometimes irregular tempo, spouting water through a large pipe to foam into a ditch on the way to the corn and tomato plants.

Robert leaned one shoulder against the wall of the cabin, thrust both hands into his pockets and eyed his family.

"Mattie," he said, "the bossman told us there ain't nothin' ready to pick here for a while. There ain't no food here neither, an' no stove to cook it on if we had some. Look like we got here too soon." He kicked a miniature fur-

row in the soft dirt, "We got to get somethin' to eat . . . an' quick!"

Mattie looked first at her husband, then at the baby. "That sure is the truth," she said. "He'll be mighty mean if I have no milk for him."

Adolphus stirred, rearranged himself more comfortably and went back to sleep. A crisis had been momentarily averted but it would come again.

To label Robert Andrew an easygoing man would be not to describe him at all. Superficially, the word would isolate one of his character traits. But there was more, much more, to him than gentle submissiveness. True, he was soft of nature, placid, easily led—or misled—and tractable to a fault.

What other manner of man would have bundled his family up at a moment's notice and blindly moved them and their beer-carton bedspread baggage, to the dead end of a backwoods farm-labor camp?

Robert was slight of stature, almost boyishly built, with slim tapered upper body and a small waistline. He was just a few inches over five feet in height and weighed not over 135 pounds.

Yet, the man was wiry and tough. Corded muscles stood out in his lean neck when he moved his head around to survey the tiny patch of the world around him. Strong, sun-blackened arms showed through his rolled-up-to-the-biceps shirtsleeves. There was every evidence that he had spent many long days at hard labor.

He was a man who, it appeared, existed for the purpose of being taken advantage of by others; but there was nothing in his manner which suggested the bitterness, the rancor which touched other men of his kind. He was a man to be told what to do—and he did it. He could be told what not to do—and he shunned it. He never entertained the thought that an order, even a suggestion, could operate to his disadvantage. It mattered only that he had been told what to do and he did, or did not, do it. His slim, youthful face was open and innocent, almost like that of a child. Every emotion, every thought, every fear —and every delight—was candidly inscribed upon his chocolate countenance. This, perhaps, was the reason that Mattie had married him. Beyond a doubt (it was clear in her tired eyes) she loved him. In the few short hours since we had met at the "loading grounds" in Homestead, I found that I had developed a special regard for him, too. Robert was truly an honest man; a man who knew nothing of vindictiveness.

I hunkered in the powdery dirt in the Robinson family circle. Roly-poly Adolphus still slept in his mother's arms, completely oblivious to all that went on around him. It was just as well. Occasionally he puckered his lips in the instinctive search of the young for a mother's breast. After a while Mattie allowed him to nurse.

The adventure of arriving at a new place overwhelmed Virginia Lee. She clung to her doll baby and her picture book as she took in the new sights. Her wide eyes left nothing unexplored. Everything in her view was a new source of amazement, an exciting discovery. She inspected the broken-down shanties, from the outside of course, and the rusting, wind-bent well digger. She listened to the ceaseless, irregular chugging of the irrigation pump.

She asked many questions of the people around her; and she was not very often satisfied with the answers she got, if she got any at all.

"Who's going to live here? Where are the other kids my momma said would be here? Where do we have to play?"

The little girl was most unlike her father. She accepted nothing at face value. Everything was to be scrutinized. The unfathomable was to be investigated.

There was one question she wanted to ask, but she didn't dare. It formed on her lips, then faded, unarticulated: Where was that school that momma said might be here?

The truth was that the child knew the answer. She had seen enough of the camp; she realized its remoteness; she knew it was abandoned, deserted. It would be the same as the last place, and the one before that. There was to be no school.

The little girl had been conditioned to disappointments and though this one hurt a little bit more than the others, she had cultivated (perhaps inherited) the rare kind of fortitude which helped her to shed the heartbreaks. She did not permit them to destroy her dreams.

The little girl broke away from the family group, head hung and silent, and shuffled around a corner in search of another part of the clearing to explore.

Her mother breathed an audible sigh of relief as she watched the child scuff through the dirt in her bare feet. She hadn't wanted to face the question;

now the inevitable answer could be postponed for a while.

The flame-red sun settled over the camp's shoulder into the trees and it became increasingly clear to Robert that the immediate problem was food. The crew leader had vanished somewhere in one of the trucks and there was muted grumbling and disorganized stirring about the camp as the men and women, and a few children, wandered aimlessly between the rows of cabins in search of somewhere to settle down.

There was no food about the place. The cabins were in no way ready for occupancy. Except for the irrigation pump, there was no water supply; nor were there toilets or other sanitary facilities. The last inhabitants of the camp had left the place in disarray, with miscellaneous debris and litter scattered around the shanties.

Robert dug a two-pound Maxwell House coffee can ("It's good to the last drop!") out of a mountain of equipment in the rear of one of the crew leader's trucks. He scooped a shallow hole in the dirt with a broken-handled hoe he found under one of the shanties. With brush and leaves and bits of paper, he built a fire in the hole, then placed four discarded vegetable tins at each corner. Over them he laid a rectangular sheet of metal roofing which he had found somewhere in the clearing.

Robert went about his task purposefully, methodically, as though he had a plan. Mattie watched as though she had seen it all done before. I watched with quiet amazement.

Despite all of his shortcomings, Robert was a resourceful man and that quality reinforced my own regard for him.

Dry wood and brush soon blazed under the sheet-metal roofing and Robert walked down the dirt road leaving the fire in his makeshift open-air stove to grow hotter. A few moments later he returned with two cabbages which he had torn from their roots in a nearby field.

He filled the coffee-can cookpot with water from the irrigation pump, then with his pocketknife, cut one of the cabbages into bite-size pieces and dumped them into the can. He placed it carefully on the stove and squatted beside it to wait.

After a time the hot water softened the unsalted cabbage and it was ready, as ready as it ever would be—the first meal for the Robinson family since they'd departed Homestead many hours —and more than three hundred miles— earlier.

Robert lifted the infant from his mother's arms to give her the first turn at the cookpot. With the pocketknife he had handed her she speared a few chunks of cabbage and put them into her mouth. She rolled them around for a moment, then began chewing slowly, reluctantly, hesitantly. At last she gave the pocketknife back to her husband.

Mattie Robinson had been weary when she climbed into Rudy Thompson's crew bus in Homestead, but now I saw a human being completely consumed by discouragement. She brushed her knotted, early-gray hair back with her hands as she fought with all the courage she could muster to hold back the tears. She locked her fingers tightly behind her back and looked away from her husband.

She pondered her plight: a long trip to nowhere, to poverty and hunger amid plenty. It was the way it had been before; it was the way it was now; it was the way it would be tomorrow.

This was the way of a migrant farm family.

At last the woman wept silently. Great tears welled up in her eyes, rolled heavily down both dark cheeks, and collected in pools in the wrinkles at the sides of her mouth. When the baby began to cry, she bent to take him from his father, and the tears fell onto the hot sheet-metal cookstove he had built.

Mattie didn't notice where her tears fell; she didn't hear them sizzle and dance and sputter away. She still wept silently, and a shudder began at the top of her head and fell like a dark shroud down over the length of her tired, sagging body.

Robert was unaware of his wife's fleeting confrontation with despair. He had been busy spearing pieces of boiled cabbage with his right hand while holding his son in his left arm.

That was the kind of man he was —and Mattie loved him.

It was the end of a punishing day, perhaps the most strength-sapping labor I had ever done. It took all the reserve I could muster just to wait in the line, then shuffle up to the bossman for my pay. Red was a few yards ahead of me and, by the time I had collected my little handful of change, he had already boarded Cowboy's bus for the trip home. When I sat down beside him, I found that he was ready to unburden himself of a few more thoughts, this time without my prodding. Though the weariness in my muscles and joints, the aches across my shoulders and back made conversation a real chore, I would not have lost a rare opportunity to share the thoughts of the slender, quiet man who thought more of his family than of the persistent cough that wracked his insides.

"You been worryin' me about the woman an' kids," he announced, "so I'm goin' to take you to see 'em. It ain't far from here, 'bout nine or ten miles up the way on the main highway. When you gits ready to leave, you can walk out to the road and ketch you a bus to Miami. Don't cost but a quarter or thirty-five cents. Ain't no space for you to stay for the night in that little shanty. Cowboy lets a whole gang of us off up at Goulds, an' he picks us up again in the morning."

By stretching imagination to the limit one might describe the place where Alonzo Fisher lived with his wife, Emily, and their five children as a single-dwelling unit in a suburban housing development. It qualified in one respect: it was just a dozen or so miles from Miami, within easy commuting distance. It sat in the midst of a cluster of similar residences on a two-acre plot of land a few hundred yards west of U. S. Highway No. 1. Scattered irregularly around the Fisher abode were ten or twelve one- and two-room shanties, all occupied, all of them of like construction. The shacks were in pretty much the same condition as Red's, which is to say that they appeared in imminent danger of collapsing into ten or twelve piles of debris. None were more than just barely habitable; their sameness also might have qualified them as part of a development, but that was as far as the projection could legitimately extend. Perhaps they had been constructed sometime in the distant past by the same builder. Or maybe they had been erected by different persons using the same plan, or no plan at all.

I arrived there with Red after a short walk from the roadside stop where Cowboy had paused briefly to let us hop off his crowded bus. We were at the tail end of a hard day's labor and the exertion had done nothing to improve the tall fellow's health. He was caught up in another coughing attack as he led me down a dirt road into a stand of pine trees. The development, nestled in a small V-shaped hollow, was shielded from view by a thick growth of wild underbrush. For anyone who didn't know the precise direction, the place would have been almost impossible to find. There was no name for the dirt pathway that led to the cluster of shanties; there was no number over Red's door, nor over the doors of his neighbors. His shack just stood there, unashamedly, the middle one in a row of three. A hill covered with waist-high foliage sloped away to the rear of the plot. You approached the Fisher place by picking your way, stumbling a little, down a small incline which was one side of the V. Beyond the crest of the other side there was a large warehouse-like building with piles of rusted road-construction machinery and bits and pieces of indistinguishable vehicles leaning against its walls. There was an air of decay and abandonment around the building, as if the owners had gone away four or five years ago with the intention of coming back and had later changed their minds. Weeds and grass had sprung up around a wheelbarrow propped against the warehouse door.

To the right of Red's shanty was a similar, though smaller, one. Its roof was of corrugated metal, perhaps zinc; its siding of red simulated-brick shingling. A hardware-store lock and a clasp anchored with carpenter's nails fastened the front door from the outside. A large washtub hung from a nail beside the door. Red's next-door neighbors, whoever they were, seemed not to be at home.

The door to the place on the left hung slightly ajar. Through it I could see a man, attired only in loafer-type oxfords and underwear, eating his evening meal. There was a loaf of grocery-store bread on the table, a stove-blackened coffeepot nearby and from a large plate the man scooped with considerable relish some manner of migrant-farm-laborer's fare. A huge black dog slumbered beneath the table, ignoring the clanking of silverware as the man busily shoveled whatever it was into his mouth in great spoonfuls, seemingly unaware of the two of us stumbling down the slope in the half-light of dusk.

From the pair of four-by-four timbers that supported the tiny porch in front of the Alonzo Fisher place hung a clothesline. From it, one quickly concluded that the family was predominantly female: rayon slips and panties of various sizes, an oversize brassiere, a half-dozen dishcloths and a bath towel or two. There was a single pair of men's work pants, and it was easy to see that they belonged to a stoop worker. They were worn thin at the knees and along the thighs there was the dark, telltale stain of the bug spray that neither scrub board nor washing machine would ever get out. Here, too, a washtub hung from a nail beside the door, and draped over the low rickety railing around the porch were a little girl's anklets and a pair of blue sneakers with white rubber soles, washed and set out to dry for wear the next day.

Four sets of cinder blocks supported the wood-frame shingled shanty at each of its four corners, elevating it perhaps two or two and one-half feet off the ground. Two additional stacks of cinder blocks somewhat precariously held up the tiny front porch. The uniformity of construction, so characteristic of housing developments, whether town or suburban, whether by accident or design, was just as evident in the back-country Dade County community where Alonzo Fisher lived with his family. Like all of its neighbors, this development was weather-worn and wind-beaten.

"Come on in," Red invited. "This place ain't nothin' special, but you said you wanted to meet the woman and them there chil'ren, an' see how we live. Ain't nothin' much to look at, but you're welcome to see. Been here 'bout two months now, since when the crops started to come in good. Season's 'mos down in this part of the country and we'll be gittin' on up the road, somewhere else."

Red's lumber - yard - brick castle measured some ten feet and a few odd inches across and twelve to fourteen feet from the threshold of the front door to the back wall. A kerosene lantern, its wick turned low to conserve fuel and minimize smoke, cast dim, flickering shadows on the walls. A blanket, hung from a clothesline, stretched across the right side of the room, dividing it into two compartments. The blanket hung to a point just short of the floor and behind it I could distinguish children's shoes and sneakers and socks and clothing under a bed.

Emily Fisher arose from her seat at the kitchen table. She was an ample woman, as striking for her girth and large bosom as her husband was for his elongated thinness. She got up slowly, leaning her full weight on the table for support, and grasping the back of a chair to pull herself erect. She was shy, reticent, even more withdrawn than her husband; the mere act of nodding her head in acknowledgment of his introduction was obviously a difficult task. I did not add to her discomfort by probing questions such as I had been putting to Red during the day.

"How ya do?" she mumbled and slid back into her chair by the table with noticeable effort, again grasping the chair back for support and resting one hand on the table. There were the remains of the evening meal: a plate of fried chicken, a pan of cornbread, a few boiled potatoes, and a green leafy vegetable.

To the left of the entrance door, immediately inside, stood a two-burner kerosene stove, a coffeepot on one burner, a frying pan on the other, its bottom covered with a film of the grease in which Emily Fisher had cooked the chicken. There was a sink next to the stove, but there were no faucets for running water. The back of the sink was mounted in some way on the wall. The two front corners were supported by wood posts which were nailed to the floor. Though a drainpipe led from the drain hole in the back of the sink through the wall to the outside, I could not find at first glance any source of water supply. Red cleared that point up when he saw me inspecting the sanitary facilities. He reached under the sink, felt around for a moment, and drew out a bucket of water. The bucket was the kind housewives generally use for scrubbing, but he dipped water from it, poured it into a glass and handed it to me. It was for drinking.

"You want some?" he inquired.

I declined with profuse thanks. The memory of the tall fellow's frequent unrelieved seizures were to remain forever etched in my mind. And there was the thought that two of his young children had the same kind of rumbling cough. . . .

A three-quarter-size mattress on a steel frame occupied most of the space along the back wall. There was a chair at the head of the bed and a slop jar, for late night toileting, at the other end. The bed was covered with a rough, off-white muslin sheet tucked and folded neatly at each corner, hospital style. A heavy olive-drab blanket was folded across the foot of the bed, but there were no pillows. There was a window in the center of the back wall directly over the bed, but a wrinkled green blind had been thumbtacked over it, so that there was no view from the rear of the Fisher shack. Another window above the kerosene stove looked out over the shanty next door, the one occupied by the man we had seen eating his dinner in his undershirt.

"The kids is asleep, all of 'em," Red declared as he draped his long frame over a chair. "You c'n see 'em if you want to, but they's all asleep. Don't wake 'em up! Look behind that blanket hangin' up an' that's where they are."

I had so much wanted to see and talk to them. I wanted to know some of the facts of a migrant-farm-worker's life through the eyes of his children, but I was reluctant to disturb their slumber. I pulled back a corner of the divider blanket and the errant rays of the kerosene lantern threw tiny fingers of light into the gloom. The three youngest children lay sleeping crosswise on one bed. It was a sagging, mesh-spring piece of antiquity and the small forms were spread-eagled wherever they could find space. The stale odor of damp, moldy cotton was mixed with the moist tang of human perspiration in the tiny space. Two other children slept close together on a narrow cot next to the larger bed. From somewhere in the dark corner nearest the right wall came the heavy, labored breathing of one of the children, gasping, fighting to fill his lungs with more air. Springs creaked as one

of the tiny forms shifted in a subconscious search for more space.

A feeling of nausea crept up from my stomach into my throat and I dropped the corner of the blanket back into place. There in the darkness of that broken-down red-shingled shack, I saw and smelled and heard the hopelessness, the futility, of one migrant-farm-worker's family. I knew the sickness that lived in one man's chest, the same agony that—along with inadequate and improper food—had already sent two of his little ones to their graves.

"Toilet's out in the back," Mrs. Fisher volunteered, perhaps detecting a look of illness on my face. "Whole lots of folks use it," she added, "so if it's busy, you go out in the woods. When we can't wait, we goes out 'hind a tree." This was a rare burst of volubility for Red's woman, but she warmed up even more: "Maybe twenty-five or thirty people uses that toilet, 'cluding a lot of kids. Most times we can tell when it's busy, 'cause the door squeaks one way when you goes in and another way when you comes out. Ain't heard no squeakin' noises in a spell, so I guess you can go if you want to."

I was anxious to get out of the heavy, foul air of Mr. and Mrs. Alonzo Fisher's shanty, but I was there as an invited guest and there simply was no escape, not for a while.

So we talked for half an hour or so and I learned that they rented the place from a landlord named Mr. Clay, but they saw him, or one of his numerous sons or agents, only on Saturday morning when the rent was due. There was no heat in any of the dwellings, with the exception of the kerosene cookstove; and there was no light except for the kerosene lanterns that each family had purchased down the road at the general merchandise store which Mr. Clay and his sons ran.

It was the lot of Alonzo (Red) Fisher to live and sleep and eat—and suffer—with his woman and his five children in this back-country Dade County suburban housing development, along with ten or twelve neighbor migrant-farm-labor families. They shared these mean quarters with an assortment of vermin, insects, and other crawling, slithering things, the true census of which no one knew. It was a pitiable environment, pregnant with all of the elements conducive to disease and early fatality; the kind of evil atmosphere in which the Fisher young ones suffered and strained for breath in their moldy, creaking mesh-spring bed behind the hanging blanket. It was marginal living in all of its shocking crudity, a dozen or so miles from plush Miami.

Alonzo and Emily Fisher's children had been conceived, born, and reared in a succession of such migrant-farm-labor settlements. So, for that matter, had Red and his wife. Demanded from them for their existence on this tiny portion of Mr. Clay's land was $13.50 every Saturday morning when one of the sons or the agents came by. It was just enough space to be born in; it was at the same time enough to lay down and die in.

Mrs. Isabelle Johnson, the mother of three, occupied the two-room unit in the center of the long building.

She shooed the flies away from an infant asleep in a cot and declared, "That child ain't got a chance. His daddy and me want to give him the best, but we can't do no better than this."

Mrs. Johnson had been a tenant at the camp for three years. She had moved there with her husband on her first visit to central New Jersey on the season.

"Well, it was like this," she explained. "My husband got laid off from his job at that sawmill near Essex, Virginia. There was this busload of people going through, so we got on. We heard all the talk about a lot of work in the fields in New Jersey at good wages. We didn't have nothing to lose, so we got on and came here.

"The first year wasn't so bad," the young mother related, "and we moved into this place kind of temporary. Me and my husband both worked in the tomato fields. Then when potatoes were ready, we picked up behind the digging machine. We even bought a second-hand car and George drove it back and forth to the different jobs he found. But I started having babies one right after the other and now we can't get out of this place. Can't find no landlords that take farm people with children, so we got to stay here."

Mrs. Johnson and her husband, George, paid $15 weekly rent for the two rooms they lived in. There was no bath, no indoor plumbing, and no sanitary facilities—only the community outhouse to the rear, which they shared with the rest of the tenants. The only time they knew that a landlord existed was when he sent a rent collector around on Saturday morning. The owner rarely appeared. The couple wanted desperately to return to Virginia with their children, where they would be with the rest of their families and friends, but because of the weekly rent, expenses for food and medicine and other necessities, they were unable to save enough for the trip.

"We're stranded here in this awful place," Mrs. Johnson lamented, "and there just ain't a thing we can do."

Another tenant, Edward Dalton, a sixty-two-year-old native of Durant, Mississippi, told a similar story. He had arrived with a migrant crew early one spring to find that the crops he had been brought in to harvest were not ready. "I left that outfit and came into the 'duck ranch.' Started working for the man who owns this place in trade for my rent—cleaning them outhouses and doing odds and ends around here like that. He don't always pay me money for the work I do; sometimes it's groceries and meat he gets from the supermarket in Riverhead after they don't want it no more.

"Sure would like to get me 'nough money together to get back to Mississippi. Won't never come back here no more."

Mr. Warner's spotlessly white grocer's smock seemed out of place in the dim, cluttered general store when I stopped in to chat with him. Crates and boxes and cartons littered the aisle, and toward the rear more cartons were stacked almost to the low ceiling. Occasionally customers who lived on the site came in for milk, or bread, or canned goods, or meat.

I asked him how his tenants were doing.

"They're all happy people here," he said grimly. "I look out for them when nobody else will. Nobody don't want these people. Some of them are on relief. I'm the only one that gives 'em a place to live. I sell 'em their food here, and sometimes they can get it on credit when they don't have the cash. Sometimes I see that they're taken care of when they're sick. What more do they need? They're all happy here. Look around for yourself and see."

I accepted Mr. Warner's invitation. I did look—and I saw. At the time of my first visit in the summer of 1961, and again in September, 1964, there was running water in only a few of the shacks and indoor toilets in almost none. The water supply, for cooking, washing, bathing, and other uses, came from several community pumps supplied by two 1,000-gallon storage tanks. Cesspools received the toilet and sink drainage in the few converted residences that had plumbing, but rainwater simply stagnated in pools around the place until it was absorbed in the sandy earth.

Tin cans, garbage, the wrecks of scavenger-looted automobiles and all manner of other debris littered the grounds. The cockroach and vermin infestation was almost beyond belief. There were no fire hydrants or other fire-fighting devices anywhere on the site, though construction of the buildings and general living conditions made them highly inflammable.

A half-naked little girl of about four hopped and skipped among the debris near Mr. Warner's general store. From the cabin where she lived with her mother, across the dirt street, came the strong, pungent odor of Southern-style cooking. The child darted and danced around the scattered, rotting lumber and rusted machinery parts. She chattered and sang to herself in obvious delight with her own game. Her playmates were a scraggly, flea-bitten mongrel, a kitten and a few chickens. Her toys: a rusty, wobbly tricycle that didn't run and a length of rope to skip. The child was enjoying herself. Clearly she was one of Mr. Warner's happy tenants.

She had been born and nursed at her mother's breast in a single room in one of the duck sheds; she slept there in a bed at her mother's side. When the roof leaked, she got wet, and on cold winter nights when heat from the kerosene stove didn't penetrate the corners of the little room, she was cold, along with her mother and her two playmates —the little mongrel and the kitten that had come along and joined in her games one day. She was happy because she didn't yet know any other way to be. Perhaps she would never know that another, far different world lay somewhere beyond the trees that surrounded the duck ranch, a world through which other folks rode on the Long Island Railroad to Easthampton and Westhampton and Southampton, even as far out as Montauk Point, then back to their comfort in the city. Perhaps the little girl would not survive long enough to learn of the things and people and places which the trees concealed from her view.

PEONAGE IN FLORIDA

Robert Coles/Harry Huge

Around October, cold spells begin to reach up North and into the Midwest, and thousands of Americans remind themselves that in a nation as large as ours, spread out over so many latitudes, a willing traveller can find summer anytime. So the trek to Florida begins. The southern part of the state begins to bulge with the rich and the not-so-rich, the owners of winter homes and the one-week guests who fill up thousands of hotels, motels and rooming houses.

Others also manage a return to Florida in October, though to get there they don't use jets or toll roads. Often they even shun our new and free interstate roads, and if asked why, they demur, or quickly assert their wish to move quietly, to attract nobody's attention. Yet, they do get attention. When they arrive at a state line, they may be met by the police and told to go right through, fast and with no stops at all; if they should try to pause here and there, to use a rest-room or enter a restaurant, they are quickly singled out and shouted

at and pushed away. The owner of one gas station in Collier County, Florida told us who these other winter visitors are: "They're dirty, the migrants. They'll come by, and I tell them to scram. They'll ruin your restrooms for good, inside an hour. Sure, we need them here, to pick the crops, but that's all they're good for, if you ask me, and I've lived here all my life and seen them come and go each year. I'll tell you—I don't even want to sell them gas. You know why? We're a first-class station, and if tourists or the regular people here drove up and saw those migrants around, they'd go somewhere else with their business, and I wouldn't blame them. You don't come from up North all the way to Collier County, only to find yourself standing next to—the likes of them."

What are they like? Where do they come from and how do they live, the some one-hundred-thousand migrant farmers who each year harvest Florida's vegetables and fruit, worth millions of dollars?

Actually we don't know all there is to know, because the migrants commonly slip by census-takers or local officials charged with recording births and deaths. Nomads, itinerants, wanderers, they live everywhere and no-

Reprinted by permission of The New Republic, © 1969, Harrison-Blaine of New Jersey, Inc.

where. Each county of each state calls them someone else's responsibility, though in all places the terribly hard and demanding work they do is considered essential. Nor has the federal government ever seen fit to step in and say, yes they will in a sense belong to all of us, for whose benefit, after all, so much of that travelling and stopping and cutting and picking is done. On the contrary, migrant farmers are denied just about every benefit that 30 years of struggle achieved for other workers —such as the right to organize into labor unions without harassment and bargain collectively with employers, and the right to get unemployment insurance or a degree of compensation for injuries sustained at work. Most migrants can't vote, are ineligible for any kind of welfare or other advantages and services that towns or counties offer their residents.

Here is how one migrant worker talked to us about his life as a virtual peon: "Well sir, I was born in Louisiana, I was; my daddy worked there on shares, and before him my granddaddy, and I guess it goes back to slavery. (My granddaddy, he'd tell us about all the slaves he used to know, and how one by one they died, and when the last slave died—I mean that was a slave before they was all set free—well my granddaddy, he said his mother said she hated to see him die, but it was just as well we tried to forget about slavery.) I guess I thought I was going to stay there, in Louisiana, but I sure didn't, I'll tell you. I was thirteen or fourteen, I think it was, and my daddy was telling us that we were in real bad trouble, because the government up in Washington was giving the bossman a lot of money, and in return he wasn't doing as much planting as before; and

what he was planting, he was going to do it all by machine and he didn't need us anymore to pick the crops. So, he told us we could stay there in the cabins, but that was all, and the sooner we went up to Chicago the better, he said, and my daddy was all set to go with us, but we got the message that his sister up there had died all of a sudden, and he got scared to go.

"I remember him saying that if we went up there, we'd all die like his sister, and if we stayed down on that plantation, we'd not last long, and so there wasn't anything to choose— except that one day a man came along, and he was going from door to door, he said, and signing people up for work, to pick the crops he said, over in Florida. And he told us, I remember, that all our worries was over, and all we had to do was go on over there with him and the others and do what we knew to do, pick some beans and some tomatoes and like that, and it wasn't any different from working on cotton, and maybe easier, he said. So daddy told us he thought we should go, and there was, I think, five or six families he got, just from our bossman's place; and of course he got others. And would you believe it that they had these buses, four of them I recall, and they put us on them, and they looked like the school buses, only they were older, much older, and soon we were on the road, yes sir; and I'll tell you, it's been a lot of that ever since, moving here and there and everywhere, until you don't know where you're at and how you'll ever stop. Believe me, sir, we wants to stop and find us a place to live, all year round, like other folks do. But if you're trying to eat, and you owe them all that money, and you have to eat while you try to get even and not be owing them, well then, you just have to go up North and come back, or else they'll have you in jail, I'll tell you that, or worse than that, much worse, they'll just go and pull the trigger, I believe some of them might, if you tried to run free of them. And I'd like to know where you could go even if they let you, and they didn't try to stop you, and they didn't call the sheriff, and they even drove you where you wanted to go. We wouldn't know where to go, because the people, they just don't want us, to use their restrooms or even buy from them. They'll tell you to 'git,' and they sure mean it, you can tell on their face by the way they looks down on you."

His story is not unusual. Thousands of sharecroppers and tenant farmers have gone North to our cities, where they frequently found no work and went on welfare. Thousands of other field hands have given their lives to constant travel and the hardest, most menial jobs, for which they are called "lazy" and "shiftless" and paid the lowest possible wages. (Only recently did farm workers come under the protection of the minimum-wage law, and their minimum wage just moved up from $1.15 to $1.30 per hour, whereas other workers are guaranteed $1.60 per hour.) Worse, migrants like the man just quoted fall victim to a kind of peonage that seals not only their fate but that of their children. They are brought to Florida, whole families or single men or single women or groups of teen-aged children. The men who bring them are called "contractors" or "crew leaders," and are paid, say, "50 dollars a head" (their words), by growers. The frightened, confused former sharecroppers and their children are housed in camps and put to work, but soon they discover that in return for long hours on their knees out in the fields they will get very little cash. For one thing, in the course of a year there are days, even weeks, when there is no work to be had. The migrants move from one camp to another, and become part of a world few outsiders know anything about. The camps have their own stores and vendors, and are often guarded by "camp boys" who walk around with guns. Migrants are told they cannot leave unless all their debts are paid; the ledgers are tallied by the men who own and run the camps.

"There's always something you owe them," we kept on hearing as we talked with one migrant after another. From Rodolfo Juarez, a new and young leader of Mexican-American migrants in Florida (they make up about half the state's agricultural workers), we heard it spelled out: "I was born in South Texas, in San Benito, and when I was about fifteen I was sold, that's right. They came and got a whole group of us and told us there was a lot of money to make up North and over in Florida, if we just went along with them, and they'll take us and even feed us. I now know they got so much money from the growers for each body they brought up from Texas. Well, we were living like animals where we were, and getting practically nothing for doing crop work in south Texas, so we thought: why not? why not? I was taken up to Indiana and Ohio, to work on farms there, and then we tried to break out, but it's hard. They tell you that you owe them for the food and the transportation and the mattress on the floor you use for sleeping, and they tell you that if you try to leave, they'll get you thrown in jail and you'll never get out until you pay your bills. How else can you pay them but by going back to work for them, and when you do that, you have to eat and you have to sleep somewhere and a lot of the time there's no work, until it's time to harvest, and so you're their property, that's what it amounts to with some of those contractors. They own people, that's what, unless they escape, like I did; but I'll tell you the truth, a lot of migrants—you know, they're Mexican-Americans like me, or black people, and a few are white, yes, but not many —they're not aware of their rights, and they're scared, and they should be. Have you seen them patrolling some of those camps? The men will ride around with guns, and the crew leaders will herd the people into the trucks to go picking. They stand them up and they look like cattle going to the market, and that's no exaggerating."

We visited the camps and the fields all through Collier County and Palm Beach County. We saw the same sites that recently shocked Senator McGovern's Select Committee on Nutrition and Human Needs: broken-down shacks, some without even windows, some nothing more than enlarged outhouses without running water or heat, a few even without electricity, all of which rent for $10, $15, even $20 a week. The drinking water is often contaminated, taken as it is from superficial wells located near garbage-filled swamps. Children are supposed to walk a quarter of a mile or more to unspeakably inadequate outdoor privies. There are no showers, no baths, no stoves and often no refrigerators. Entire families live in one room, sleep, if lucky, on mattresses, live on soda pop and bread and grits and fat-back and cheap candy. Yet, Collier County has no food-stamp program, no commodity food pro-

gram, and no welfare program for migrants, who have been called by local officials "federal people," or "not our people." In Collier County's Immokalee, an Indian word which ironically means "my home," we saw children not only hungry and malnourished, but obviously and seriously ill, yet never seen by physicians. Born "on the road," brought up on buses and trucks, or carried from farm to farm in cars, left to themselves in the fields and, when twelve or thirteen, quietly put to work in the fields, they nevertheless have to be considered fortunate if they are still alive, since the infant mortality rate for such children in places like Collier County is estimated to be about five times that of other American children. The children are badly frightened and confused. They live unstable, chaotic lives and feel at loose ends, worthless, virtually dead.

One of us spent two years studying migrant children in Belle Glade and Pahokee, Florida, and we recently went to see some of those children, a little older now but still to be found (through a minister) in one of the camps: "Yes, we're soon to be going north again," a ten-year-old boy told us. "I'm afraid each time that we won't get back here, but we do." How did school go for him this year: "Well, I didn't get there much. We moved from place to place, and I helped with the picking a lot, and the schools, when you go to them, they don't seem to want you, and they'll say that you're only going to be there a few weeks anyway, so what's the use." What does he want to do when he gets older? "I don't know. I'd like to stay someplace, I guess, and never have to leave there for the rest of my life, that's what. I could have a job—maybe it would be where they make cars and trucks and planes. I could make plenty of money, and bring it home, and we'd all live on it, my brothers and my sister. But my mother says someone has to pick the crops, and we don't know what else there is to do, and they'll come and beat you and throw you in the canal, the crew leaders, if you cross them; and then you'd be dead in one minute. So, we'd better stay with the crops; because my mother is probably right. I hope I never fall in one of those canals. You can never get out. They're deeper than the ocean I hear. I've never seen the ocean, but I know it's not far away."

The ocean is indeed nearby—Palm Beach and all its glitter to the east, and to the west the more sedate but no less wealthy Naples, the seat of Collier County's government. One can drive the major roads of Palm Beach County or Collier County and get no idea what is happening down those dusty pathways that lead to fields and camps and "loading zones" where human beings are picked up and left off. "There's no end to it," a migrant mother said to us in Immokalee, "you just hope you'll die in between picking-time, so you're resting. I'd hate to die on the road, yes sir; my children, they'd never find their way back to Florida. I guess that's our home, yes sir. We spend more time there than in the other states; but I'll say this, they're not very good to us there, if you ask for anything."

What has she asked for? What does she need that Collier County might supply, particularly since the county's officials have publicly acknowledged that without migrant workers like her its huge farms and its dozens of well-equipped packing houses would be worthless? She is, of course, rather modest when she talks about her needs.

She'd like good food for her children, particularly during those weeks when she is waiting for work. (The migrant's average annual income is $1,700 a year.) She would like to be paid in full for her work. (Migrants repeatedly claim they are short-changed—given, say, five dollars at the end of a day and told that for "meals and transportation" they have been charged another five.) She would like to find decent housing and pay a reasonable amount of rent: "In Immokalee a few white men own everything. They push us into those little rooms, one for each family, and you pay $20 a week. If you go to the camps, after they deduct the rent you've got no money left, and they tell you that you owe them some, on top of it."

She is not about to fight things out with Collier County's officials. We saw a little of what frightens her—those "camp-boys" and labor contractors driving pick-up trucks fitted with gun racks that hold three or four rifles. We saw a jail in Immokalee, only recently abandoned, whose cramped and primitive quarters must rival anything that ever was or is in Siberia. On the other hand, we met up with a fine group of lawyers who are fighting hard for that woman and others like her under a program called the South Florida Migrant Legal Services, begun in April, 1967 under an OEO grant. Lawyers cannot by their exertions alone bring social and economic justice to a group of people variously called in the last two or three years, not a half century ago, "the slaves we rent" or "serfs upon the land" or "America's wretched of the earth." Yet, every day migrants feel themselves victimized, cheated, deceived; and they have no past experience with lawyers, no money for them, and no belief that a law suit will lead to anything. Now, for the first time, some of those Florida migrants have found out that there are intelligent and compassionate men who know the law and are ready to represent the interests of people who haven't a cent to offer for legal fees. No social revolution has occurred in Florida, but at least a few complaints on behalf of the migrants are being made—and as a result the growers and crew-leaders and labor contractors and real estate groups that employ migrants and herd them about and rent shacks to them have become convinced that the South Florida Migrant Legal Services must be brought to an end very soon, when the OEO grant runs out. Florida's political leaders are putting strong pressure on OEO to refuse another grant, and though the agency's staff reportedly has high praise for the program, the real test will come not only when (and if) refunding takes place, but after Governor Kirk exercises his expected veto, and OEO's new chief, Donald Rumsfeld, decides either to stand firm and override the veto or allow one of the agency's best programs to be killed. It is, too, a program that aims to change things through legal action, through reliance on court orders and "due process," those quiet, slow, patient maneuvers we are daily urged to respect.

Meanwhile, Senators come and are horrified and ashamed. Tourists drive by and if they see anything, shake their heads and wonder how many miles to the next Holiday Inn. People like us quickly find ourselves out of Collier County's Immokalee and safely in Collier County's Naples—where we can eat well and take a swim, and give vent to our confusion and sadness and most galling, our frustration: how can our words do justice to the misery and heart-ache we have seen, and how can we describe and make unforgettable the worried, pained faces of boys and girls whose bodies are thin and covered with sores and bites and covered also with Florida's rich muckland, whose crops those children have harvested? Back in Immokalee we were offended, disgusted; later in Naples there was the tropical green water and the soft sand and a long, long pier where we could stand and discuss things with Michael Foster and Michael Kantor, two resourceful young lawyers who work for the South Florida Migrant Legal Services in Collier County and every day try to get housing codes enforced, and money paid to people who have bent and stooped from dawn to dusk, only to be denied their rightful earnings, or who have gone for weeks without work, without unemployment compensation, without relief payments.

We stood on the pier for a long time and looked at sworn affidavits that had been taken six months ago and sent up to the Justice Department, affidavits that spell out the details of peonage: "From October 17, 1968 until late in November 1968, I was only paid wages of $5.50. I went to the camp authorities to ask why I had been paid so little and they merely responded they had paid three doctors bills for me and that I was not due any money at this time. To the best of my knowledge I did not have three doctor bills while I was at Camp Happy." During her stay she "had many problems" with the camp guards. She was beaten, thrown across a room, told she might be killed. When she asked to leave, one of the camp's guards said "I could not go because I owed $25 to the company." What is more, others kept on arriving to share her fate: "On January 11, 1969, a bus with forty-two people arrived from the state of Mississippi. . . . Around half of these persons were under sixteen years of age and were not accompanied by adults. The man who brought the children to the camp was paid $15 for each person he brought." And finally, so that everybody at Camp Happy was kept happy, "persons also used to come from Fort Myers and sell narcotics at the camp. I did not know the names of these persons. They carried on their activities with the full consent of those who operated the camp."

What is to be done? The two lawyers told us they could only keep trying, keep pressing matters through the courts—though even that method has caused an uproar among Florida's political leaders. We said we could report on what we had seen and learned, even though we know that in past decades reports have been written and written—and the evident futility of all those words must haunt those who wrote them. Perhaps, we speculated, the only answer to the problem is one suggested by a tough, angry "community organizer"—an "outside agitator," no doubt about it, we met near Immokalee: "Look, you people can do your lawyering and your doctoring and your writing, but a lot of good it will do these people. They're in bondage, don't you see that? They're treated like animals— in a country that's the richest, fattest country in the world. They have no constituency, that's the problem. They don't even have the kind of constituency the

blacks do in Mississippi—you know, the Northern liberals, with the voting laws they've put through, and like that. These people have nothing to fall back on but the conscience of the nation, and a lot of good that's done for them. I'll tell you, there's only one way to change things here in Florida, in Collier County. Over there in Naples there's Roger Blough of United States Steel, and there's the president of Grant's department store, and there's the president of Eli Lilly, and all the rest. They have it nice here in Florida. There's no personal income tax, and there's no tax on the corporations. I'll bet if the migrants started marching down that highway 846 to Naples, and fought their way to that Gulf Shore Boulevard there—well, I'll bet the people who live there would call in those sheriffs and county commissioners, and they'd call in the politicians who do what they're told to do, and say to all of them: boys, give them a bigger slice, because we don't want any more trouble here. You hear that! And then the migrants would be a little better off and you guys, you'd praise yourselves and all your attitudes and say like you always do: democracy, it's wonderful!"

We are in no danger of the kind of middle-class self-congratulations he scornfully described—the kind that follows a successful uprising of the poor. For there's no danger the migrants will be causing anyone much trouble. They will roam the land, follow the sun and the crops, harvest our food, and go on getting just about nothing.

MEXICAN AMERICAN YOUTH

Excerpts from

MEXICAN AMERICAN YOUTH: FORGOTTEN YOUTH AT THE CROSSROADS

Celia S. Heller

DISTINGUISHING CHARACTERISTICS

In physical appearance Mexican American youth are far from homogeneous. As George Sanchez describes them, "Biologically, they range over all the possible combinations of, first, their heterogeneous Spanish antecedents, and, then, the *mestizaje* resulting from the crossing of Spaniards and various indigenous peoples of Mexico. . . ."[2] To this, one could add that insofar as they are predominantly American born, they are also apt to show some physiological effects of the American environment. An anthropological investigation

has discovered that, similar to the children of other immigrant groups in the United States,* the American-born sons of Mexican-born fathers display such physical changes as increase in stature, hand length, and decrease in nasal index.[3]

The *differentia specifica* between the Mexican American and the Anglo American youth is not United States birth but rather non-Mexican origin. Because of common misconceptions, it should be stressed that nine out of ten Mexican American youths (ages 15 to 19) are native born, and that both parents of six out of ten were born in the

* In 1912 Franz Boas first demonstrated that American-born descendants of immigrants undergo bodily changes, but the cause of such changes, apart from the increase in stature, is as yet unknown. (See: Ashley Montagu, *Human Heredity*, New York: Mentor Books, 1960, pp. 101–2.)
[3] Marcus S. Goldstein, *Demographic and Bodily Changes in Descendants of Mexican Immigrants*, Austin: University of Texas, Institute of Latin-American Studies, 1943; M. F. Ashley Montagu, *An Introduction to Physical Anthropology*, Springfield: Charles C Thomas, 1951, p. 423.

Footnote 1 does not appear in excerpt.
[2] Carey McWilliams, *North from Mexico—The Spanish-Speaking People of the United States*. Philadelphia: Lippincott, 1949, p. 42.

United States. Thus the majority are at least third-generation American.[4]

Whether they are first, second, or third generation, their principal language, especially in interpersonal relationships, seems to be a form of American Spanish, that is, a local Spanish dialect heavily intermingled with hispanized English terms and anglicized Spanish words. The Texas Spanish, for example, is known as "Tex-Mex."[5] A highly specialized dialect is *Pachuco*, but since it is mainly the language of delinquent youths, we shall describe it in Chapter Five, which focuses upon this subject.

Many of the children were first introduced to English in school. That the schools largely fail in their minimal function of teaching the native tongue to Mexican Americans is reflected in the language difficulties with which these youths are plagued. Although no systematic studies of their language pattern have been conducted in recent years,* various writers have emphasized their language handicap and have noted that a foreign accent in English is common among second- and third-generation Mexican American youths.[6] This is a cause of considerable embarrassment and often results in their feeling self-conscious when in contact with Anglo Americans. Frequently Mexican American youths are deficient in informal English: they do not know how to "kid" or use "small talk," so important in everyday encounters. Still, they do not, as a rule, seem to encourage the rare efforts of Anglo Americans to speak Spanish to them, but tend to respond in English. It is likely that they perceive such attempts as a way of "talking down" to them. Also, they seem embarrassed by their "poor Spanish."

The language problem of the Mexican Americans, however, is not insurmountable. Both common sense and available research[7] indicate that language does not necessarily have to be a permanent intellectual handicap for children born into foreign-language-speaking homes. Furthermore, any programs geared to overcoming the English language difficulties of Mexican American children would have in their

---

[4] Calculations based on 1960 Census figures which appear in: *Persons of Spanish Surname*, Final Report PC (2)—1B, Washington, D.C., 1963, Table 2.

[5] Muzafer Sherif and Carolyn W. Sherif, *Reference Groups—Exploration into Conformity and Deviation of Adolescents*, New York: Harper and Row, 1964. p. 169, Table 2.

* The latest work is that of George C. Barker, "Social Functions of Language in a Mexican-American Community," *op. cit.*, pp. 185–202. The recent Racine and Pomona studies do report on the language of Mexican Americans but they are based on the questioning of adults about their own and their children's language rather than on observation. Furthermore, the language of the children in Racine and Pomona may lean more toward English as compared with the children of the Southwest in general. (See: Shannon and Krass, *op. cit.*, p. 299; Penalosa, *op. cit.*, pp. 104–20.)

[6] Ossie G. Simmons, "Anglo-Americans and Mexican-Americans in South Texas." Unpublished Ph.D. dissertation, Harvard University, 1952, pp. 407, 419–20; Richard G. Thurston, "Urbanization and Socio-cultural Change in a Mexican-American Enclave." Unpublished Ph.D. dissertation, University of California, Los Angeles, 1957, p. 205; Leonard Broom and Eshref Shevky, "Mexicans in the United States—A Problem of Social Differentiation," *Sociology and Social Research* 36 (January and February 1952), p. 153; Margaret Clark, *Health in the Mexican-American Culture*, Berkeley: University of California Press, 1959, pp. 24–25.

[7] Leona E. Tyler, *The Psychology of Human Differences*, New York: Appleton, 1956, p. 305.

favor the factor of Mexican heritage of verbal articulateness. Verbal mastery is a highly cherished value among Latin American males of all classes and finds reflection in the fluency of language and extensiveness of vocabulary even among those of humble origin and position.[8]

One of the few programs is the campaign started by LULAC, a Mexican American voluntary organization (League of United Latin American Citizens), to teach children going into elementary school four hundred basic English words. The campaign was subsequently taken up by the state authorities in Texas.[9] But apart from such programs, distinct changes are coming to the forefront. These should be noted especially because the preservation of the Spanish language by Mexican Americans has been interpreted as "a persistent symbol and instrument of isolation."[10] It has been observed that from the Anglo point of view the wide use of Spanish is the primary symbol of the "foreignness" of the Mexican Americans, but from the latters' viewpoint it is the primary symbol of loyalty to La Raza.[11] And yet one notices the

beginning of a new pattern of language behavior among Mexican Americans today which manifested itself among other immigrant groups in the second generation. Parents speak American Spanish to their children and the children respond in English. In Pomona, for example, 65 percent of the interviewed Mexican Americans who had children reported that their children spoke only English to them.[12] (Of course, one must keep in mind that the Mexican Americans of Pomona are more acculturated than those in many other parts of the Southwest.) Then, too, there is a growing awareness among Mexican Americans that language skills are necessary for socioeconomic advancement.[13] An increasing number of parents are forcing themselves to speak English at home so as to "make it easier" for their children. For instance, Margaret Clark quotes a Mexican American woman: "Since my husband and I knew that our children would probably have teachers who don't know our language, we were always careful to speak some English around the house so that the children would have an easier time in school."[14]

FAMILY SIZE AND ITS IMPLICATIONS

To this day probably most Mexican American parents continue to be un-

[8] John Gillin, "Ethos Components in Modern Latin-American Culture," American Anthropologist, 57 (June, 1955), p. 497; Oscar Lewis, The Children of Sanchez, New York: Random House, 1961, p. xxii.

[9] Jane MacWab Christian and Chester Christian, Jr., "Spanish Language and Culture in the Southwest," in Joshua A. Fishman, ed., "Language Loyalty in the United States," A Final Report to the U.S. Office of Education, Language Research Section, Vol. 3, p. 38.

[10] Leonard Broom and Eshref Shevky, "Mexicans in the United States—A Problem of Social Differentiation," Sociology and Social Research, 36 (January–February, 1952), p. 153.

[11] William Madsen, Mexican-Americans of South Texas, New York: Holt, Rinehart and Winston, 1964, p. 106.

[12] Funado Penalosa. "Class Consciousness and Social Mobility in a Mexican-American Community." Unpublished Ph.D. dissertation, University of Southern California, 1963, p. 120.

[13] Arthur J. Rubel, "Social Life of Urban Mexican Americans." Unpublished Ph.D. dissertation, University of North Carolina, 1962, p. 49.

[14] Margaret Clark, Health in the Mexican-American Culture, Berkeley: University of California Press, 1959, p. 55.

aware of the extent to which each child's chances for advancement are hampered by the large number of siblings. There is little room for dispute that, in general, the size of a family is inversely related to its upward mobility.[15] My recent study of Mexican American high school seniors supports the contention that Mexican Americans are no exception to this general relationship—students with fewer siblings had more means for realizing their occupational aspirations than others. Moreover, there was as much as ten points of difference in the average I. Q. scores of Mexican American boys with only one sibling or none and those who had four or more siblings. As many as 43 percent of the former but only 14 percent of the latter pursued an academic course of study. Furthermore, three times as many boys with up to three siblings anticipated finishing college or pursuing graduate studies as those with four or more siblings.

This study suggests the idea that an important factor in the slow upward mobility of Mexican Americans, which has not been sufficiently explored, is their high birth rate. The importance of family size in this respect is supported by the finding that, while the avenues of mobility of Mexican American students differed significantly with size of family, they did not differ much with parental occupation, education, or country of birth.[16]

[15] S. M. Lipset and R. Bendix, *Social Mobility in Industrial Society*, Berkeley: University of California Press, 1962, pp. 240–41.
[16] Celia Stopnicka Heller, "Ambitions of Mexican-American Youth—Goals and Means of High School Seniors." Unpublished Ph.D. dissertation, Columbia University, 1963, pp. 114–15, 141, 164–67. For an analysis of the data about Anglo American high school seniors in Los Angeles, see: Ralph Turner, *The*

Table 2

PERCENTAGE DISTRIBUTION OF FAMILIES WITH OWN CHILDREN UNDER EIGHTEEN YEARS OF AGE, BY NUMBER OF CHILDREN: 1960

Number of Children	"White" Families in the United States	Mexican American Families * in the Five Southwestern States
1	32.8	23.6
2	32.5	24.2
3	19.2	19.4
4 or more children	15.5	32.9
Total	100.0%	100.1%

* Mexican American stands for families with Spanish surname

Sources: U.S. Census of Population: 1960, *Families*, Final Report PC(2)–4A, Table 5; U.S. Census of Population: 1960, *Persons of Spanish Surname*, Final Report PC(2)–1B, Table 5.

A glance at Table 2 shows clearly that Mexican American youths as a whole come from much larger families than those of the "white" segment of the population. The proportion of families with four or more children (of the total families with children under 18) is twice as high among Mexican Americans as among "whites" in general. Such large families constitute one third of all Mexican American families with children under 18. Although there are no known studies specifically devoted to this subject, some evidence exists that the family among Mexican Americans

Social Context of Ambition, San Francisco: Chandler, 1965. The data about Mexican Americans, which he collected but did not utilize, he generously made available to me.

has not become smaller in size than has the family in Mexico, nor does it vary in size with generations in the United States.[17]

HOME SOCIALIZATION

Not only in size, but also in organization, the Mexican American family displays an unusual persistence of traditional forms. It continues to be an extended type of family with strong ties spread through a number of generations in a large web of kinship. These ties impose obligations of mutual aid, respect, and affection. The kinship ties are extended even beyond genetic links by the institution known as *compadrazgo*. The *compadres*, not blood relatives, assume what are in fact family obligations in a religious ceremony establishing ritual kinship. For example, parents and godparents are *compadres* and have a right to seek help and advice from each other.

In its authority structure, the family is also highly traditional. Family authority within the nuclear unit is vested in the father or, in case of his absence, in the oldest male wage earner.[18] According to the traditional norms, the husband is regarded as the authoritarian, patriarchal figure who is both the head and the master of the family and the mother as the affectional figure in the family. In the words of Oscar Lewis,

"His prerogatives are to receive the obedience and respect of his wife and children, as well as their services." Actually, the wife exercises a considerable amount of control within the home, especially concerning the children, since "husbands keep aloof from the petty details of the household."[19] In the Mexican American home the division of labor between the sexes is sharply defined, resting on a sexually based dichotomous set of cultural expectations: throughout life males are accorded higher status than females.[20]

The kind of socialization that Mexican American children generally receive at home is not conducive to the development of the capacities needed for advancement in a dynamic industrialized society. This type of upbringing creates stumbling blocks to future advancement by stressing values that hinder mobility—family ties, honor, masculinity, and living in the present—and by neglecting the values that are conducive to it—achievement, independence, and deferred gratification.

Of particular importance in forging family ties is the sense of responsibility that the child acquires toward his younger siblings. From the age of five or six, a child may be responsible for his younger brother or sister. With this

[17] Richard G. Thurston, "Urbanization and Socio-cultural Change in a Mexican-American Enclave." Unpublished Ph.D. dissertation, University of California, Los Angeles, 1957, pp. 51, 211.

[18] Robert C. Jones, "Ethnic Family Patterns: The Mexican Family in the United States," *American Journal of Sociology*, 53 (May, 1948), p. 450.

[19] Oscar Lewis, "Husbands and Wives in a Mexican Village: A Study of Role Conflicts," in Olen E. Leonard and Charles P. Loomis, eds., *Readings in Latin American Social Organization and Institutions*, East Lansing: Michigan State College Press, 1953, pp. 23, 29.

[20] Munro Edmonson, *Los Manitos—A Study of Institutional Values*, New Orleans: Middle American Research Institute, Tulane University, 1957, p. 32; R. Fernandez Marina, E. D. Maldonado-Sierra, and R. D. Trent, "Three Basic Themes in Mexican and Puerto Rican Family Values," *Journal of Social Psychology*, 48 (November, 1958), pp. 167–81.

responsibility also comes a growing authority of older over younger, approximating parental control.[21] Younger children are usually as much in awe of an older brother as they are of their parents.

This early training finds full expression in the adolescent boy's assumption of the role of guardian and protector of his sisters, both younger and older, and of his younger brothers. The role of the brother—similar to the situation in Mexico itself—begins, in a sense, as the extension of the father's role. In Mexico the father's position is invested with great authority over his wife and children, and some of his power is extended to the "grown sons." But in the Mexican American family in the United States the "grown boy's" role, which begins in adolescence, and particularly that of the oldest son, has a quality distinct from that of the father's role. He is the link with the outside world and acts as mentor in the American outlook and American practices for his younger siblings. Thus he "becomes protector, orderer, and forbidder, in short a foster parent schooled in American ways." [22] In acting out this role, the Mexican American boy may even commit acts which bring him to the attention of the police.

This role is colored by the image of the ideal male personality which is held up before the male child, irrespective of the social position of the family. This image includes sexual prowess, physical strength, adventurousness and courage, male dominance, self-confidence, and verbal articulation.[23] Ruth Tuck notes that "Boys and girls are given a differential upbringing. The girl is trained for the home, the boy for the world." [24] This differential socialization is consistent with their future adult roles. The norm is that the husband, being a male, cannot be expected to remain faithful to his wife, but the wife owes the husband absolute sexual fidelity and is expected to regard the peccadillos of her husband with tolerance. Male children are indulged, and boys are given a good deal of freedom of movement for which they are not expected to account to their parents. Their outside activities are considered part of the process of becoming a man. Such indulgent attitudes of parents have been shown by David McClelland and others to hamper in their sons the development of the "need of achievement" in educational and occupational endeavors.[25]

On the other hand, girls are closely supervised and taught that their place is in the home,[26] although there is some

---

[21] Ralph L. Beals, "Culture Patterns of Mexican-American Life." *Proceedings of the Fifth Annual Conference, Southwestern Council on Education of Spanish Speaking People,* Pepperdine College, January 1951, p. 11; Florence R. Kluckhohn and Fred Strodtbeck, *Variations in Value Orientations,* New York: Row, Peterson, 1961, p. 197.

[22] Norman D. Humphrey, "The Changing Structure of the Detroit Mexican Family: An Index of Acculturation," *American Sociological Review,* 9 (December, 1944), p. 625.

[23] Ossie G. Simmons, "Anglo-Americans and Mexican-Americans in South Texas." Unpublished Ph.D. dissertation, Harvard University, 1952, p. 75. Arthur J. Rubel, "Concepts of Disease in Mexican-American Culture," *American Anthropologist* (October, 1960), pp. 810–14.

[24] Ruth Tuck, *Not with the Fist,* New York: Harcourt Brace Jovanovich, 1946, p. 124.

[25] See: David C. McClelland, *The Achieving Society,* Princeton: Van Nostrand, 1961, p. 356.

[26] John H. Burma, *Spanish-Speaking Groups in the United States,* Durham: Duke University Press, 1954, p. 11.

indication that the norms of feminine behavior may be changing in the direction of more freedom.[27] However, this seems to be not so much a result of changes in early home socialization as a product of the adolescent girl's revolt against female confinement at home.

The theme of honor, like that of *machismo* (manliness), is predominant in the orientation the Mexican American child receives at home. Honor in this conception is tied to an inner integrity which every child inherits as part of his Mexican American birthright and which he is to guard jealously against all. It manifests itself in "extreme sensitivity to insult"[28] displayed so often by Mexican American youths. Their reactions, consistent with their concept of honor, seen from the Anglo American standpoint, often appear as "touchiness."

Tied to the values of honor and respect is the emphasis which the home places on respectful conduct. It is a sign of *persona educada* and is stressed as behavior to be learned by all, irrespective of social class. The individual who lacks it is *bruto* or *burro,* an out-model of which the child is often reminded. Both boys and girls are urged to show respect, obedience, and humility in their behavior toward parents and elders and are drilled in courtesy.[29] In many homes, for example, the child is taught to respond to the parents' or elders' call of his name with the phrase *mande usted,* at your command. As Ruth Tuck observes, "Good manners stand high in the list of desirable attributes for children, even in humble homes."[30] This value is reflected in the everyday behavior of Mexican American youth, which is marked by extraordinary courtesy and politeness as compared, at least on the basis of casual observation, with that of Anglo American youth of the same socioeconomic status. It should be noted that Mexican American youths do not think of this kind of behavior as "good manners" but rather as "being respectful." When questioned whether their home stresses good manners they tended to answer in the negative and point to school as the place where they are stressed. Yet the same boys related at length how they were taught at home to be respectful and how they try and do conform to this rule.

But honor and politeness are not strategic values for young people in the development of mobility aspirations, which require a more direct orientation toward the goal of occupational success. Mexican American children do not receive this kind of training at home. Parents, as a whole, neither impose standards of excellence for tasks performed by their children nor do they communicate to them that they expect evidence of high achievement. The parents' great love for their children is not conditional: it does not depend on the child's level of performance as compared with his peers—a widely reported trait among middle class Anglo American parents.[31] Although conditional love is not the only known mechanism

[27] Arthur J. Rubel, "Social Life of Urban Mexican Americans," *American Anthropologist* (October, 1960), p. 213.

[28] Ossie G. Simmons, "Anglo-Americans and Mexican-Americans in South Texas." Unpublished Ph.D. dissertation, Harvard University, 1952, p. 115.

[29] Rogelio Diaz Guerrero, "Neurosis and the Mexican Family Structure," *American Journal of Psychiatry,* 112 (December, 1955), p. 414.

[30] Ruth Tuck, *Not with the Fist,* New York: Harcourt Brace Jovanovich, 1946, p. 124.

[31] Florence R. Kluckholn and Fred Strodtbeck, *Variations in Value Orientations,* New York: Row, Peterson, 1961, p. 197.

for early socialiaztion in achievement, other mechanisms with that function, comparable, for example, to that of "shame" among Jews and Japanese, are also lacking. Unlike some children in these minority groups, the Mexican American child is not prodded to achieve or risk bringing shame on himself and his family.

This lack of emphasis upon "making good" in conventional terms is consistent with the themes of fatalism and resignation which run through Mexican American culture. What it lacks is the idea, so characteristic of modal American culture, that the individual can command the future to serve his own ends. The contrast between the former's present-time orientation and the latter's future-time orientation is striking, borne out in the conspicuous fact that the Mexican American home does not cultivate in the children the ability to defer gratification which, according to many contemporary studies, is conducive to upward mobility.[32]

The combination of stress on work and rational use of time to which Anglo American children, especially in families sharing middle class values, are exposed at home forms little or no part of the Mexican American socialization process.[33] Time tends to be disregarded when it interferes with other values, such as rest, thought, and enjoyment. Mexican Americans have retained the conception of work as, at best, a necessary concession: the child learns at home that work, although the common

lot of the people around him, is a necessity, not a virtue. Also stressed in his home environment is the notion that inactivity and leisure are dignified and worthwhile goals, and these values are reinforced by the inculcation of supportive attitudes. There is the consequent learning of "lax" habits and the failure to develop habits of self-discipline and time manipulation.

The home also fails to provide the kind of independence training that, as brought out in various investigations, is highly functional for achievement.[34] This is the sort of training in which parents communicate to the child that they expect him to be self-reliant and grant him relative autonomy in decision making situations. In contrast to this orientation, as Florence Kluckhohn notes, Mexican American children are "vigorously trained for dependent behavior as the average Anglo-American child is schooled for independence." It is not surprising, therefore, that these children seldom show initiative or freely express their own ideas.[35]

Finally, few Mexican American homes stress higher education or intellectual effort. That parental influence and pressure to go to college are an important determinant of whether a working class boy will obtain a higher

---

[32] See, e.g.: Louis Schneider and Svere Lysgaard, "The Deferred Gratification Pattern: A Preliminary Study," *American Sociological Review*, 22 (February, 1957), pp. 67–73.

[33] John H. Burma, *Spanish-Speaking Groups in the United States*, Durham: Duke University Press, 1954, p. 9.

[34] See, e.g.: Bernard C. Rosen, "Race, Ethnicity, and the Achievement Syndrome," *American Sociological Review*, 22 (February, 1959), pp. 48–60; Bernard C. Rosen, "Socialization and Achievement Motivation in Brazil," *American Sociological Review*, 27 (October, 1962), pp. 612–25; D. C. McClelland, A. Rindlisbacher, and R. de Charms, "Religious and Other Sources of Parental Attitude Toward Independence Training," in D. C. McClelland, ed., *Studies in Motivation*, New York: Appleton, 1955, pp. 389–97.

[35] Florence R. Kluckhohn and Fred Strodtbeck, *Variations in Value Orientations*, New York: Row, Peterson, 1961, p. 197.

education has been convincingly demonstrated by Joseph Kahl in his article on " 'Common Men' Boys." [36] And this mode of parental behavior is largely absent in the homes of Mexican American youth. Mexican American boys have often complained to me that they lacked encouragement from their parents, especially their fathers, to continue their schooling. This may be in part an indirect product of tension and conflict between father and son over authority. As we have seen, the authority of the son in the American setting is no longer simply an extension of the father's authority but rests on his being the mediator between the Mexican and American cultures. The father-son relationship seems to be profoundly disturbed in many of the Mexican American homes as the sons assume positions of dominance or of equality with their fathers.

The lack of parental encouragement to pursue a formal education may also be directly tied to the parents' belief that higher education is useless for their children and would not result in achievement but rather lead to frustration and humiliation. To help their children avoid this situation, some parents cite those Mexican Americans who have received a college education but who have nevertheless failed to move into occupations for which they are technically qualified.[37] One young Mexican American, for example, told me: "My father always says: 'you don't need to

go to school. You will have to work anyway.' "

The questionnaire responses of the recent Racine study seem to be consistent with the above observations based on qualitative data. Mexican American as well as Anglo American and Negro parents were asked how much schooling they would "like" their children to have. Only 25 percent of the Mexican Americans, in contrast to 50 percent of the Negroes and 67 percent of the Anglo Americans, mentioned college. When questioned whether they would be satisfied with various levels of education actually reached by their children, more Mexican Americans said that they would be content with a minimal amount than did either the Anglo Americans or the Negroes (37 percent of the Mexican Americans but only 6 percent of the Anglo Americans thought that they would be satisfied if their children received only a junior high school education). And finally, a substantially higher percentage of Mexican Americans than either Anglo Americans or Negroes felt that it would be "practically impossible," considering their financial condition, to keep their children in school beyond the ninth grade.[38]

To be sure, a change is beginning to take place in the attitudes toward education among Mexican Americans. Some parents are now encouraging their sons to continue their schooling. I recall, for instance, a young student who, during my interview with him, gave this reply to my question as to

[36] Joseph A. Kahl, "Educational and Occupational Aspirations of 'Common Men' Boys," *Harvard Educational Review,* 23 (1953), pp. 186–203.

[37] Ruth Tuck, *Not with the Fist,* New York: Harcourt Brace Jovanovich, 1946, pp. 189–90. Florence R. Kluckhohn and Fred Strodtbeck, *Variations in Value Orientations,* New York: Row, Peterson, 1961, p. 248.

[38] Lyle W. Shannon and Elaine M. Krass, *The Economic Absorption and Cultural Integration of Immigrant Mexican-American and Negro Workers,* Iowa City: State University of Iowa, Department of Sociology and Anthropology, 1964, pp. 240–44.

what prompted his decision to go to college:

> I guess I've always wanted to go to college. There was much value placed on education at home. . . . My father, in his uneducated way, was always reading to us kids, and I remember a game he used to play with the dictionary, in which he would read words and let us guess their meanings. He would then give us the dictionary and let us quiz him. As he would rattle off how much he knew, I can still remember the look on his face of great proudness of what he had learned.

But such parents are still the exception among Mexican Americans.[39] Generally, their children experience a kind of socialization that, on the one hand, reinforces traditional values and, on the other, is dysfunctional for achievement in conventional terms. Thus, in examining the Mexican American youth of today—both the ambitious and the delinquent, as well as the majority who fall between these polar types—we should keep in mind the fact that they have first entered school having already acquired a relative inability for and disinterest in the success tasks that are commonly set in school.

THE SCHOOL EXPERIENCE

Our public school philosophy is based on the assumption that education is not the sole responsibility of parents but that at a certain point society, or rather its agencies, must step in and take over the task of educating its members. This being the case, it is important to examine to what extent schools realize this aim, especially with such groups of children as the Mexican Americans whose homes do not prepare them for adequate functioning in our society.

Many Mexican American parents recognize their inability and failure to develop in their children the facility to deal with the non-Mexican environment. However, they do not seem aware of the fact that the schools, too, fail the Mexican American children in this respect. These conclusions, based on conversations with parents, are supported by the findings of the Racine study. When asked: "Where do children learn more—in school, in the home, or when they go to work?" 22 percent of the Mexican Americans, but 62 percent of the Anglo Americans, mentioned home, or home and other factors. As many as 74 percent of the Mexican Americans, compared with 29 percent of the Anglo Americans, named the schools only.[1]

Scholastic Performance

As has been shown, Mexican American children enter school without the kind of experience on which school life is based. Under the circumstances, it would not be surprising if their scholastic performance were poorer than that of Anglo American children at the start of their schooling. Yet, several studies have shown that Mexican American children tend to start out on much

---

[39] Claire L. Peterson, "When the Migrant Laborer Settles Down—A Report of the Findings of a Project on Value Assimilation of Immigrant Laborers," mimeographed, University of Wisconsin, 1964, p. 25.

[1] Lyle W. Shannon and Elaine M. Krass, *The Economic Absorption and Cultural Integration of Immigrant Mexican-American and Negro Workers,* Iowa City: State University of Iowa, Department of Sociology and Anthropology, 1964, p. 223.

the same level as the Anglo American children both in I. Q. scores and scholastic achievement. It may, however, seem tragic that the longer Mexican Americans stay in school, the less they resemble the other children in these endeavors.[2] One of the most recent investigations, that of Los Angeles high school seniors dramatically reinforces these these findings. Here is a group of Mexican American students, products of public schools, who were so highly motivated to continue their education as to resist the prevalent tendency to drop out of school before their senior year. After twelve years of schooling, their I. Q. distribution did not correspond to the "normal I. Q. curve." Almost half of them, in contrast to 13 percent of the Anglo Americans were below average in I. Q. Only six percent of the Mexican Americans but 28 percent of the Anglo American high school seniors scored above average.[3]

What are the schools like which these Mexican American children have been attending? Until the late forties, Mexican American children were *formally* segregated in separate buildings or separate schools. The rationalization was that these children knew little or no English on entering school,

could not compete on an equal basis with Anglo American children, and it was therefore best for both groups to be separated. In California, in 1947, the courts decided, in the *Mendez* case, that enforced segregation violated the United States Constitution. A similar decision, in the *Delgado* case, was rendered in Texas in 1948.[4] Today, the schools attended by Mexican Americans are located in the poorest areas and thus are largely segregated on a *de facto* basis.

These schools generally do not make the first exposure to American values and skills the exciting experience it could be. As a rule, no designs have been worked out and incorporated into educational programs to enhance the early experiences in school or to facilitate the transition from the Mexican home to the American school. According to a recent study, most teachers were found to believe that the same type of curriculum would essentially satisfy the needs of both Mexican American and Anglo American children.[5] As George Sanchez put it 25 years ago— and it still seems to apply today—the school program generally proceeds on the fallacious assumption that all children come from homes with American cultural standards and traditions.[6]

Teacher-Student Relations

The blame for the poor scholastic record of Mexican American children has often

[2] Thomas R. Garth and Harper D. Johnson, "The Intelligence and Achievement of Mexican Children in the U.S.," *Journal of Abnormal Social Psychology*, 29 (1934), p. 224; Nathaniel D. M. Hirsch, "A Study of Natio-Racial Mental Differences," *Genetic Psychology Monographs*, 1 (1926), p. 24; H. B. Carlson and N. Henderson, "The Intelligence of American Children of Mexican Parentage," *Journal of Abnormal Social Psychology*, 45 (1950), p. 548.

[3] Celia Stopnicka Heller, "Ambitions of Mexican-American Youth—Goals, and Means of High School Seniors." Unpublished Ph.D. dissertation. Columbia University, 1963, p. 143–57.

[4] James W. Vander Zanden, *American Minority Relations*, New York: Ronald Press, 1963, p. 231.

[5] Horacio Ulibarri, "Teacher Awareness of Sociocultural Differences in Multi-Cultural Classrooms," *Sociology and Social Research*, 45 (October, 1960), p. 52.

[6] George I. Sanchez, *Forgotten People—A Study of New Mexicans*, Albuquerque: University of New Mexico Press, 1940, p. 327.

been placed on the teachers. It appears in almost all the writings about Mexican Americans which touch on the problem of their low educational achievements. The "explanations" range from the general claim that teachers simply do not understand the Mexican American children to the specific charge that the teachers are hostile toward them. The latter is illustrated by the following statement made by Carey McWilliams:

> Notoriously bad linguists, Anglo-American teachers have been known to show an unreasoning irritation over the mere sound of a Spanish word or phrase. . . . This irritation is often reflected in a hostile attitude toward Spanish-speaking students. Over a period of many years, I have heard Anglo-American teachers of the Southwest complain bitterly about the "stubbornness" of Mexican-American youngsters who will persist in speaking Spanish. . . .[8]

Even if one were to dismiss this as based on single experiences rather than rigorous evidence, the former observation that teachers generally fail to understand Mexican American children is supported by a number of studies. For example, Richard Thurston noted that

none of the teachers in the community he investigated ever visited the neighborhood where their Mexican-American pupils lived.[9] Again, a more recent study by Horacio Ulibarri found teachers to show little awareness of sociocultural factors affecting the classroom behavior of Mexican American children. These teachers were quite sensitive to the obvious fact of the pupils' English language deficiency but largely unaware of such basic issues as the meaningfulness, or lack of it, of the classroom experience for Mexican American children.[10]

Teachers today still tend to regard assignment to a school in a Mexican American district as an inferior one, bordering on punishment (as do teachers who are assigned to schools in areas heavily populated by Negroes). Their numerous complaints about the difficulties of teaching Mexican American children become more understandable in view of their ignorance of the children's background. For example, a teacher who, perhaps unknowingly, offends the Mexican American boy's sense of honor may find it very difficult to control him. As one perceptive Anglo American high school teacher noted, it was much easier for her to gain the cooperation of Mexican American boys by using, in her words, "extra-polite" language.

Lack of such knowledge and understanding may not only make it hard for teachers to instruct Mexican Amer-

---

[7] Louisa G. Sanchez, "The 'Latin-American' of the Southwest: Backgrounds and Curricular Implications." Unpublished Ph.D. dissertation, University of Texas, 1954, pp. xviii, 208; Carey McWilliams, North from Mexico—The Spanish-Speaking People of the United States. Philadelphia: Lippincott, 1949, p. 299; Proceedings of the Conference on the Education of Spanish-Speaking People, sponsored by the California State Department of Education, March, 1953, p. 20; Florence Kluckhohn and Fred Strodtbeck, Variations in Value Orientations, New York: Row, Peterson, 1961, pp. 250–51.

[8] Carey McWilliams, North from Mexico—The Spanish-Speaking People of the United States, Philadelphia: Lippincott, 1949, p. 299.

[9] Richard G. Thurston, "Urbanization and Socio-cultural Change in a Mexican-American Enclave." Unpublished Ph.D. dissertation, Los Angeles: University of California, 1957, pp. 51, 211.

[10] Horacio Ulibarri, "Teacher Awareness of Socio-Cultural Differences in Multi-cultural Classrooms," Sociology and Social Research, 45 (October, 1960), p. 55.

ican children, but also to proceed in a way that would make it easier for the children to identify with their teachers. One college student, during an interview, had this comment about his fellow Mexican Americans during his high school days: "They don't take the teachers seriously. To them, when the teacher talks, she talks from the other side of the fence." Mexican American boys seem rarely to identify with their teachers. Thurston relates that, in the community he studied, "Reports of school experiences by Pueblo children . . . were predominantly negative or neutral. There did not appear to be much idealization of teachers." [11]

This situation merits further systematic study, since the teacher probably occupies a strategic position for influencing Mexican American upward mobility. One gains insight into the potential importance of this position when talking with Mexican Americans who have been occupationally successful. Careful questioning reveals that there is almost always an individual, often a teacher or principal, whom such mobile persons credit for their accomplishments. For example, a Mexican American college graduate described his school history: "I was discouraged about even going to elementary school until I reached the fifth grade. . . . I had been kicked out of four schools already as a problem child. In the fifth grade, at the California Street School, the principal, without asking any questions as to why I had transferred, asked whether I wanted to be a Safety Monitor. . . . From then on I became inter-

ested in school in spite of the fact that I was afraid the other boys would razz me for being a school stooge." [12] Another Mexican American, a student at the University of California, testified: "As long as I live I will never forget a sixth grade teacher I had. . . . Her encouragement made me want to make something of myself. She planted the seeds of college in my head. . . . Words of encouragement and acceptance meant a great deal to me." [13]

In this connection, Florence Kluckhohn, in her study of a Mexican American community, Atrisco, also points to the potential influence of the teacher on the acculturation of Mexican Americans. She describes one sympathetic teacher who was sought out by young and old alike for advice and support, and concludes that, had the community had more such teachers, "it is probable that a degree of familiarity with the Anglo dominated outside world would have been gained and gained without resentment." Not only were there no other teachers with her understanding and insight, but "even she was hampered in what she could do by a formal educational program which was not designed to meet the adjustive needs of Spanish-Americans." [14]

School Curricula

School guidance personnel, in addition to teachers, have been subjected to con-

[11] Richard G. Thurston, "Urbanization and Socio-cultural Change in a Mexican-American Enclave." Unpublished Ph.D. dissertation, Los Angeles: University of California, 1957, p. 202.

[12] "Interviews Given by the Panel on Values of Scholarships for Students of Mexican-American Ancestry," Los Angeles School Journal, 34 (April 2, 1951), p. 20.
[13] Proceedings of the Conference on the Education of Spanish-Speaking People, sponsored by the California State Department of Education, March, 1953, p. 53.
[14] Florence Kluckhohn and Fred Strodtbeck, Variations in Value Orientations, New York: Row, Peterson, 1961, pp. 250–51.

siderable criticism by individuals interested in the educational problems of Mexican American youth. The charge is often made against them that they deliberately guide Mexican American students into nonacademic subjects and thus limit their possibilities of reaching college.[15] The fact is that a much smaller proportion of Mexican American than of Anglo American high school students pursue an academic course of study. Thus, Ralph Turner's data on Los Angeles high school students show that one fifth of the Mexican Americans, as compared with one half of the Anglo Americans, followed an academic curriculum. But both school guidance personnel and teachers usually believe that they are merely being objective, citing the low I. Q. scores of Mexican American youth, in advising and encouraging them to pursue "practical" rather than academic programs. They do not see these scores for what they really are: products of peculiar social and cultural circumstances and indeed indicators of deficiency in schooling itself.[16]

Perhaps as often as being pushed by school personnel into industrial and vocational courses, Mexican American children simply drift into them. As one youth, who managed to finish college despite having followed an industrial high school course, explained: "Taking the industrial course was the easiest thing to do. It was the line of least

resistance."[17] The "line of least resistance" may be a common pattern for the other Mexican American students who are handicapped in some of the things that go into achieving an adequate I. Q. score.

Dropouts

Another common pattern is to stop attending school as soon as possible. Thus the proportion of Mexican American youths, between 16 and 19 years old, who do not attend school is considerably higher than that of Anglo Americans. According to the 1960 Census, in the Southwest 66.9 percent of 16- and 17-year-old Mexican Americans, as against 83.6 percent of Anglo Americans of the same age, were enrolled in school. For those 18 and 19 years of age, the respective percentages were 33.2 and 43.3.[18]

The dropout problem is especially acute among Mexican Americans, but has not been studied sufficiently. Only one pilot study is available on this subject and its main concern is the extent of the problem. This investigation, conducted in three high schools of Los Angeles, shows that, between 1955 and 1957, 31 percent of the Mexican Americans, as compared with 19 percent of the other students, dropped out of school before high school graduation.[19]

In trying to account for this high

[15] Proceedings of the Conference on Educational Problems of Students of Mexican Descent, Los Angeles: University of California, March 26, 1955, p. 28.

[16] Celia Stopnicka Heller, "Ambitions of Mexican-American Youth-Goals and Means of High School Seniors." Unpublished Ph.D. dissertation, Columbia University, 1963, pp. 128–32, 143–57.

[17] Proceedings of the Conference on the Education of Spanish-Speaking People, sponsored by the California State Department of Education, March, 1955, p. 30.

[18] U.S. Bureau of Census; Persons of Spanish Surname, op. cit., Table 4; State Volumes, Tables 94 and 101.

[19] Background for Planning, Los Angeles: Research Department, Welfare Planning Council, 1963, p. 61.

dropout rate, only bits of information exist from studies directed at other problems. Thus one analysis of attitudes toward education reports that Mexican American junior and senior high school students are more likely to consider dropping out of school as desirable than Anglo Americans even when social class and I. Q. are held constant.[20] Another investigation, focused upon problems of health, brings out the Mexican Americans' tendency to leave school because of their embarrassment about being poorly dressed and having little spending money as compared with Anglo American students. The author of this study also refers to the feeling of scholastic inadequacy which characterizes Mexican American students,

illustrating this reaction by quoting a university graduate who made the following comment about dropouts: "It was very hard for Mexican students . . . the teachers would run them down for being so dumb all the time. Most of them just got sick of it and dropped out of school." [21]

It remains to be seen to what extent the current national programs aimed at coping with the dropout problem in general will succeed in reducing the rate of dropouts among Mexican Americans. To summarize the situation as it exists now, Mexican American children are not prepared at home for the experiences which await them in school and the schools are not prepared or equipped to receive and hold these children.

[20] George D. Demos, "Attitudes of Mexican-American and Anglo-American Groups Toward Education," *Sociology and Social Research*, 46 (August, 1962), p. 255.

[21] Margaret Clark, *Health in the Mexican-American Culture*, Berkeley: University of California Press, 1959, pp. 59–71.

Excerpts from

SPANISH-SPEAKING CHILDREN
OF THE SOUTHWEST

Herschel T. Manuel

I was born in a coal mining camp. I attended the . . . County grade school for one year. This was my kindergarten. I was much older than the rest of my schoolmates, but in county schools they don't mind if you are younger or older, just as long as you go to school. In 1948 my father was run over by a train. I was 7 at the time, and I have never forgotten it. We came to D___ and I started school. I was much older than my schoolmates; so the principal transferred me to the second grade. I adjusted very fast to my schoolmates. I was the only Spanish girl in the whole school, I think, and I found out then that no one cared what color I was.

I made friends all through grade school, and I was a leader in most of my activities. I think that I was very well accepted; in fact, I was chosen or rather elected to be the president of some tree club. I was in student council all through my grade school years, and

Herschel T. Manuel, Spanish-Speaking Children of the Southwest (Austin: University of Texas Press, 1965), pp. 92–93, 101, 105. Reprinted by permission.

I was president of my fifth- and sixth-grade class.

When I went to junior high, I didn't like my seventh grade at all. I was very skinny and more Mexican people attended [that school]. Gangs were forming and I didn't know what way to turn. I started to stick around with [English-speaking] girls and boys, and the Spanish people would call me a "Paddie lover." I didn't care because I knew that they were the foolish ones by not mixing.

In the eighth and ninth grades, I was elected to student council. I was president of the Red Cross and editor of the school paper, and I attended leadership camp twice. I held a lot of offices in junior high.

In high school, I was very lost. I kept up my grades, and success followed. I was in Sophomore Council and Junior Council. After I was admitted to the local honor society, I tried for National Honor. After I was in National Honor, I ran for several offices, and I got them. I was chosen the senior of the year, and I was vice-president of the All-Girls Club, vice-president of the Pep Club, and secretary in the Future Teachers of America. I won a scholarship to . . . College for four years.

[Now] I have a very good job as secretary, and there is no racial prejudice at all in the office.

Supplementing the account of her school experiences, she made some interesting comments on the Spanish-speaking population of the city in which she lives. Among the comments are those which suggest the tremendous social pressures under which these young people live.

Many Mexicans are embarrassed by poverty, language difficulty, or the feeling of difference from other pupils, and quit school early. This gives the Mexicans a bad reputation because they are left to wander in the streets or get jobs that no one else would take.

The name "Mexican" has turned into a dirty word for those of that origin. It means "hoodlum," one who is stupid, dope addict, clown, and a drunk. Some movies always have the Mexican play the dumb guy.

I'll never forget the time when someone called me a "Dirty Mexican." Of course, this bothered me to the extent that I began to cry. What was I crying for? Not for the name itself, but for the meaning behind this name.

You are what you are and you have to learn to accept it and be proud of it, whether you are black, brown, fat, thin, tall, short, pretty, or ugly. What can you do about it? With acceptance comes tolerance.

Another thought that is in the minds of Mexicans is, "Everyone is against us." This is not true. If a person would stick around with [English-speaking] people, he would find out that they don't call him down. You are always asked to do what they do. They consider you part of them. You are part of them.

To be Spanish is to be from a "better" country, of lighter complexion, and a nice kid; so, naturally, everyone wants to be "Spanish." If you would ask a Mexican [living here] what he was, he would tell you that he is Spanish. Why are they ashamed to tell you they are from Mexico? One of the reasons might be when the first Mexicans came they worked in beet fields, and when the season was over, they were left with nothing; so they had to steal to exist. People turned this into a "racial" bias, reinforcing the anti-Mexican feeling. If some of the present Mexicans who deny their race were to go back to Mexico, they would find out that Mexico is a "fantablous" nation. [She explains that "fantablous" is a slang expression meaning that something is extra superb.]

I do not think that I was born under a black star, just because my skin is darker than others. I think that if people would live and let live, there would be no racial prejudice at all. All Mexicans should mix and at the same time work together [with other people]. "All Mexicans must stick together"; this shouldn't be true, because in order to make things better, you should do something about the present situation instead of making it worse.

While I attended elementary, there were not too many Anglos; so not many difficulties in race were present. After entering junior high there was little tension. But I could feel just a little dislike toward me because I spoke Spanish. No one actually said it but somehow I felt a little dislike. The way it is with Spanish-speaking students is that they feel that the Anglos hate them. When a Mexican mixes with Anglos naturally they are criticized by their own race; so they avoid the Anglos as much as they can. Personally, no one ever said anything about it, until I got to high school. They would call me "Mexican" in a way that did not sound so good and later came "wetback." It may have been a joke.

Concerning teachers, there are few who seem to dislike Mexicans and I have nothing to say about them. However, people that offer jobs will be silent just for a second or two when I say [my name]. It may be my imagination, I'm not sure.

As to some suggestions which I might have, there are few. One thing for sure is that the language which their parents speak is not right at all. This only shows that Spanish is not considered good enough to be spoken in an American school and yet they teach it in school. I think the textbooks describe Pancho Villa and other Spanish heroes as being the lowest class in the world. Maybe they were, but not according to what people say in Mexico. There could be better relations among the Anglos and Mexicans by allowing Mexicans to accept responsibilities, for I am sure that there are a few who would be qualified. How that can be established I don't know.

I was born in a Latin-American neighborhood. Consequently I spoke no English until the summer before I started school. That summer we moved into an Anglo neighborhood. There, with the help of Anglo children I learned a few necessary words. As I progressed in school, so did my ability to speak better English. A number of teachers were interested enough to further help me with outside work.

At the age of ten . . . my family moved into a poorer-than-average Latin neighborhood. I was at first resented and disliked. I found that I could win their favor if I behaved as bad as they did. This, of course, got me into trouble. After a number of brushes with the police, I changed acquaintances and habits.

I really enjoyed junior high. Once again I made a number of acquaintances among Anglos. Among my acquaintances was a pretty girl. I finally got enough courage to ask for a date. She was surprised and angered; with what seemed a terrible tone in her voice, she told me that she would not go out with a "greaser." About this time, I also noticed that my Anglo friends started drifting away. After a number of painful experiences, I gathered that my Anglo friends did not want much to do with me. An interesting observation I made at that time is that people coming from intelligent and educated families hold no specific dislike against Latins.

In senior high, the rift between Anglos and Latins is more noticeable.

THORNS ON THE YELLOW
ROSE OF TEXAS

Robert Coles/Harry Huge

About as much cotton is grown in Texas as in India, which is the world's second largest producer. Texas sends the most beef to our markets. It offers up our chief supply of oil (about half the country's yearly supply). A huge chemical industry flourishes near Houston. Wheat production is very substantial; the same goes for corn, rice and peanuts. Texas is a large turkey-raising state; its land is grazed by thousands and thousands of sheep and goats; it yields enormous amounts of magnesium, sulphur, natural gas and bromine. In large cities like Dallas and Houston, the state has institutions that accompany all that wealth: well-run banks and insurance companies, well-known theaters and private museums, well-supported medical centers and private secondary schools, prosperous department stores whose buyers travel to London, Paris.

There's an unusual richness of social and cultural traditions as well. Counties along the Rio Grande are heavily Mexican and Catholic. The

Reprinted by permission of The New Republic, © 1969, Harrison-Blaine of New Jersey, Inc.

southeastern section is very much a part of the South. A quarter of the nation's rice is grown there. Near Corpus Christi millions of waterfowl from all over North America choose to winter. The people on the Gulf Coast and to the north, in the so-called "piney woods" section, are also Southern: Protestant, tied to one another the way rural people are, but also deeply divided racially. Further north and to the west, white, Anglo-Saxon Protestant fundamentalism loses whatever softening a warm and wet climate provides. The land becomes dry, the countryside more austere, and the people sternly, insistently Baptist. In Waco, right in the center of the state, 66 Baptist churches are needed by a population of about 100,000.

W. R. Poage, Chairman of the House Agriculture Committee proudly calls Waco his home. The 11-county district that he has represented in Washington since 1936 is doing just fine. His counties and dozens of others in Texas don't need a lot of new-fangled social legislation meant to feed the hungry and give them money and work. In Poage's words: "From my limited knowledge of nutrition I would assume that it was true that many Americans suffer from an improper diet, but the problem there is one of education and of personal decisions. It differs greatly from the inability of citizens to secure either through gainful employment or public relief enough nutrients."

William Robert Poage wrote those words in a letter to county health officers all over the nation. He asked whether those health officers have "any personal knowledge of any serious hunger" in their counties, the kind of hunger that is "occasioned by inability of the individual to either buy food or receive public assistance." The replies came back from all over, and in a chorus they said no, there isn't any serious hunger or malnutrition among Americans. One doctor in Texas didn't mince words: "I am very sorry that the poor have become a political football, because the kicking around does them more harm than good. I am persuaded that it is only by learning and working that people can better themselves. Giving them 'things' and doing things for them can only make them weak." In Limestone County, part of Poage's district, the health officer shunned such long, philosophical discussions. His reply was the shortest one received: "I have had no cases of starvation or malnutrition reported to my office." The health officer of Milam County, also in Poage's district, insisted that "the general health of the people in the county is good and that in my private practice I have not had the opportunity to treat any patient with any of these conditions." He had earlier said: "Not a single death [in the county] was *ascribed* [italics ours] to malnutrition or any disease caused by any dietary deficiency."

Recently we traveled around Poage's district. We went to Milam County and Limestone County and Robertson County (which connects them). We went to Waco, in McLennan County and to small towns nearby or not-so-nearby—Sunrise, Hearne. We started in San Antonio, which is only a few hours' drive from Mr. Poage's territory. Located midway between the Atlantic and Pacific, San Antonio is the first large city north of the Rio Grande, and in 1960 its some 700,000 people were about half "anglo" and half of Mexican descent (41.7 percent) or black (7 percent). There's an excellent system of freeways, a fine new library, a new convention center, new office buildings and hotels, a river that works its way through the heart of the business district and is lined with cafes, restaurants, stores and even an outdoor theater, all very European in atmosphere; and not the least, a few old and graceful buildings in the Spanish missions (San Jose, Espada) whose arches, courtyards, aqueducts and beautifully wrought facades remind us that not all "culture" comes from England by way of New England.

There is another San Antonio, much of it on the city's West Side, which is predominantly Mexican-American. No outsiders like us have to come there and make a lot of mean, wild, reckless charges; the office of San Antonio's city manager has bluntly and extensively described the *barrios* in an application to the Department of Housing and Urban development "for a grant to plan a comprehensive city demonstration program." The city officials acknowledge that there is a "San Antonio where 28 percent of the families have incomes of less than $3,000 a year, and where over 6 percent of the families have annual incomes of less than $1,000"—the latter figure almost incredible for an urban center. "The need for physical improvements . . . may best be described as total," the city manager says. "The environmental deficiencies have their effect on every aspect of the residents' lives."

What San Antonio's officials spell out we saw: unpaved, undrained streets; homes without water; homes with outdoor privies; homes that are nothing but rural shacks packed together in an urban ghetto that comprises only 8 percent of San Antonio's land area but whose residents must put up with far higher percentages of suffering—32.3 percent of the city's infant deaths, 44.6 percent of its tuberculosis and well over half of its midwife deliveries. After we had gone from home to home on one street we began to realize that in almost every way thousands of people are walled off—as in the ghettos once present in Europe. The white people we met, rarely go "over there," as one lawyer put it, and the Mexican-Americans rarely leave except to seek out work, which often enough they don't find: "Yes, we came up here to San Antonio because we thought surely in a city we could find work, but we can't. My husband looks all over but finds work nowhere. He is sad, very sad, and sometimes he says life is not worth living. We would all starve to death if I didn't go wash the floors, in the bank, and thank God for my mother, that she is here to care for my children. You ask how much money we have for ourselves every week. I'm afraid not enough: sometimes it is $25, and sometimes less and sometimes up to $40, when my husband and me both can find something to do. My sister, she's here, too; and she is very sick with her lungs and can't work. If the priests didn't help her and her children, they would all starve

to death. Her husband can't find work, and they told him to go home, the welfare people did, and keep looking for a job. Maybe if our men left us, we could get relief, but they won't leave. I pray every day that it will all get better, but I'll be honest and tell you, I don't believe there is much hope, no sir, not until the Next World. I've lost three of my children, and when I cry about it, I quickly remind myself that they must be happier where they are. No, a midwife helped me out, right here. I don't think I've ever seen a doctor for more than a minute. I haven't the money, and they're not around here to see; and the hospital is way away, and how can we get there; and if it's life-or-death, like with my babies it was, each time, because they were sick—well the priest, he got us there, but it was too late, and the nurse, she said we should take better care of ourselves, and go get some help someplace, though she didn't know where."

Albert Pena is one of Bexar County's four Commissioners (San Antonio is in Bexar County) and was born in those barrios and still lives there. We asked him where this woman could go for help. "There's nothing the poor here can do," he said, "except try to make their voices heard, and it's not easy by any stretch. They've gerrymandered the city so that the Mexican-Americans have one Congressman and the rest of the city shares two others. They won't let our children speak Spanish in school; instead they tell them right away, in the first grade, they have to learn English and be graded by the way they speak it—mind you, the children are six or seven and have been speaking Spanish all their lives. The children are scared and confused; soon they drop out, by the thousands they do. As for welfare and public assistance, it's almost unbelievable. Over 100,000 people in the county make below $2,000 a year, but only about 20,000 people get public assistance, and *less* than that have been allowed to take part in the Agriculture Department's food program."

We went to see Joe Bernal, the only Mexican-American in the state's senate. (There are a million and a half Mexican-Americans in Texas.) An active, outspoken, basically joyful man, he gave us a stern and somber lecture. He reminded us that Texas, unlike any other state, sets a constitutional limit on the amount of funds that can be spent for public assistance. Despite the natural population growth, despite inflationary pressures that have reduced the value of the dollar, there is no way to increase welfare payments or even hold payments to their present levels without excluding all new applicants —unless the voters agree to raise the ceiling on welfare funds, which in 1968 the voters refused to do. As a result grants to the poor are going down and will be going down further—the latest cut to go into effect May 1. Estimates of what is to come have a family of 4 or more children getting under $100 a month. Since rents are fixed and often half or more of that figure, the amount available for food is obvious. Families get no supplemental allowances—no money to travel to a hospital, no money for drugs, no clothing issues, bus tokens, shelter provisions.

Senator Bernal told us about another one of his state's laws. Section 288 of the Texas Penal Code, passed in 1933, makes it illegal for teachers, principals and superintendents to teach or conduct school business in any language except English, except when they are teaching a foreign language to English-speaking students. All textbooks must be in English. The state's two voices of enlightenment in Washington, D. C., Senator Ralph Yarborough, who authored the first bilingual education legislation introduced in the Congress, and Rep. Bob Eckhardt of Houston, recently cosponsored and helped become law the Bilingual Education Bill. It aims to help schools in, say, Texas or California teach Mexican-American children how to read and write English as well as Spanish. Next to California, the various school districts of Texas have sent in more requests for funds under this new Bilingual Education Law than districts in any other state—but all to no avail unless the state legislature acts.

Men like Commissioner Pena and Senator Bernal are intelligent, tough, and lonely. Few of their people have risen high in office; every day there is a new indignity, a new outrage to fight: the Texas Rangers, a virtual law unto themselves, and the way they intimidate and manhandle farm hands trying to follow the lead of Cesar Chavez; the absurd welfare laws; the severe unemployment among Mexican-Americans; the insulting educational practices that lead to almost unbelievable statistics— for example, 52 percent of all Mexican-Americans in Texas over 25 finished only 4 years of school, and a mere 11 percent went to high school. The city manager of San Antonio admits that 44.3 percent of the Mexican-Americans under his jurisdiction are "functionally illiterate." The 1960 census showed that 20 percent of adult Mexican-Americans in Bexar County: "have not completed any years of school at all."

Things are changing, though. We

met a number of young men who intend to follow the lead of Albert Pena and Joe Bernal, who speak of *La Raza* (roughly, a prideful way to signify the Mexican-American "people") and insist upon the rights and power that must be won for some five million citizens who live mainly in the Southwest. One youth put it this way: "We've been quiet. A lot of us have been afraid to speak up. We've been content to go to church and pray, and be happy we have our family together, as bad as it is. Some people here, if you talk with them, you find they're afraid they'll be sent to Mexico, or something like that, if they start protesting like the black man has been doing. But something is happening, I can tell you. If you look into it, you'll see that our people are organizing—in Los Angeles and New Mexico and here in Texas, too. They're breaking loose from the anglos, and from our own bosses, who work with them and are just as bad as the anglos are. It won't take as long as some people think before we're really on the march."

North of San Antonio one meets up with gently rolling hills, small but full rivers, scrub oaks. Austin rises out of the prairie, but a few moments later the countryside is once again quiet, even desolate except for cows and chickens and an occasional scarecrow. We approached Congressman Poage's territory from the south and west. In Hearne we interviewed some of the Congressman's constituents: Mexican-Americans, blacks, whites. "Up here we're white, not anglo," a grocer told us. "You know why? The Mexicans are thinning out, and the Negroes, they're getting thicker. I've been through Alabama and Mississippi, because I was

stationed there during the war, in Montgomery, and I'll tell you, around here it's like there—not completely, but a lot so. To tell the truth, I prefer it like that—rather than like you find it up in New York and Philadelphia. I've also been to both of those places, and the colored there, they're fat and sassy. They think they own the world, that everything's coming to them for free. You see it on television all the time, the way they're pushing on us, pushing all the time. I'll say this about our colored folks down here, they're a lot better. They'll only do what they *have* to, of course—but at least they're not marching down our streets asking for this and that and everything."

Actually, the blacks and Mexican-Americans of Hearne have a hard enough time walking down their own streets, which are unpaved and on occasion hard to drive through, let alone march down. Near the 79 Hi Cafe we crossed the railroad tracks and entered the city's black section. The inevitable shacks were there—mounted on cement blocks, full of cracks, lucky if tin roofs covered them and if a somewhat decent privy stood nearby and if a boardwalk made the last steps into or out of the house a half-way easy job. An earlier rain had settled into muddy ditches, which were everywhere. We asked a number of people how things go for them, and from one man heard the following: "We don't have heat here, except for the stove; and no water running, not inside the house, only in the streets. Plenty runs there though—yes it does. So, I guess it's hard, but isn't it always? The first thing I remember my mother told me, it must have been 35 years ago or so, was never to expect much, just be glad if you stay alive.

That's what I tell my kids. No sir, we don't have food stamps, but there's commodities, if you're good and lucky and they says it's o.k., the welfare people. I don't get welfare, and I don't want it if I can help it. I try to get by through the small jobs I get, one this week, then maybe one the next. If it's a good week I'll get $50, but most of the time, I confess, it's half that. You don't get rich that way, I guess; but there's no use complaining. There's no one to complain to, anyway. You go downtown and they'll throw you in jail fast as can be if you do that."

Downtown, the town of Hearne has railroad tracks and railroad cars and a bank called The Planters and Merchants State Bank and a movie-house which featured *Night of the Living Dead* and a black business section in which one sees Pentecostal churches and men walking the streets in overalls and cowboy hats. Not far away is the large Hearne Cotton Compress Company, which receives cotton from gins in Robertson County and presses the bales and ships them out.

It is all very interesting and educational for people like us, but not so good for thousands of people whose way-of-life does perhaps explain why Rep. W. R. Poage of Texas and Rep. Jamie Whitten of Mississippi think and vote so much alike and become similarly enraged when those bleeding-heart liberals from the North start talking so emotionally about "hunger" and "malnutrition" and all the rest. In Robertson County, just outside Hearne, and again in Limestone County, we asked several members of the middle class who should know (because each runs a grocery store) whether children go hungry and become malnourished because their parents cannot afford the right amount and kind of food. "Well sir," replied one grocer, "I don't think they're really hungry. No, they get a lot of coke and they love Kool-Aid. They take to starches, too. I'm not sure which is the cart and which is the horse, though. The cheapest things are your soft drinks and your starches—bread and things like that. It *is* expensive to buy meat and fresh vegetables, especially in the winter time. We don't have food stamps here, just the commodities, and I'll admit, I couldn't get my family to eat that stuff day after day, all that flour and cornmeal. I think a lot of those people are just lazy, but if you ask me where they can find good jobs here, I'd have to admit it's not so easy. I know, because my kid brother came back from Vietnam and he didn't just find work ready and waiting, and he's —well, he's not a nigra and not a Mexican. I'll admit it's easier for us, but in this country if a man really wants to work, he'll go and do it. He'll sacrifice and pray hard and somehow he'll get ahead. I believe that. Of course, if a child is hungry, and he's not getting the right food, then he should be fed. But his parents owe it to him to get off their rear ends and work, and if they can't find any, they should go some place else and get a job there. My father, he came here from Louisiana. Yes sir, there wasn't work there, so he came here, that's right."

We found him kind, helpful, even generous with us. He wanted to tell us about the town, his county, even show it all to us—the rich land, the flowers just beginning to appear, the open, courteous quality of the people he brought us to meet. Meet them we did— and found them sturdy, stubborn, God-fearing, possessed of a curious and almost uncanny mixture of pride, aloofness and friendliness. They all fought as hard with themselves, with their conflicted sensibilities, as we did with the logic of their various assertions. Yes, children are innocent and need to be fed; but no, we cannot coddle people. Yes, there is plenty of misery around; but no, special "favors" (we heard that word over and over again) simply cannot be granted. Yes, some people really do need help; but no, the only help we ought to get has to come from God and our own exertions.

So we left and drove on, past signs that urge each and every driver to "Get Right with God," signs that straddle twenty centuries, like "Christ Is the Answer-Wrecking Service." In Waco and the rest of McLennan County, Congressman Poage's home county, it is the same story—prosperity and misery. ("Waco is in trouble . . . Almost 30 percent of Waco's buildings are substandard," says the city's chief official in his Model Cities application to the federal government.) Once again the blacks are found living near the railroad tracks, on unpaved Harlem Ave. Once again the effort is made to speak with reasonably prosperous white people, and once again they reach out for understanding and compassion, but suddenly stop and with a remark or two summarize this nation's ambiguities: "Why can't we get rid of our slums, here in Waco and every other place? I believe in justice, and so does everyone I know. You'd think a lot of our poor folk, they'd be doing better by now, with all the prosperity we've had since the Depression. Maybe they just don't care, don't really *want* to better themselves."

The masked lady of justice—scales in hand—stands on top of the McLennan County Court House in Waco, there to be seen for miles around. Nearby the Baptist churches fight it out with Sophia Loren, one of whose movies is in town for the weekend. Nearby, people live decently and comfortably, and live lives that eventually get to make up a bundle of dry statistics: in Limestone County almost half the population makes less than $3,000 a year, and a quarter makes less than $2,000, but only 1,681 people get public assistance and 1,947 get commodity foods—and the infant mortality rate is 42.4, double the nation's rate. In Robertson County the same figures hold. In McLennan County —because of Waco it is called 80 percent urban—nearly a third of the population makes less than $3,000 a year, 7 percent less than $1,000, but only one-sixth of those who make less than $2,000 are permitted to take part in the commodity food program.

There are, other statistics, more encouraging ones. The *Texas Almanac* declares that the same Limestone County has been found to have one of the state's major oil fields, with an estimated volume of over 100-million barrels. All that oil makes money, of course, and the Securities and Exchange Commission has on file the earnings of some oil companies that operate in Texas. Texaco had a net income of $754,386,000 in 1967; Gulf managed to reap $578,287,000 that year and Sinclair Oil Company a modest $95,322,000. At the same time, as of November 1968, Texas—whose large cities and industrial wealth make it comparable to Michigan and Pennsylvania—ranks 47th among states in welfare payments per recipient, ahead of only South Carolina, Alabama and Mississippi, which have no such wealth. As for Mr. Poage's

Congressional district, during 1966, $244,000 in food assistance money came into the 11 counties from the Agriculture Department, but one-tenth of one percent of the people in the district—a handful of rich farmers—managed to get $5,318,892 in various benefits from that same Agriculture Department. Still, as the grocer insisted, "oil and crops are our big, important businesses here, and you've got to support them. You can't interfere with them, because then you're down the road to socialism."

We have travelled hundreds of miles down the roads of that grocer's native state, and it turns out he has nothing to worry about. The miserable, wretched roads and the first-rate, well-paved ones cover different territory, and few people in Texas are interfering with anything very big or important.

AMERICAN INDIAN
YOUTH

CUSTER DIED FOR YOUR SINS

Vine Deloria, Jr.

Chicago has seen the rise of Indian nationalism by younger people. In addition to the established centers and clubs, young people have started to move the urban Indian structure toward a more militant stance in regard to urban programs available through the mayor's office. Denver has recently seen the organization of another Indian club that is avowedly more militant with regard to programs being administered by the city. Omaha has a group of younger Indians which threatens to begin to move city Indians toward community involvement.

Because there is such a mushrooming movement among urban Indians, old ideas and traditional policies have become woefully outmoded. In the past, tribal councils have largely determined national Indian policy. Many times the Bureau of Indian Affairs has been able to apply pressure on certain tribes to hold back militant stands by Indian people. It learned to effectively play one

Reprinted with permission of the Macmillan Company from Custer Died For Your Sins by Vine Deloria, Jr. Copyright © 1969 by Vine Deloria, Jr.

tribe against another until the tribes were confused and disheartened. Then it would appear to compromise and tribes would eagerly agree to whatever was placed before them. When one recalls that every tribe had to have approval of the BIA to lease its lands, to travel, to get legal counsel, it is a wonder that tribes have been able to get anything done.

While the BIA still has to approve basic tribal operations, it no longer has the resources to keep track of everything happening in Indian Affairs today. Other agencies are continually calling conferences which take tribes from one end of the country to another. Pressuring individual tribes has become too risky because of the great competition between government agencies to appear more active than competing agencies.

Urban Indians have a great advantage over reservation people. They have no restrictions on the way they raise or spend money. The bureau has no means by which it can influence decisions made by urban Indian centers. Thus, if it is to influence urban Indians at all, it must be by offering them something. Urban Indians have nothing to lose and everything to gain, so initial success breeds deeper thought and more comprehensive planning for the next go-round.

Nor do the emerging non-federal eastern Indians have anything to lose. In many cases, in many states, they are busy compiling the documentation to prove their claims. The tribes of Maine are moving incredibly fast in pressing their claims against Massachusetts. And Massachusetts may have its hands full with other tribes such as the Wampanoag and Narragansett before it is finished with Indian people.

The great weapon which the eastern tribes have is invisibility. No one believes they exist, yet back in the statutes and treaties lies the key to their eventual success. The Montauks are a good example. At the turn of the century the tribe was thrown out of court because the Montauks lacked standing to file suit. They were wards of the state of New York. Well, people argue, if they were wards of the state of New York, what has the state been doing for them?

At present there is tremendous potential awakening in the cities and among the non-federal tribes of the East. At least three-quarters of the national Indian population lives in the cities and eastern United States. A new coalition of eastern Indians and urban groups could force a radical change in existing federal policy toward Indian people. These people generally vote more than reservation people. When they organize for political purposes, they will be able to exert more influence than they have at present.

Many non-reservation Indians are scattered in states and Congressional districts that have yet to produce a Senator or Congressman who has taken an interest in Indians. When these groups organize for effective action they will begin to make Indian Affairs a concern of interested non-Indians who would like to assist Indian people. Thus there is every indication that eastern and urban people will be able to bring up issues which reservation people have not been able or willing to raise.

Tragically, Indian Affairs within the Bureau of Indian Affairs is today exclusively oriented toward individual reservations. Little concern is shown for program development on a regional, state, or inter-area office basis. Thus the BIA is extremely vulnerable to unexpected pressures from regional groups which combine urban concentrations or urban centers and reservations.

Excerpts from

THE NEW INDIANS

Stan Steiner

In the process the last hope of communicating with his conqueror was lost. The years on the old-style reservations sealed the lips of the tribal Indian. His thoughts then turned inward, and his stoic resignation became his image. His voice was not listened to when he tried to speak and those agency Indians appointed by the government spoke for him.

"Our Indians in the Creek Nation were fearful, they were afraid," the Creek prophet, Reverend Clifton Hill, said. "It seemed as though they couldn't speak for themselves. Or do anything. Because all through the ages, all through the years, the white men were always telling the Indians they couldn't do nothing."

Reverend Hill thought that the Indian was not mute; he had been deliberately rendered voiceless: "Any time an Indian spoke up for himself and his justice, the white men, and the white Indians, who worked for him, they stood up and said, 'We don't want it that

From pp. 84–86, 93–95 in The New Indians by Stan Steiner. Copyright © 1968 by Stan Steiner. Reprinted by permission of Harper and Row, Publishers.

way.' They were the ones that always smothered what Indians really thought and wanted. That has held us back. That has been going on for years. That was a Great Giant. That was a Mountain.

"Like that Tower of Babel, that had to fall. It had to come down. It could not go on. Our Indians had to learn how to shake up that Tower of Babel. And they will. They have."

The awe of the Tower of Babel no longer overwhelms some of the young Indians. Some of them have climbed the tower. Some speak the languages of confusion. "If someone asks me, condescendingly, whether I talk 'Indian,' I usually answer in French," said the Cherokee girl Mary Lou Payne. From the top the tower does not loom so large as it did from the bottom. And some of the elders of the tribes, seeing their youth climb upward, are no longer as fearful of it; it does not seem so formidable an obstacle.

Has the Tower of Babel fallen? Not quite.

Coming home from the schools and the cities and the military services the Indians of the new generation loom larger in their own self-esteem. It is this contagious pride that they have brought back with them to the reservations. Moreover, they now know more than merely how to speak the language of the conquerors. They know how to speak it in a way that the white man knows how to listen to. And it is this, their articute voices, in swinging and university-toned English, which they have brought to the tribal elders, that more than anything else has scaled down the size of the unmountable mountain.

The effect of this change on the Cherokees of Oklahoma was told by Clyde Warrior: "The unrest and resentment has always existed through all the age groups of Indians. But the elders did not think anything could be done.

"Now they have young people coming home who are somewhat verbal [in English], who have some knowledge of how the mechanics of government and American institutions work. They have begun to utilize these rebellious young people. It's a kind of happy meeting of elders, with power in the community, and these young people who have some idea of how urban America works."

In this way the young Indians are becoming the spokesmen for the unspoken thoughts of their fathers. So many things unsaid and uncommunicated for years have begun to be voiced with that "vehemence" and that "expressive, concise, emphatical, sonorous, and bold" eloquence that James Adair heard two hundred years ago.

And yet the white man, long soothed by the seemingly supplicant and seemingly stoic Indian, is reluctant to give up that comforting image. He prefers, of course, not to listen.

The tribal Indians are undergoing so intense and complex a process of rediscovery of their beliefs and strengths that they do not know how to make

their voices heard. Nor do they know what to say. Young Vine Deloria, Jr., of the National Congress of American Indians, thought his own path of self-discovery that had led through two universities and governmental offices and Congressional hearings and national politics was not atypical.

His path "was just a little longer," Deloria, Jr., said: "In the college where I went there was a professor who had just discovered the 'crisis of identity.' He would sit in seminars and ask us: 'Do you have this "crisis of identity"?' What he meant was, 'Do you have a crisis in identifying with the mainstream of my way of life?' He should never have asked that question!

"There were a number of us, young Indians, who thought about it and discovered that we did not identify with his way of life. We identified with our Indian way of life.

"Lots of young Indians have been educated in this way, in colleges, in the last ten years. They understand the so-called mainstream. They look at the mainstream, and what do they see: ice cream bars and heart trouble and neurosis and deodorants and getting up at six o'clock in the morning to mow your lawn in the suburbs. They see that in the mainstream the urban and suburban men are trapped; once you get a job it's climb, climb, climb. If you get heart trouble it's the price you pay.

"It's a strange thing. When you get far enough away from the reservation, you can see it's the urban man who has no identity. So he gets money. Or power. To feel secure, to protect himself. But he hasn't any roots, any land, any soul.

"In the beginning, when the Indians first went on the reservations, they were brainwashed by do-gooders, people who taught them Western culture. For a long time the older people accepted those things as 'truths.' These were the 'truths' brought to them by the missionaries, by the Bureau of Indian Affairs. And the Indians adjusted to this. But, at the same time, these people in their urgency to get the Indians into the mainstream began to educate them.

"You can educate a brainwashed Indian just so far. And then he begins to think for himself. He decides that he can accept, or reject, these 'truths.' That's where they made their mistake.

"The young Indians know these are not 'truths.' It is a pattern of behavior you are forced into because you live in a certain way. So you find lots of Indians, educated Indians, rejecting this way of life, and going back to the old people and saying: You have kept the tribal values under wraps, and you've never dared express them. Well, it's all right to express them. We have been out in the white man's world. We have been educated. We have read Plato and all his philosophers. And we see that the Indian ways are better. So the old people shouldn't be afraid to be really Indian."

Deloria, Jr., thought it was not just the younger Indians who spoke of these changes. Their fathers, so long silenced by hopelessness and the burdens of the past, were becoming as outspoken. In the once somnolent reservations more and more of the elders of the tribes were beginning to say, truthfully, in public what for so long they said only in private.

Rebellion of the youth; but with a difference. The temper, the mood, the philosophy, of the new Indians voiced no rebellion against their fathers, the tribal elders. Rather it was their guard-ian—the Great White Father—they were rebelling against, and they were returning home, to the home of their fathers, their spiritual fathers. "You *can* go home again" was their motto.

One of them was Professor Jim Wilson, an Oglala Sioux. He had a doctorate in education, but he was thinking now of going home to his reservation. He remembered when, as he was growing up on the Pine Ridge Reservation in South Dakota in a back-country hut, "the yellow school bus had kidnaped him"; and he began his wandering in pursuit of education. He was one of "the select club" of Indians, he said, who "had made it." Wandering the nomadic trail of academia in search of a career, he had encamped at various universities before becoming chief of the Indian Division of the Office of Economic Opportunity in Washington. Where could he go from there? His odyssey was leading him, it seemed, back to his people. His tribal trek was, he thought, typical of his generation.

"I am enough of a Red Muslim to think I've got to speak out!" Dr. Wilson said. "Many of these young people who are getting educated and finding employment are going back [to their tribes] and reviving some of the things that were almost lost during the past generation. The young Indian finds in going back for the second time, with more time to devote to it, with a better understanding of the learning process, that he can take his heritage back into himself to a greater extent than if he had grown up in a condition of poverty. He might have had these things around him before, but to a large extent they were unnoticed. It is like studying something new.

"Many of the concerns of the traditional Indians about the changing values of the young Indians were relieved when these young Indians found that they could be productive members of this society, and still be Indians in every sense of the word. This was the real breakthrough for a lot of us."

And the "breakthrough" was growing wider, thought Vine Deloria, Jr., who like his fellow Sioux tribesman Dr. Wilson had spent several years in Washington, D.C., as the director of the National Congress of American Indians.

The cultural turnabout of the young Indians had begun to affect even the student elite, Deloria, Jr., said. Recently the United Scholarship Fund of Denver, Colorado, under his direction, had assisted more than forty Indian boys and girls in attending exclusive prep schools.

"When I was working with the prep school program," Deloria, Jr., said, "and getting these kids accepted, their first reaction to the testing and all that was to be as good white Indians as the missionaries and local school districts had taught them to be. These kids weren't in prep school for six weeks before they were the most violent nationalists you ever saw. These kids began to write me all the time: Send us books on Indians. We want to learn the legends of our tribe. Here they were, in the perfect setting for painless acculturation, and they were racking their brains, twenty-four hours a day, to remember the Indian words they used to know. They began to write the old people at home to find out the Indian words they had forgotten.

"I think these kids suddenly realized that outside of hula hoops and Cadillac fins, the white society had nothing, absolutely nothing, to offer them spiritually. They became really proud to be Indians. They had a culture, something of their own that their classmates did not have. Holden Caulfield was a sad cat to them."

"These young Indians have their sawdust leaking out," said the Cherokee anthropologist Robert Thomas. "And they are going to build the barricades on which to fight out the battle of their Indianness, out of their own sawdust, if they have to. But they are going to make themselves Indian. Every three years there is a new generation. And every new generation is more Indian than the last. Youth leaders of the National Indian Youth Council, who were hotshots three years ago, are considered by the new new Indians to have cooled it, to be conservatives."

The older generation of new Indians, the generation of a few years before, sensed the change in the newer generation. Clyde Warrior said: "Five years ago those of us who started off the Youth Council were called the most radical of radicals. Those of us who headed the movement five years ago now are considered Uncle Tomahawks. There is a more and more angry bunch of kids coming up. Which I like. When we started five years ago I said: It wouldn't be us that do anything. It'll be the ones that come after us. They will be angrier and madder. It's happening. It has happened."

Herbert Blatchford, in his calm Navajo way, reflects: "It is time to face the fact that the Indians are skeptical of the Anglo-American culture."

LO, THE POOR INDIAN

Ralph Nader

The cry of "Lo, the Poor Indian" resounded once again from Washington this month—this time in the form of a special presidential message to Congress. Like a torrent of previous statements on the "Forgotten American" flowing from the Department of Interior, the President said most of the right things and used most of the compassionate adjectives. As in former years and former Administrations, emphasis was placed on self-help, self-determination, a higher economic standard of living, better education, improved health care, manpower training, new roads and a bill of rights for the 400,000 reservation Indians.

Is there anything new here, other than further action-displacing sympathy that has bred a hard skepticism into most Indians long resigned to poverty in perpetuity? Clearly, a direct White House commitment to Indian betterment, for the first time, gives the mission greater visibility and importance. There is a 12 percent increase in overall Indian appropriations requested of Congress for fiscal year

1969. But beyond that, the President's message avoided dealing with the enduring organizational dry rot upon which these programs are being advanced, namely, the Bureau of Indian Affairs (BIA).

One hundred and nineteen years ago, the BIA was established in the Department of Interior with both presumed and actual missions. The former dealt with improving the lot of the Indian; the latter with facilitating the encroachment on or exploitation of Indian lands and resources. Under the Bureau's aegis and congressional directive, the Indian land base shrunk from 150 million acres to the present 53 million acres—about the size of New England. For generations the Bureau presided over people without a future. Indians were called "wards," were culturally devastated, physically pushed around and entwined in the most intricate web of bureaucratic regulations and rulings ever inflicted anywhere in this nation's history. They still are.

In the meantime, the BIA has prospered, growing to its present size of approximately 16,000 employees providing the services of a federal, state and local government in one administrative bundle. Together with smaller programs in Indian health (under the Public

Health Service) and antipoverty programs (in OEO), current fiscal year appropriations for Indians totaled about $460 million or an average income per reservation family of some $5,600 if paid out in cash. (The average family income is $1,500 per annum.)

The Indian budget has been increasing at a rate that has doubled in the past decade. Yet the picture on the reservations is drab and grim. The present poverty tally is a 40 percent unemployment rate (with much underemployment), grossly dilapidated housing, at least 30 percent illiteracy, two-thirds the life expectancy and less than a third of the average income of other Americans, rampant disease including a tuberculosis incidence seven times the national average.

Anyone who has followed Indian affairs finds these figures to be a dreary redundancy of past recitations. With the exception of some advances in Indian health, reservation conditions remain as bad or worse than 10 or 20 years ago. In the past decade a new dimension of despair has emerged in the form of 200,000 Indians in city slums such as Los Angeles, Denver and Minneapolis. But the BIA continues to exude fads of hope—whether it is relocation away from the reservations, tourism, mineral development and the latest unfilled expectation—bringing industry to the reservations.

Prior to the President's message, the White House rejected the major recommendation of the President's Task Force on American Indians to transfer primary responsibility for Indian affairs from the Secretary of Interior to the Secretary of Health, Education and Welfare. The Task Force, in its still secret 104-page report completed in 1966, urged the shift to HEW on the

grounds that 75 percent of total Indian appropriations is allocated to health, education and welfare functions. About 53 percent of the BIA budget ($250 million in fiscal 1968) goes toward its education function on the reservations. With responsibility for Indian health services already in HEW, the Task Force diplomatically concluded by emphasizing that "HEW program emphasis on conservation and natural resources."

Beneath such a placid rationale was the disgust and despair felt by many of the Task Force's members at the performance of the Bureau. The Task Force report took note of the widespread impression that "too many BIA employees were simply time-servers of mediocre or poor competence who remained indefinitely because they were willing to serve in unattractive posts at low rates of pay for long periods of time; that too many had unconsciously anti-Indian attitudes and are convinced that Indians are really hopelessly incompetent and their behavior reflects this assumption."

Building on numerous previous government (Hoover-type) critiques of the BIA's changeless ways, the Task Force ticked off a list of "discoveries" which shocked it: "The Bureau has no really hard data on population dynamics, income, employment, education . . . grossly inadequate data on which to base development plans. *The Bureau does not even have one trained statistician on its staff at the present time* [its emphasis]. . . . A related matter, equally shocking to the Task Force, was the total absence of any R & D funds in the BIA budget."

The Task Force, were it not divided into a majority and small minority position over shifting the BIA's functions to HEW, might have made a far stronger case against the BIA. Illustratively, Senator Robert Kennedy's subcommittee has pointed attention to the failure in quantity and quality of BIA reservation schools. Since these schools breed despondency, cultural inferiority and alienation, it is not surprising that the dropout rate exceeds 50 percent. Mismanagement of BIA's supervisory responsibilities over land, timber and water resources is legion. Last year BIA negligence led to major forest fires including one on the Mescalero Apache Reservation in New Mexico and another on the Quinault Reservation in Washington. BIA has managed to oversee the leasing and franchising of valuable reservation property rights and income opportunities into predominantly non-Indian hands. Even busboys in the restaurants on the Cherokee reservation are non-Indian; while Indian boys stand or sit idly by the roadside. Still, the BIA will not supply inquirers with a list of all the franchises given non-Indians on the reservations.

Secrecy in the BIA has bordered on the Byzantine. The complexities of the government-Indian trust relationships, the undisclosed details of trust funds held in the Treasury Department, and the fractionated land heirship problem on reservations are all wrapped up in the BIA's endemic secrecy. It is not even possible to receive from the Bureau a reliable estimate as to the number of Indians on the reservations who are not serviced. Moreover, services are uneven in any given program and a few reservations become BIA "favorites" for one program or another, depending on the needs of Indian politics.

By not dealing with the fundamental malaise of the BIA, the White House will see its slightly refurbished proposals consigned to a limbo of resonant rhetoric. Quite possibly, the Administration did not want to upset the intricate relationship which BIA has built up with grazing, timber, mining interests in the West, on the one hand, and its Indian associates on the reservations whom young Indian reformers call derisively "Uncle Tomahawks." Moreover, many Indian chiefs, fearing that change could place them at a greater disadvantage and perhaps activate the semi-dormant federal termination of the reservation policy approved by congressional resolution in 1953, cling to the Bureau as the best bulwark against change. They could not be more accurate in this estimate of the Bureau's molecular inertia as well as the omnipresent pressure from several congressmen for renewing the termination policy whereby reservations would be dissolved. Completed terminations on the Klamath reservation in Oregon and Menominee in Wisconsin have had terribly adverse effects on Indians and their local economies. Without a land base, Indians will soon cease as distinct cultures.

Until the recent hearings by Sen. George McGovern of the Senate subcommittee on Indian affairs, there have been no meaningful hearings on Indian poverty. There is no indication, however, that the Bureau will be subjected to a probing congressional oversight hearing. Criticism directed at the Bureau has been for *not* terminating reservations fast enough. James Gamble of the Senate subcommittee staff, with the apparent knowledge of Senators Henry Jackson (D, Wash.) and Clinton Anderson (D, N.M.) has long been the chief congressional worker for termination of Indian reservations and assimilation of the Indian into the mainstream of American life. The intensity of his animosity toward what he considers the privileged position of Indians and the BIA, which he says has a vested interest in this position, is almost startling. Not until 1967 did the Indian affairs sub-committee in the Senate and House lose their total grip on matters Indian. Both Senators Robert Kennedy and, to a lesser extent, Abraham Ribicoff (D, Conn.) held hearings during the past year on Indian urban ghettoes and Indian education. Such a trend may lead to a fresh approach toward understanding at least the dimensions of the Indian problem and the priorities in policy-making.

For example, Professor Gary Orfield of the University of Virginia believes the key focus should be in providing the Indians with jobs. Employment, he believes, would radiate the kinds of self-confidence and options that offer freedom of choice and break the vicious circle of poverty. "Even allowing for the rapid population growth, it is obvious that the basic economic problem of the Indian communities could be solved by the provision of 40,000 jobs. This would seem a small demand for a nation where civilian employment has increased an average of 723,000 each year from 1955 to 1965, and where the last five years the average increase has been almost 1.5 million per year." Analysis after analysis of the reservations' economic potential points to what has to be done to achieve this relatively modest objective. Provision of adequate loan funds to finance tribal enterprises and incentives to attract industry are often recommended. Conservation projects, recreational site developments, public housing construction and other community improvement projects can be more immediately implemented. There is solid precedent for success in job creation in the Indian Emergency Conservation Work program during the thirties. Some 15,000 men were put to work in a few months time.

Excerpts from

OUR BROTHER'S KEEPER:
THE INDIAN
IN WHITE AMERICA

Edgar S. Cahn, Editor

THE BUREAU OF INDIAN AFFAIRS: THE LESSER OF TWO EVILS

The Indian tolerates his present impotent and unjust status in his relations with the Federal Government because he sees the Bureau of Indian Affairs as the lesser of two evils. The BIA is all he has, and every promise to replace it with something better has been broken.

Those new to Indian problems and enraged by the conduct of the BIA, and even those long acquainted with the Bureau's impenetrable bureaucracy often reach an obvious conclusion: why not just do away with the Bureau and, in the words of a U.S. Senator, "free" the Indian?

The easy answer is the wrong an-

Edgar S. Cahn, Editor Citizens' Advocate Center, Our Brother's Keeper: The Indian in White America (Washington, D.C.: New Community Press, 1969), pp. 14–23, 27–36, 38–45. Reprinted by permission.

swer, and the Indian knows it better than anyone else. Those who would abolish the Bureau to "help" the Indian will find as their most vehement opponent the Indian himself. He knows that he must, even at the cost of his liberty, preserve the Bureau—because the Bureau and only the Bureau stands between the Indian and extinction as a racial and cultural entity. Only the Bureau stands between the Indian and total, unilateral renunciation of all federal treaty obligations. The Bureau has been and only the Bureau remains the special protector of the Indian and his champion, at times, against predatory interests. The Bureau and the solemn promises of the Federal Government are symbolically synonymous in the mind of the Indian. To destroy one is to destroy both.

The Bureau has done a terrible job; it has compromised the Indian time and again; it has permitted, tolerated, even assisted in the erosion of Indian rights and the whittling away of the Indian land base. Still, to the Indian, it is *his*. In the light of wisdom gained from long years of bitter experience, the Indian knows that a threat to the Bureau, an attack on the Bureau or any change in its structure is to be resisted as a threat to his own survival.

Thus, in April, 1969, newspapers around the nation carried stories of atrocities, brutality, mismanagement and professional incompetence at the Chilocco Indian School in Oklahoma. The accounts were based on disclosure of a report by BIA staff investigators.

Yet, a few days later, the newspapers told of rallies by Chilocco students to defend it against these attacks and "save our schools." Were the rallies instigated by Bureau school officials? Perhaps, in part. The fact is, however, that Indian students at Chilocco know despite alleged abuse and its faults, the school is preferable to the total isolation, the prejudice, the humiliation, and the degrading condescension which they meet in public schools. Standards may be low and conditions almost intolerable, but students and graduates at Chilocco at least are permitted to retain an Indian identity. Because of that identity, they develop a solidarity and a sentimental attachment to a school which at least shields them partially from the cultural assault they experience elsewhere.

Similarly, those who try to make changes in the Bureau will find themselves met with substantial opposition from Indians. Thus, a proposal in 1964 to shift the education functions of the Bureau over to the Office of Education in the Department of Health, Education, and Welfare was resisted violently by Indians who saw it as a first step toward dismantling the Bureau, abrogating federal responsibilities and turning over Indian education to state education agencies.

The much heralded Omnibus Bill of 1967 which provided, among other things, sorely needed capital funds for economic development and land consolidation, was defeated in part because the Indians perceived it as an attempt to facilitate the withering away of federal obligations.

A proposal adopted in May 1969 by the National Congress of American Indians to streamline the Bureau by abolishing the middle tier of unresponsive bureaucracy, was coupled with an expression of fear: "If the Bureau of Indian Affairs is abolished or its services fragmented, it will again jeopardize, and in many cases it will terminate the present services of the Federal Government. It will be termination in disguise."

Indians can and often do criticize the Bureau, but they do not necessarily regard the non-Indian critic as an ally. They know that criticism can play directly into the hands of their worst enemies—those who wish to end the special relationship which exists between the Indian and the Federal Government.

Even the truth is to be resisted, if it is a truth which can endanger their protector, the Bureau. The Bureau plays upon this fear to stimulate Indians, and particularly tribal leaders, to attack and deny any report which seeks to tell the truth—although the same Indians privately will admit the truth of the charges, and even cite examples.

The Indian not only tolerates the injustice of the system; he helps insulate it from scrutiny and criticism, because history has convinced him that an attack on the Bureau will lead to the destruction of his special status as an Indian, and to the death of his people. This fear takes a particular form—fear of "Termination."

TERMINATION—*An end to the special status of the Indian, and with it a disavowal of his trusteeship and protection arrangement with the United States Government.* Fear of termination pervades Indian thinking. It colors the Indian's appraisal of every proposal, suggestion and criticism.

Termination refers to that policy officially adopted by the Federal Government in the 1950's, "freeing" the Indian from the BIA's paternalism. But to the Indian, termination is just the latest and most deadly in a series of policies of destruction which has prevailed for nearly two centuries. Earl Old Person, a leader of the Blackfeet Tribe, points out:

"... (I)n our Indian language the only translation for termination is 'to wipe out' or 'to kill off.' We have no Indian words for termination. . . ."

The threat of termination remains strong and reduces the Indian's limited options still further.

"... (H)ow can we plan our future when the Indian Bureau constantly threatens to wipe us out as a race? It is like trying to cook a meal in your tepee when someone is standing outside trying to burn the tepee down. . . . "In the past 190 years, the U.S. Government has tried every possible way to get rid of the troublesome Indian problem. . . . First the Government tried extinction through destruction—where money was paid for the scalps of every dead Indian. Then the Government tried mass relocation and containment through concentration—the moving of entire tribes or parts of tribes to isolated parts of the country where they were herded like animals and fed like animals for the most part. Then the Government tried assimilation—where reservations were broken up into allotments (an ownership system the Indians did

not understand) and Indians were forced to try to live like 'white men.' Indian dances and Indian hand work was forbidden. A family's ration of food was cut off if anyone in the family was caught singing Indians songs or doing Indian hand craft. Children were physically beaten if they were caught speaking Indian languages. Then termination was tried by issuing forced patents in fee [fee simple title] to Indian landowners—land was taken out of the trust relationship with the U.S. Government and an unrestricted patent in fee was issued to the Indian whether he wanted it or not or whether he understood what was going on or not." [1]

The Indian was correct in his appraisal of termination as annihilation rather than emancipation. Events of the past decade have more than confirmed his worst fears. The Menominee Tribe of Wisconsin, terminated in 1961, symbolizes the nightmare come true. Members of the tribe were proud and relatively self-sufficient people with good schools, community services and a tribal-owned sawmill. Once terminated, their reservation became incorporated into a county, and today it is the most impoverished county in the state. State Public Assistance costs in Menominee County soared from $121,686 in 1961 to $766,601 in 1968. Menominee County ranks at or near the bototm of Wisconsin's Counties in income, housing, property value, education, employment, sanitation, and health. The median income for the Menominee is below $1,000. Much Indian land has been sold at auctions because Indians were unable to pay the state property

[1] Statement by Earl Old Person, Chairman of Blackfeet Tribe, in testimony before Indian Leaders Conference. Bureau of Indian Affairs, Spokane, Washington, pp. 15–16, October 17–19, 1966.

taxes to which their land became subject after termination.[2]

The State of Wisconsin has neither the money nor the inclination to assume the responsibilities abandoned by the BIA. The tribal sawmill, inefficient and outmoded, could not provide enough jobs. The county tax base is too small to support decent schools and health services. The Menominee hospital, one of the best for Indians, was forced to close. Indians even lost the right to hunt and fish on their own lands without paying for a state permit—until the Supreme Court decided that the Menominee still hold that right because Congress had "forgotten" to abolish it.

In February 1965, 11 years after termination, a BIA report to Congress gave an accurate portrayal of the effects of termination: ". . . The impact of developments since 1961 on the people of the county cannot be simply characterized. Some Menominees seem to be as demoralized as any poverty-stricken people anywhere. Others, far from demoralized, are highly and vocally indignant."

Professor Gary Orfield, in a study of the tribe conducted at the University of Chicago, commented: "Freedom was the fundamental objective. . . . The failure to extend the real freedom of the tribe has been almost total. . . . The Menominee tribe is dead, but for no good reason."[3]

The Klamath Indians of Oregon fared no better after their emancipation from BIA paternalism. Senator Ralph W. Yarborough of Texas gave this summary: "Their reservation was terminated . . . the lands sold and money distributed. And now . . . somewhat less than 10 years later, the number who finished high school is very small compared to the number who finished high school when they had the reservation. Suicides have increased— this is among the adults—at a terrific rate, drunkenness at a terrific rate, and criminal records are a serious problem."[4]

Similar results from forced termination can be found among the Utah Paiutes. In no case can it be shown that a tribe gained in self-sufficiency after termination: most ceased to exist as cohesive communities with their own culture and history. Even today there is unrelenting pressure to terminate the Colville Indians in Washington state, and in California members of the Agua Caliente Bands are being pressured unscrupulously to abandon the trust status of their land.

Indians were not given any choice about the termination policy of the 1950's. During this period, BIA commissioners were appointed who supported the idea of ending federal-Indian relations. One was Dillon Myer, who gained his government experience as the head of the War Relocation Authority, the agency which directed the internment of the Japanese in the Western U.S. during World War II.

Typically, termination has been forced down the throats of the Indians —by unilateral dictation, deception,

---

[2] "The Status of the Termination of the Menominee Indian Tribe," A Report to the Committee on Appropriations, House of Representatives by the Department of the Interior, Bureau of Indian Affairs, February 1965; CAC telephone interview with Wisconsin State Welfare Office, June 11, 1969.
[3] Gary Orfield, A Study of the Termination Policy, pp. 15, 23.

[4] Hearings on the Education of Indian Children before a Special Subcommittee on Indian Education of the Senate Committee on Labor and Public Welfare, 90 Cong., 1 and 2 sess., Part V, p. 2160, October 1, 1968.

and fraud. An assistant commissioner explained, "We did not feel that it was necessary for us to go back to the tribe . . . and start trying to draft a new program. . . ."[5] Fear of termination and continuing intense Congressional pressure for it forces Indians to defend the very agency which wrongs them. This fear paralyzes the Indian and mutes his efforts to change his way of life.

Although termination has been officially discarded as federal policy by the Kennedy, Johnson and Nixon Administrations, the Indian has sound reason to believe that termination lies behind each new reform which the Government poses for Indians. He need only examine the statements at a 1967 Senate hearing of Robert Bennett, the first Indian Commissioner of the BIA in this century and a supposed champion against termination, to see how rhetoric changes, but the underlying purposes persist:

Senator Hatfield: ". . . What is the basic philosophy of the Bureau of Indian Affairs at this time?"

Mr. Bennett: ". . . The basic philosophy is that the Government has made commitments to the Indian people . . . and the Government should carry out these commitments. . . . When the Government has carried out these commitments . . . in the way of their educational level, health level and so forth, then I feel, as Commissioner of Indian Affairs, I have a

responsibility to report this to the Congress, and that the Congress, as the policymaking body, will then determine whether or not our services shall be withdrawn and terminated or whether for reasons that the Congress may decide they shall be continued. . . ."

Senator Hatfield: "In other words, termination is the basic philosophy that we are moving toward as each group is brought to a place where they are considered to be self-supporting and self-sufficient; is that correct?"

Mr. Bennett: "Yes, sir. Then the tribal leaders have said when Congress gets through and has carried out their commitments, then they will all have to face this question."[6]

The Indian knows that termination takes many forms. He can be flooded out of his reservation; he can be relocated; his reservation can be sold out from under him if he cannot meet taxes to which it is subject. His limited power to protect himself on the reservation from local prejudice and discrimination can be wiped away by the substitution of state laws for tribal law, and state jurisdiction for tribal jurisdiction. All of these, the Indian knows, are variants on one basic truth: the United States Government does not keep its promises. Sometimes it breaks them all at once, and sometimes slowly, one at a time. The result is the same—termination. When the Indian is asked to forsake his status under the Bureau in

[5] Statement by Rex Lee, Assistant Commissioner of Indian Affairs. *Joint Hearings on the Termination of Federal Supervision over Certain Tribes of Indians*, 83rd Cong., 2nd sess., Part VI, p. 610, quoted in William A. Brophy and Sophie D. Aberle, *The Indian: America's Unfinished Business*, p. 200, 1966.

[6] Testimony by Robert L. Bennett, Commissioner, Bureau of Indian Affairs. *Hearings before the Subcommittee on Indian Affairs of the Senate Committee on Interior and Insular Affairs*, 90 Cong. 1 sess., pp. 25, 27, June 8, 1967.

exchange for cash, for promises of technical aid, for public works improvements and industrial developments, he has learned to expect two things:

—*That the promises will not be kept.*

—*That even if they should be kept, they will prove inadequate to maintain the Indian at even his reservation level of deprivation.*

As Wendell Chino, President of the National Congress of American Indians, stated, "We American Indians are tired of proposals which offer limited assistance and exact, as the price, the risk of losing our traditional protections afforded by our federal trusteeship." [7] The Indian has learned that he is better off with the Bureau than with the substitutes which have been offered in the past.

A 1969 White House report on Indian problems noted, "The termination issue still 'poisons' Indian affairs and causes almost every proposal and act of government in the field of Indian affairs to be viewed by the Indians, first, with suspicion and a genuine concern for possible termination motives or results." [8]

For all these reasons, any report which is critical of the BIA places the Indians in a difficult spot. Criticism, even when valid, can backfire. Criticism can be misused to increase the pressure for eliminating the BIA, and with it the special obligations of the nation to the Indians. Criticism can bring termination, and termination in any of its

[7] "Weekly Report," *The Congressional Quarterly*, Vol. XXV, No. 21, p. 889, May 26, 1967.
[8] Alvin M. Josephy, Jr., *The American Indian and the Bureau of Indian Affairs—1969: A Study with Recommendations*, p. 5, February 1969.

forms is evil. It has wrought only havoc, misery, increased deprivation, and total destruction. Termination, in all of its forms, has been a way to break promises, not fulfill them.

Until reform and termination are separated in the reformer's schemes as well as in the Indian mind, the Indian will continue to defend his Keeper. In that world, the Indian suffers a slow death, but he still can cling to hope. That is the lesser of two evils.

EDUCATION AS WAR

Education for the American Indian today follows a pattern of "cold war," modeled on a time-tested formula. Its components:

—*Promises made and promises broken.*

—*The long trek from home to the white man's wasteland.*

—*Unremitting pressure toward total submission, leading to personal, cultural and ethnic annihilation.*

Promises are cheap. A treaty signed a century ago between the United States Government and the Navajo nation included this pledge:

"The United States agrees that for every 30 children . . . who can be induced or compelled to attend school, a house shall be provided and a teacher competent to teach the elementary branches of an English education shall be furnished. . . ."

In 1969, 40,000 Navajos—nearly a third of the entire tribe—are functional illiterates in English.

Rupert Costo, President of the American Indian Historical Society and a chairman of the Cahuilla tribe of California, says Indians have always considered education crucial to their survival. "In our contact with the whites, we have always and without fail asked for one thing. We wanted education. You can examine any treaty, any negotiations with the American whites. The first condition, specifically asked for by the Indian tribes, was education." [1]

In spite of that and in spite of periodic reassertions by the Government of its commitment to education, the product—through BIA-operated boarding schools and day schools and through contract arrangements with local public school districts—is abysmally poor.

The Bureau of Indian Affairs operates 77 boarding schools, scattered throughout the nation, and 147 day schools located on or near reservations. In recent years, the Bureau has sought to transfer much of its responsibility for educating Indian children to local school districts, entering into contracts with the states. In 1969, 57.4 per cent of all Indians attending schools were in public schools, attending classes with non-Indians. Two-thirds of the remaining youngsters, or some 35,000 children, are sent to boarding schools. BIA day schools serve only 16,000 children, or about 14 per cent of the Indians in school.

In 1966, more than 16,000 Indian children of school age were not attending any school at all.

—*The average educational level for all Indians under federal supervision is five school years.*

—*Dropout rates are twice the national average.*

—*Indian children score consistently lower than white children at every grade level, in both verbal and non-verbal skills according to national tests, administered in 1965. The longer the Indian child stays in school, the further behind he gets.*

—*More than one out of five Indian males (22.3 per cent) have less than five years of schooling.*

—*The Cherokees of Oklahoma today have reached an educational level one year behind the state's Negro population of 10 years ago and 2.2 school years behind the Negro population of present-day Oklahoma.*

It is the same bleak story, no matter whether one studies national Indian statistics, a single BIA school, or even the public schools serving Indians and receiving special federal funds. (If any distinction is to be made, the public schools receiving special BIA funds may have done even worse. The BIA has abdicated responsibility—even though its funds and its trust obligations are involved.)

The human needs of children are "swept away when [the Indian child] is put in a BIA boarding school situation, where there might be as many as 100 to 150 other children under the care of a single matron. She is supposed to provide a substitute environment to become a parent-substitute for him." [2]

---

[1] *Hearings Before a Special Subcommittee on Indian Education of the Senate Committee on Labor and Public Welfare*, 90 Cong., 1 and 2 sess., Part I, 242, January 4, 1968.

[2] Statement by Dr. Daniel J. O'Connell, Executive Secretary, National Committee on Mental Health. Indian Education Subcommittee Hearings, 90 Cong. 1 and 2 sess., Part I, p. 53, December 14, 1967. See also Dr. Robert L. Bergman, "A Second Report on the Problems of Boarding Schools," reprinted in the Indian Education Subcommittee Hearings, Part III, p. 1130, March 30, 1968.

"I many times stay up late at night holding a girl's head on my lap while she is crying," a boarding school staff member lamented, "but when you have 100 students in a dormitory it is impossible to comfort all those who need comforting." [3]

Senator Walter Mondale of Minnesota, a member of the Senate Indian Education Subcommittee was advised by the BIA recently that "there is one psychologist in the whole BIA [school] system and only two or three social workers." Most counselors and dormitory aides are unprepared for the difficult tasks that face them at Bureau boarding schools. They often perceive their roles as that of guards rather than substitute parents. Those few who are skilled and dedicated have little time to devote to helping the children with special problems, because of overcrowding and understaffing. One boarding school counselor said he spends most of his time retrieving AWOLs, supervising housekeeping and other "general service tasks," but spent *none* of his time counseling—even though he works a 10 to 16 hour day.

> "There is a tendency—a pronounced tendency—to 'herd' rather than guide. The boys and girls are yelled at, bossed around, chased here and there, told and untold, until it is almost impossible for them to attempt to do anything on their own initiative—except, of course, to run away." [4]

[3] Statement by Dr. Robert L. Leon, M.D., Professor and Chairman of the Department of Psychiatry, University of Texas Medical School. Indian Education Subcommittee Hearings, 90 Cong., 1 and 2 sess., Part IV, p. 2152, October 1, 1968.
[4] Letter from a boarding school teacher to the late Senator Robert F. Kennedy; Chairman, Indian Education Subcommittee. Indian Education Subcommittee Hearings, 90 Cong.,

The entire BIA educational system is plagued by mediocrity: an over-burdened and sometimes insensitive staff, inadequate physical facilities, out-of-date texts and supplies, little money for innovation. Teachers' salaries are not competitive with the public schools. The pay may be the same, but the BIA hires on a year-round basis requiring 12-months work while public school teachers work about 180 days a year. Educational specialists confirm the observation of a 1966 Presidential Task Force that "too many BIA employees were simply time-servers of mediocre or poor competence who remain indefinitely because they were willing to serve in unattractive posts at low rates of pay for long periods of time."

Teachers who come to the reservation day schools often know little about the children they are going to teach (only one per cent of the reservation elementary teachers are Indian). Teacher orientation and training sessions pay scant attention to Indian cultural values or to problems which the teacher may encounter with children who speak little or no English, have different values and know different experiences. Instead, orientation concentrates on housing, pay, and civil service fringe benefits.

Widely publicized innovations and crash programs have slight impact on the BIA schools. For example, an experimental program to teach English as a second language was implemented to make it easier for Indian children to learn English, but a national report has shown that the program often is ignored. One teacher left the materials untouched because she "did not believe

1 and 2 sess., Part III, p. 1118, March 20, 1968.

in the new system of teaching English."

A former Assistant BIA Commissioner of Education, Dr. Carl Marburger, remarked: "The Education Division is isolated from the research, program development, evaluation and dissemination activities in education so that the educators in the Bureau are severely out of touch with the practices in the field."

"I was in Alaska," reports Congresswoman Julia Butler Hansen of Washington, "and I saw 'John and Jane went to the store,' or 'John and Jane had a cow,' as reading examples in the textbooks. This was the Far North, just below the Arctic Circle. They had never seen a cow and they may never see a cow. . . ."

The sterility of the curriculum is typically matched by the bleakness of the facilities. Dr. Robert Bergman, a child psychiatrist with the Indian Division of the Public Health Service, noted:

"Dormitories are usually large barrack-like structures with no provision for privacy, and usually no space that is each individual's to control as he sees fit. Only occasionally is there opportunity for the children to decide on the decoration of any of their living spaces."

At the Chilocco boarding school in Oklahoma, one dormitory room contained exposed heavy duty electrical wiring at the head of one youngster's bed. A BIA report on conditions at the school admitted, "the possibility of that girl being electrocuted in her sleep was evident." The two-room Gila River Indian Day School in Arizona is a rebuilt garage. It serves 130 children, 60 of them in a room which should hold 29.

A survey of BIA teachers in 1965 revealed that 25 per cent would rather be teaching whites than Indians. Still

another survey showed that while Indian students saw jobs and college as their long-range educational priorities, their teachers believed an ability to get along and assimilation were more important traits for Indians to absorb.[5]

It was the Indian's great misfortune to be conquered by a people intolerant of cultural diversity. The Indian looked different, spoke a different language, had his own religion and customs; Americans saw him as an anathema and were chagrined when he refused to conform to "civilization." Indian education policies were formulated—in the words of a Commissioner of Indian Affairs—". . . to prepare him for the abolishment of tribal relations, to take his land in severalty and in the sweat of his brow and by the toil of his hands to carve out, as his white brother has done, a home for himself and his family."[6]

The Long Trek—from Homeland to Wasteland

The Indian child's trek to school, measured in miles, becomes a Trail of Tears, a form of compulsory and permanent expatriation, especially for the 35,309 children attending BIA boarding schools. In 1968, 9,000 of the children in Indian

[5] James Coleman, "Equality of Education Opportunity," quoted by Senator Robert F. Kennedy at Indian Education Subcommittee Hearings, 90 Cong., 1 and 2 sess., Part I, p. 5, December 14, 1967; Abt Associates, Inc., Systems Analysis Program Development and Cost-Effectiveness Modeling of Indian Education for the Bureau of Indian Affairs, Sixth Monthly Progress Report, p. 11, December 14, 1967.

[6] Brewton Berry, "The Education of American Indians: A Survey of the Literature," prepared for the Indian Education Subcommittee of the Senate Committee on Labor and Public Welfare, 91 Cong., 1 sess., p. 17.

boarding schools were less than nine years old.

In Alaska, where 15 per cent of the national Indian population resides, there are not enough schools, nor is there room for all the Indian children in public schools. As a result, Indian children are shipped as far away as Oklahoma, 6,000 miles from their parents.

Even where the Indian children attend day schools or public schools, the journey can be a rugged one. In Utah, Indian children wake up at 4:30 a.m., walk three to four miles over rough terrain to the bus and then ride 65 miles to the public school. In New Mexico, high school students walk two miles to the bus every day, and then ride 50 miles to school.

Once in a boarding school, the children are effectively cut off from their families. Parents cannot visit often because of the great distance and because many schools are located where roads are impassable for much of the year. Boarding school officials do not offer transportation or accommodations for parents who might want to come. Even when the school is convenient to the reservations, parental visits are discouraged because the children often become hard to manage after parents leave and sometimes run away.

Permission to see one's own parent is not a "right." It is often granted as a reward for good behavior—or denied as a form of punishment. "If [the child] has been a 'problem' (e.g. has run away) parents are often not allowed to take him until he has 'learned his lesson.' This may take up to a month to accomplish." [7]

Education becomes a forced journey to alien institutions: on the Navajo reservation, BIA schools are called *"Washingdoon bi oltka"* which means "Washington's schools." From the Indian's point of view, the public schools seem the longest way from home. The Navajos refer to them as *"Beligaana bi oltaka,"* the "little white man's schools."

The journey to school takes on many meanings. But above all it expresses the white man's judgment of rejection and disdain for the child's home and way of life. The message is not subtle. At one boarding school, a child was heard to pray:

"Dear Lord, help me not to hate my mother and father."

At another, a school teacher exclaimed in a fit of anger: "If you want to live in a hogan for the rest of your life just don't bother to study." One student left school precisely because she did want to live in a hogan for the rest of her life. [8]

Boarding schools serve "students with marked educational retardation based on either delayed school entrance or past social and behavioral problems, and . . . students who have unsatisfactory home conditions or social-emotional problems," as well as children who have no schools available near their homes. Poverty is regarded as an unsatisfactory home condition. Many boarding school students are welfare referrals; the schools are used to avoid providing increased family assistance and parents are penalized for

[7] Letter from a boarding school teacher to the late Senator Robert F. Kennedy, p. 118.

[8] Dr. Robert L. Bergman, "Boarding Schools and Psychological Problems of Indian Children," reprinted in Indian Education Subcommittee Hearings, 90 Cong., 1 and 2 sess., Part IV, p. 1122, April 16, 1968.

being poor by having their children shipped off to distant boarding institutions.

Senator Barry Goldwater showed some understanding of the problem: "I try to picture myself as an Indian parent and try to sense what I might feel when my child was sent to school either close by or many, many miles away to a boarding school, knowing that the child would come back, yes, speaking English but also having forgotten the religion of his tribe, the ancient ways of his tribe. . . ."

The day school is just as explicit a rejection as the boarding school. Its function is to save the child from his own home and family. One school principal states bluntly:

> "When the mothers ask me what they can do to help their children, I tell them: 'Don't do anything.' "
>
> "It isn't that they should fear authority but that they should respect the authority that is doing things for their own good." [9]

A Pueblo day school teacher expressly rejects the child's home by ruling it off limits professionally:

> "My business and my concerns extend only as far as this fence"—pointing to the fence around the school—"what happens outside of these school grounds is none of my business." [10]

The significance, relevance, and even the existence of the Indian world

and its values is systematically denied by school administration. The Indian child is kept in deliberate ignorance of his culture, history and heritage. He is taught, simultaneously, that he should be ashamed of it.

Textbooks, in dealing with the Indian, often are appalling. A history text, recently in use in California public schools, gave this description:

> "The Indians who lived in the Stanislaus area were known as the 'Diggers,' although they were the Walla Tribe. They were stupid and lazy and it is said they were given their name because of their habit of digging in the earth. They dug roots for food, and they also dug holes in the ground for shelter. The squaw was required and expected to provide all of the food for her husband and family." [11]

The late Senator Robert F. Kennedy of New York related this experience:

> "We were in Idaho the other day and I was asking the superintendent of schools, where they had 80 per cent Indian children, whether they taught anything about Indian history or Indian culture. The tribe was a very famous tribe, the Shoshone, which had a considerable history, and he said, 'There isn't any history to this tribe;' this has a tremendous effect on the children. So I asked him if there were any books in the library where all these children could go and read about Indian history, and he said, 'Yes,' and we went to the library. There was only one book and the book was entitled, "Captive of the Delawares.' It showed a white child being scalped by an Indian."

The teachers are not trained to counteract these distorted accounts of the Indian's history. In California,

[9] Murray L. Wax, *et al.*, "Formal Education in an American Indian Community," *Social Problems*, Vol. 11, No. 4, Spring 1964, reprinted in Indian Education Subcommittee Hearings, 90 Cong., 1 and 2 sess., Part IV, pp. 1391, 1403, April 16, 1968.

[10] Statement by Dr. Alfonso Ortiz, Anthropologist, Princeton University. Indian Education Subcommittee Hearings, 90 Cong., 1 and 2 sess., Part I, p. 64, December 14, 1967.

[11] Statement by Rupert Costo. Indian Education Subcommittee Hearings, 90 Cong., 1 and 2 sess., Part I, p. 242, January 4, 1968.

which has the second largest Indian population in the country, teacher training in the colleges devotes "something like six-and-a-half pages of the required reading . . . to . . . Indians, and about five-and-a-half of these six pages are very detrimental to the Indian child." [12]

The Lower Brule Sioux Tribe of South Dakota reports that at their day school "students seldom hear anything about Indian culture or history" and "pride in their heritage is not encouraged." The Mesquakies of Iowa set up an art class in an abandoned farmhouse when the instructors at their day school refused to permit Indian art in the classrooms.

The official business of the school is teaching middle-class values and skills to "culturally deprived children." The BIA's *Curriculum Needs of Navajo Pupils* states that the Navajo child:

> "Needs to begin to develop knowledge of how the dominant culture is pluralistic, and how these people worked to become

[12] Statement by David Risling, Jr. Indian Education Subcommittee Hearings, 90 Cong., 1 and 2 sess., Part I, p. 240, January 4, 1968.

the culture which influences the American mainstream of life . . ."

> "Needs to understand that every man is free to rise as high as he is able and willing . . ."

> "Needs assistance with accepting either the role of leader or follower . . ."

> "Needs to understand that work is necessary to exist and succeed . . ."

These "needs" are defined and centered within the cultural universe of the non-Indian world. The possibility that the Indian child may need an education which helps him function as an Indian, or that Indian parents might want such an education for their children, is not considered.

Instead of family-type cohesion based on respect, the schools encourage market relationships to enforce rules. At one boarding school, a program of "behavior modification" has been instituted. A child may earn points for good behavior and use them to purchase items he may want. A can of deodorant sells for 150 to 200 points. A frisbee, a 50-cent toy children toss in the air, goes for 500 points. But a child who maintains a "perfect" record can only earn 60 points in any week.

INDIAN SCHOOLS

Daniel Henninger/Nancy Esposito

Senator Edward Kennedy has taken over the chairmanship of his late brother's Indian Education Subcommittee, which is soon to release a report recommending basic changes in the ways we educate Indian children. It's about time. The Bureau of Indian Affairs spent $86 million of its $241 million budget in 1968 on the education of 55,000 Indian children, and there's little to show for it.

Nearly 60 percent of these youngsters must attend BIA boarding schools, either because there's no public or federal day school near their home or because they are "social referrals" (BIA jargon for anything from a bilingual difficulty to serious emotional disorders and juvenile delinquency). One percent finish college. In Alaska there is only one federal high school, so two-thirds of the Alaskan Indians are sent to a boarding school in Oregon; 267 others go to school in Chilocco, Oklahoma. The Navajo nation comprises one-third of the BIA's responsibility, and 92 percent of its children are in boarding

Reprinted by permission of The New Republic, © 1969, Harrison-Blaine of New Jersey, Inc.

schools. The schools have a 60 percent dropout rate, compared to a national average of 23 percent.

Assimilation has been the aim of the Bureau of Indian Affairs since the early 1800's. But it no longer expresses that purpose in the embarrassing language of a World War II House subcommittee: "The final solution of the Indian problem [is] to work toward the liquidation of the Indian problem rather than toward merely perpetuating a federal Indian Service working with a steadily increasing Indian population." From the BIA's Curriculum Needs of Navajo Pupils" we learn that the Navajo child "needs to begin to develop knowledge of how the dominant culture is pluralistic and how these people worked to become the culture which influences the American mainstream of life . . ."; "needs to understand that every man is free to rise as high as he is able and willing . . ."; "needs assistance with accepting either the role of leader or follower . . ."; "needs to understand that a mastery of the English language is imperative to compete in the world today . . ."; "needs to understand that work is necessary to exist and succeed. . . ."

Often the government places children in federal boarding schools at the age of six or seven; over 9,000 under the age of nine are so placed. That quite a few parents resist having their young taken from home for a year is indicated by a 1966 HEW survey: 16,000 Indian children between the ages of eight and 16 were not in school.

The Indian school curriculum is standard: ancient history, European history, American history, geography, arithmetic, art, music (an Indian "needs training in proper tone production in order to properly and effectively sing Western music"). Not much about *their* history. The Interior Department investigated Indian schools in Alaska last spring and found that "education which gives the Indian, Eskimo and Aleut knowledge of—and therefore pride in —their historic and cultural heritage is almost nonexistent. . . . In the very few places where such an attempt is made, it is poorly conceived and inadequate." Most of the boarding school teachers are aware of the variations in language, dress and customs of their students, but their sensitivity to the less obvious differences in Indian values, beliefs and attitudes is peripheral and by the way. Most Indian children speak English poorly or not at all, communication between teacher and pupil is difficult or impossible. Yet Bureau schools conduct *all* classes in English.

It doesn't take long to discourage young, dedicated teachers: "Most of the teachers came to Chilocco because of humanitarian reasons," said a former teacher at the Oklahoma boarding school. "They saw the pitiful situation and truly wanted to help, but after months of rejection and failure, they either quit or they began looking at it as an eight to five job with no obliga-

tion to their students." A teacher at an Arizona school wrote the BIA last year, suggesting that the inclusion of courses in agriculture and native crafts might arouse his habitually unresponsive students. "This idea [didn't] set well with many of the 'old hands' among the administrators," he later said. "The only thing that came out of it were some dark days for me, and a label as a trouble-maker." The turnover rate among teachers is double the national average. To an Indian child, the teacher is a stranger passing through. An obvious remedy is to enlist more Indian teachers. At present only 16 percent of the Bureau's teachers are Indian, and with only one percent of the Indians graduating yearly from college, there is little chance that the percentage will rise.

Estranged from his family, confronted with an alien culture and unable to talk to his teachers, the Indian's academic performance is predictably poor. What is harder to explain is the "crossover phenomenon." For the first few years of school, Indian achievement parallels that of white children and then slowly but persistently regresses. An Indian starts to fall behind between the sixth and eighth grades, and if he doesn't drop out finishes high school with a 9.5 grade education. Despite this regression, a boarding school student is never held back for academic failure; at the end of each year, he is promoted to the next grade whatever his performance. Summer school programs are scarce. Bureau teachers are contracted by the year, and one-third go on educational leave during the summer while the rest clean up the schools, take inventory and so on. As a result the typical high school class contains highly intelligent students as well as many who should still be in grade school. The teacher tries to compensate by aiming his instruction somewhere between the two extremes, so much of the class drops off to sleep or stares blankly at books.

One would think that after school the children could find some release from this dreariness, in the dorms or in some extracurricular activity. Life at a federal boarding school, though, is regimented and arbitrary. Seen from the air, many of the schools look like military installations—complexes of one-color, one-texture buildings set in the middle of otherwise barren areas. The impression of physical isolation mirrors the cultural isolation in the classroom. The building-complex usually includes dormitories (boys and girls), classroom buildings and housing for the staff. Many of the buildings are in disrepair. In a number of places (Tuba City, Arizona, for example) condemned buildings are still in use. The Fort Wingate Elementary Boarding School in New Mexico uses old Fort Wingate, once commanded by Douglas MacArthur's father. Forty years ago, the Brookings Institution's Merriam Report declared this plant unsuitable.

Even the new buildings are designed to reinforce the numbing sterility. Long, narrow, lifeless dormitories house row upon row of double-deckered iron beds and little else. Windows are sometimes barred. Floors are bare; the vivid personal decorations that are so much a part of many Indian communities are discouraged. Dress, too, is strictly regulated. The system makes individualizing one's appearance or environment fairly impossible. Beneath all the regulation is the Bureau's implicit concept of the children: all Indians are alike. In reality

some children are at boarding schools because there is no alternative schooling available, while an increasing number, the "social referrals," come to the schools with serious emotional problems. Dr. Anthony Elite of the Public Health Service's Indian Health office in Phoenix has said that "with this great change in the profile of the student body, there has not been a concomitant change in staffing skilled workers or training existing personnel to cope with these problems."

Each hour of a child's day is planned by the clock, with strict schedules posted in the dorms. Classes, meals, study periods, chores, free-time, bed—the routine never varies. Frequent head-counts are taken to quickly identify runaways or "AWOLS" as the Bureau calls them. Demerits are handed out for breaking the rules. The demerits can be removed by performing extra chores or by sacrificing privileges like TV, a school movie or snacks. At the Chinle Elementary Boarding School each child has a punchcard fastened to the end of his bed with punched holes representing demerits on one side and merits on the other. A little boy proudly displayed his card to a visitor. He was especially proud of the large number of holes he had accumulated. Most of the holes were on the demerit side. He didn't know the difference. At another school two small boys were seen sitting on the floor, tearing up old textbooks as a punishment.

Dr. Robert Bergman, a PHS psychiatrist on the Navajo Reservation said, "the somewhat limited social opportunities of the boarding high school give the adolescent students few protected ways of exploring boy-girl relationships. The sexes are pretty well kept separate most of the time, and even casual contact between them is looked on with some suspicion by school officials anxious about possible scandal. A hostile rebellious attitude develops in the students, and they make their own opportunities away from the potential help of adults. Many students make a very abrupt transition from no dating at all to sneaking out to drink and make love." The administration's response to such behavior is more repression and school officials at a number of boarding schools cite discipline as their most important problem. Asked what he would do if given more money, the superintendent at Chilocco said he would build a jail and hire more guards.

To maintain discipline, the schools eliminate as many outside or uncontrollable influences as possible. A visitor is discouraged from talking to the children. A child "caught" talking to a visitor gets a sharp warning glance from a school official. Authorities address the children in English and discourage using native language in both the classroom and dorms. Dr. Bergman relates the rather bizarre results of this policy: "I often encounter [dorm attendants] who pretend not to speak Navajo. They have become so convinced that speaking Navajo is a bad thing to do that they often won't admit that they can. [Most attendants are themselves products of boarding schools.] The children learn that what they say in Navajo is effectively kept secret from the authorities even if one of the Navajo-speaking members of the staff hears them, because the Navajo staff member will be too ashamed of having understood to tell anyone."

School authorities in effect dictate when children may go home for weekends and when parents may visit the schools. The Bureau has a de facto policy of discouraging such visits, because the children are noticeably upset and troublesome afterwards, and the number of runaways invariably increases. To reach the school, parents must travel long distances over roads that are impassable most of the year. The schools afford them neither accommodations nor transportation. At the easily accessible Fort Wingate school, signs on the dormitory doors announced that no child would be permitted home for two weekends prior to Thanksgiving. A teacher at the Tuba City Boarding School wrote of the problem last year to Sen. Robert Kennedy, then chairman of the subcommittee on Indian Education: "Most children on the reservation starting at age six only see their parents on occasional weekends, if that often. At these times parents are usually allowed to check out their children— if the child's conduct in school warrants it, in the opinion of the school administration. If he has been a 'problem' (e.g., has run away) parents are often not allowed to take him until he has 'learned his lesson.' " The students' most visible emotional problem is boredom— the deadening routine of marching in line to meals and class, the lack of recreation or an interesting diversion. The letter to Sen. Kennedy summarized the emptiness of life at a boarding school: "The children search everywhere for something—they grasp most hungrily at any attention shown them, or to any straw that might offer some escape from boredom. You can't help but see it in their faces when you visit the dorms of the younger children. At the older boys' dormitories, they are used to the conditions—you can see that, too. They no longer expect anything meaningful from anyone."

Their reaction to this gradual dehumanization is extreme. Recently on the Navajo Reservation, two young runaways froze to death trying to make it to their homes 50 miles away. Escape through glue-, paint- and gasoline-sniffing is as common as chronic drunkenness at the boarding schools. On Easter morning two years ago, authorities at the Chilocco school found a Crow boy who had apparently drunk himself to death. More recently a runaway at the Albuquerque Boarding School was found frozen to death after an alcoholic binge.

Suicide among young Indians is over three times the national average and an even greater problem at the boarding schools. Yet the Superintendent of the Albuquerque school said he had never seen an Indian suicide in any school in his 28 years of experience. Testifying before Sen. Kennedy's subcommittee, Dr. Daniel O'Connell found evidence to the contrary: "The situation as far as suicide is concerned is especially acute among the boarding school children, particularly in high school. . . . In the Busby School in the Northern Cheyenne Reservation, for example, with fewer than 250 students, there were 12 attempted suicides during the past 18 months."

The closest thing the child has to a surrogate parent is the so-called instructional aide or dormitory attendant. Aides are responsible for the children in the dorms and supervise their routine activities—dressing and washing the smaller children, housecleaning and free time. Psychologically, the instructional aide is the most important member of the staff, since the dorm is the closest thing the children have to a home life. But he is the lowest paid and has the lowest status in the school hierarchy. Each aide is expected to care for 60 to 80 children. At a conference with Dr. Bergman, an aide asked for help in getting her 75 first-graders to put their shoes by their beds at night. Every morning is mass hysteria as seven-year-olds scramble for a missing right or left shoe. Night attendants are responsible for 180 to 260 children, so there is rarely someone to comfort a youngster having a normal childhood nightmare.

The instructional aides are not encouraged to take a personal interest in the children. An aide was severely reprimanded for inviting some girls to her room to make Navajo fry-bread. The authorities would prefer that the system's few professional guidance counselors handle the children's problems. The present ratio of students to counselors is 600 to one. One counselor complained that 30 to 40 percent of his time is spent retrieving runaways, another 30 percent supervising housekeeping, leaving little time for serious counseling.

For its more serious problems—the suicide-prone, the alcoholics, the psychotics—the BIA employed one full-time psychologist last year for the entire federal school system. A rebellious or uncooperative student gains a reputation as a "troublemaker" and is expelled from one school after another until he is old enough to drop out. A Fort Hall boy who has attempted suicide six times was sent to Chilocco last fall for lack of anywhere else to send him. Among the Indians, Chilocco is considered the end of the line.

The Rough Rock Demonstration School in northeastern Arizona is a welcome anomaly in this chain of dead-end desert schools. Jointly funded by the Office of Economic Opportunity and the BIA, the Navajo boarding school is innovative in that it is run by Indians. The seven Indians who comprise the school board set school policy, hire and fire teachers and manage the school's $700,000 budget. The curriculum includes daily instruction in Navajo culture, history and language, and the school's Cultural Identification Center attracts talented Navajo artists and translators to produce meaningful texts for Indian children. Nor is the built-in bleakness of dorm life found at Rough Rock. The school has 10 counselors, and parents are invited to live in the dorms for eight-week periods (reducing the child-adult ratio to 10 to one). The parents work as dorm aides, with pay, and attend adult education programs, since many are less-educated than their children. Students are encouraged to go home on weekends and the school provides transportation for those who would otherwise have to stay at school. The school's teachers make periodic visits to the children's homes to let the parents know how their children are doing. (The parents of many children at other schools haven't the slightest idea of what grade their children are in.) Of the school's 82 full-time employees, 62 are Indians, and for many it is their first permanent job. It is too early to say whether Rough Rock's community-involvement approach is *the* answer to Indian education. The experiment is expensive ($2,500 per student) and the school will have to look elsewhere for support after OEO funding expires in June. What the Indians at Rough Rock have proved is that given effective control of the immediate forces that shape their lives, they can be a success, qualified in measurable achievement, total in terms of self-respect.

TAMA INDIANS FIGHT
FOR THEIR OWN SCHOOLS

P. Boyd Mather

HIGH-HANDED CLOSING

Rejecting the Indians' protest, the Bureau of Indian Affairs has closed down the primary school which it had operated since 1938 at the Mesquakie Indian settlement on the Iowa river just west of Tama, Iowa. The 56 first-through-fifth graders have been assigned to South Tama community school centers as out-of-district, tuition-paying pupils. Headstart and kindergarten pupils and students in grades six through 12 were already attending the South Tama schools on that basis.

The Indians raise three primary objections to the closing: (1) They see it as just one more instance of the B.I.A.'s making a decision they think should rest with the tribal council. (2) They say their children have experienced considerable discrimination in the white school system. (3) Though they agree with B.I.A. officials that vast

improvement in Indian education is called for, they want their children to be educated in an Indian rather than a white setting.

Unless the B.I.A. reverses its decision, the Indians will apparently choose between compliance and protest through direct action while seeking legal redress through the courts. That a middle ground is not possible became obvious at a meeting of the tribal council with B.I.A. officials on July 19, at which a grave lack of communication was evident. For instance, the B.I.A. officials refused to answer direct questions about whether the bureau's school in the settlement was actually closed. Nine days later Otto Knauth of the *Des Moines Register* reported that a B.I.A. official in Minneapolis had confirmed the closing in a telephone interview, but that "for reasons not immediately apparent" neither tribal leaders nor local B.I.A. officials had been notified.

In several previous conflicts between bureau officials and Indians the Tamas have conceded to white power. This time many Indians believe they cannot concede without endangering the very fiber of their tribal structure. Chairman

111

Columbus Keahna of the Mesquakie tribal council, the other six council members and the clan leaders are unanimous in opposition to the closing. The Indians consider the council, not the B.I.A., the legal local government of the tribe, and they resent the by-passing of the council on this and many other matters.

SPECIAL BACKGROUND

The Mesquakie settlement occupies an unusual position in Indian affairs. The Mesquakies, a part of the Fox group, are the only tribe still in Iowa among the 17 that once lived here. They are here because in 1856 their leaders returned from Kansas and at great personal sacrifice bought 80 acres of land. Gov. James Grimes served as trustee in that land purchase and sponsored enabling action in the Iowa general assembly. Through other purchases the settlement has grown to 3,000 acres. The population is about 430.

In 1896 the federal department of the interior took over administration of the tribe and, as Knauth wrote in the *Register,* "the Bureau of Indian Affairs has since sought to control tribal affairs as if the settlement were a reservation." Yet the settlement differs from a reservation in that the latter consists of land set aside from the public domain, while Tama land was bought from private owners. That is why the Indians believe the council should control tribal and settlement affairs, why they deeply resent the B.I.A.'s paternalism. (At the July 19 meeting, for instance, government officials called Keahna by his first name, reserving "mister" for white men.) The school closing has added fuel to ru-

mors that the B.I.A. intends to dissolve the settlement, possibly distributing the commonly owned property to individual families.

The tribal council has voted unanimously "never to agree to the complete transfer of all students from the Indian school." Chairman Keahna commented, "It looks like the only way we can apply pressure is by keeping our children out."

DISCRIMINATION

The Mesquakies believe, and they illustrate their belief with many personal impressions and experiences, that they are discriminated against in the white schools. Tom Knight, a VISTA worker at the settlement until mid-August when he was transferred to Montana, offers two illustrations: In one class in which four Indian children were present a white teacher told the pupils that she was "tired of paying taxes so the Indians can live off the fat of the land." Another teacher baited Indian pupils "to get them mad because the only time they will talk about their religion is when they are mad." (Incidentally, Knight was sent to the settlement without the Indians' consent, though he did not know this until he arrived. But he was soon accepted by them, and it was over their objection that he was transferred.)

Whether or not such incidents are verifiable, the Indians clearly believe that how their children fare depends on the lightness or darkness of their skin. "The lighter they are the better they get along," said one grandmother; "the darker, the more trouble they have." In this connection it is interesting to note that the Mesquakies have a deep appreciation of their own redness. I quoted to one young Indian the probably correct assertion of Glenn R. Landbloom of the B.I.A. that it is easier for Indian children to make the adjustment to white society when they are young, and that attending public school will facilitate that adjustment. In reply the young Mesquakie held out his bare arm and said proudly, "I am colored."

The B.I.A. asserts that the South Tama county officials are willing and ready to assume the responsibility of providing quality education for all children of the settlement, and have geared their educational program for the transfer. Everyone agrees that the schools have adequate physical facilities and over-all educational program. The schools do not, however, offer any systematic teaching of Indian history, legends or customs, nor are they likely to teach the Mesquakie language, an educational element the Mesquakies consider essential.

Because the settlement is not part of the South Tama school district, which completely surrounds it, the Indian pupils have no official relationship to the public school board, which makes decisions and sets policy. Moreover, since the government funds last year fell about $8,800 short in paying Indian tuition, one wonders how long the district will be willing to accept the settlement children.

NEED FOR IMPROVEMENT

The one point of agreement between the B.I.A. and the Indians is that the quality of Indian education needs improvement. Points out Don Wanatee, an early alumnus of the bureau school: "It has taken the B.I.A. 70 years to admit what we have known for a long time: they've been giving us an inferior education." The Indians want the present facilities in the settlement developed into a "model school" for Indian education. They are not clear as to all details of what that model should be, but it would certainly be one that would preserve the Indian language and culture while providing a basic education, that would remain federally financed and that would be under tribal control.

The importance of the Mesquakie language to the Tama Indians cannot be overestimated. Mr. Wanatee told me: "If you take away our language, you take away our religion. If you take away our religion, you take away our tribe. The three go together." Mrs. Wilson Brown, one of the mothers, explained: "We don't want our children at 35 or 40 years of age doing what we have seen other Indians doing—scrambling around trying to find out what their language and their religion are, when no one can remember." And she had another observation: "Our situation is similar to that of the Amish: we want our own schools, but we want fully accredited teachers, the best available—which we have never had—so we can get the best education possible."

In seeking to retain Indian identity the Mesquakies follow in the tradition of their great Chief Maminwanika, who was their leader for over 30 years before their return to Iowa. It is written that while he advocated peace with the whites, he steadfastly opposed adoption of the white man's customs, dress or education. Today's Mesquakies do not reject the 20th century, but they do seek to continue the distinctive heritage preserved for them by Maminwanika.

At least twice before in this century the Mesquakies and the B.I.A. have come to a showdown on the education of the children in the settlement. Each time the Mesquakies have won, but they still have not won the war to estab- lish the quality of education they want. Each previous time *part* of the issue has been whether the education was to be "red" or "white." Perhaps that is *the* issue in 1968.

APPALACHIAN YOUTH

from *Voices in the Classroom*

THE SCHOOLS OF
APPALACHIA

Peter Schrag

Goldie Bell is an experienced American elementary school teacher who has never been asked about phonics, the new math, or the college potential of her pupils. The Scuddy School, where she works, can be reached only by crossing a muddy creek from an unpaved road which winds its way into one of the many blind valleys of eastern Kentucky. Down the road from the school live the coal miners—many of them now unemployed—who would be eligible for the Scuddy School PTA, if the school had one.

Mrs. Bell teaches five grades—fourth, fifth, sixth, seventh, and eighth—in her half of the wooden building that comprises the school. In the adjacent room a younger woman teaches grades one, two, and three. The walls are painted gray and brown, bare bulbs provide light, and a pot-bellied, coal-burning stove affords an uneven heat in the winter. There is a constant murmur in the room; most of Mrs. Bell's thirty-eight children must work on their own, the older ones helping the younger, the faster giving aid to the slow. One child has no shoes, many have no socks, and several look prematurely old. They are the children of some of the poorest people in America. A few are reading a story:

Jane and Spot were going up the street as fast as they could. So were Jack and Jim. [Jane is blond and wears a blue dress; two boys follow on roller skates.]

"Get out of the way," called the boys. But just then Jane stopped. The boys stopped, too.

"Look boys," said Jane. "See what I have in my pocket."

"Pennies!" said Jack.

"What are you going to buy with them? Is it a toy for Spot?" [Later in the story they go for a spin in the family's green and white cabin cruiser.]

As they read, Mrs. Bell is asking another group about a different story.

"Who is it that's driving the big tractor?" she asks.

"Jack," says one of the pupils.

"What's the girl doing?"

"Washing dishes."

From *Voices in the Classroom* by Peter Schrag. Reprinted by permission of the Beacon Press, copyright © 1965 by Peter Schrag and the Saturday Review, Inc., copyright 1965 Saturday Review, Inc.

"What would she like to do?"

"Be out with the boy."

"They had one of those dishwashers," Mrs. Bell says. "Not many of us are lucky enough to have one of those."

The Scuddy School is one of twenty-odd one- or two-room schools in Perry County, and one of several thousand in Appalachia; many have been closed in recent years, but hundreds will remain because transportation over the "hollows" is difficult and because—strangely enough—local pride and suspicion of the world outside demand that they be kept open. Many are built of wooden slats, though some have been replaced since World War II with cinder block structures—usually because the "old school burned down." The pot-bellied stove and the outdoor privy are the only standard pieces of equipment. A miscellany of old desks, benches, tables, and chairs comprise the furniture; decorations come from old magazines and calendars.

The one-room schools of eastern Kentucky are staffed by a mixture of people—some, like Mrs. Bell, are dedicated veterans, others are women who have not met certification requirements, and still others are persons who once taught in the better consolidated schools but who were "sent up a hollow" for an academic or, more commonly, a political offense. Teachers are rarely fired, but if they identify themselves with the wrong faction in a local election, they will be sentenced to an inferior school, sometimes as much as fifty miles from home.

The presence of the one-room schools, and the fate of some of the teachers, are symptoms of the problems that plague education in Appalachia. In eastern Kentucky, which has never had a tradition of public education beyond the three R's, schools mean jobs as bus drivers, teachers, and lunchroom employees; they mean contracts for local businessmen, and they represent power for county politicians. In Breathitt County, for example, Mrs. Marie Turner has been superintendent of schools since 1931; her husband held the office for six years before, and several in-laws controlled it before that. The Turners own the building in which the Board of Education is located, and they take rent from the Board. According to the *Lexington Leader*, which ran a series of articles on school politics in Kentucky—with little apparent effect—the Turners have profited from the school's purchase of coal, gasoline, and school buses, and from the deposit of school funds in local banks. Elsewhere in Kentucky school boards purchase real estate from the sons and daughters of board members, and hire each other's children and wives as teachers. In Perry County, where Goldie Bell teaches, and where the Board followed common practice by naming a new school for the superintendent, Dennis G. Wooton ("We don't wait till they die," someone said), Mr. Wooton's son-in-law, Curtiss Spicer, is principal of the Wooton School, and his daughter, Mrs. Spicer, is one of its teachers.

This kind of nepotism is almost inevitable in an area as ingrown as eastern Kentucky: of the nineteen pages in the Hazard telephone book, the Perry County seat, two are filled with listings for people named Combs, four persons named Combs teach at the Dilce Combs High School, and recently a high school science teacher named Combs was exiled to a one-room school for supporting a school board candidate named

Combs against an incumbent named Combs. Virtually all the teachers in the Perry County Schools grew up in the county, or within a few miles of its borders, and many are teaching in the classrooms where they sat as students not many years before. Even if an outsider wanted a job in eastern Kentucky —and few do since the average salary is just over three thousand dollars—he would have difficulty obtaining one. "Outsiders just wouldn't be happy here," said one of the county superintendents.

The consequence of the inbreeding is that few new ideas have reached the schools of the area. Even the consolidated high schools operate largely with antiquated equipment, irrelevant textbooks, and obsolete material. Although many teachers sincerely strive to teach children in the best possible way, the years of previous miseducation make the task difficult. Sharon Barnett, a young, attractive English teacher at M. C. Napier High School near Hazard (Napier was superintendent when the school was built) spends the first semester in her senior course diagramming sentences; in the second semester she hopes to have her students read Macbeth. She knows that such an undertaking is difficult, but she desperately wants to bring something of the culture of the outside world to her community. She has come back to teach in Perry County because "my life is here," because "I love these people." And she knows what she's up against. "We could do so much more for these kids if their background were not so poor," she said. "They've had poor teaching in the country schools; some of the teachers are disliked so much that the kids are determined not to learn in order to hurt the teacher."

Yet despite all efforts—and there are other teachers like Sharon Barnett —the schools remain irrelevant for most of the students. Of those who started first grade in Perry County in 1948, about 12 per cent graduated in 1960. Many boys drop out, as a teacher said, "to get a job, a car and show off," and the girls quit to get married. A substantial number leave school and do nothing other than stand on the street corners of the towns. In Perry County, where the unemployment rate is about 17 per cent, the children fall into two groups: those who are ambitious and want to go north, especially into Ohio and Indiana, and those who see no value in any education, and have given up. When a grade school teacher recently asked her pupils what they wanted to do when they grew up, several answered, "to get on the welfare."

The content of the school curriculum provides little incentive for academic effort. Students are rarely challenged to work on their own, laboratory equipment is scarce and rarely used, and the courses in social studies are largely devoted to the clichés of American history and American life. The required civics book in Perry County proclaims, characteristically:

> Our economic system is founded on these basic principles: free private enterprise, competition, the profit motive, and private property. Businessmen and others must compete against one another in order to earn profits. These profits become their private property. This system is known as *capitalism*. By means of our capitalistic system we have built the most productive economy bringing Americans the highest standard of living that the world has ever known.

Since the county does not furnish free books in the high schools, students who use the civics text are not only required to read it but to pay for it. When relevant issues come up they fall outside the formal curriculum. In a discussion of civic responsibility and community planning, a high school teacher told his class: "In case something goes wrong in city government, the citizens should protest, they should write letters, and keep the officials on their toes."

"My uncle says he'll lose his job if the Democrats don't get in," a student exclaimed. Another student interrupted to say "In Hazard they don't care . . . if they cared they'd fix it up."

"It's not that bad," a third student said. "You just don't appreciate what we have."

"That's because there's nothing to appreciate. . . ."

"All the money goes to the hifalutin' big shots. You know the clothes they sent in after the flood, it didn't go to the people that needed it. They got a little bit so they could take pictures for the newspapers."

Discussions like this are rarely encouraged or channeled. Some teachers are nervous because others have been exiled to one-room schools, and because the community tolerates few heresies. The textbooks are safe and therefore irrelevant—the best teachers will admit privately that "we're not giving the kids what they should have."

Many teachers and principals are now making serious efforts to keep children in school. Sharon Barnett challenges her students to visualize themselves in ten years. "I ask them about what kind of job and home they think they'll have, and I tell them that the drunks on the street once had dreams like theirs. They've been protected by their parents and by the mountains. They don't know what the world is like.

The mountains are terribly high." These efforts sometimes mean that a principal must find shoes for a boy who has none, or a loan for this year's books, repayable at twenty-five cents a week, or a special trip to a cabin in a ravine to convince a family that staying in school is important.

Many of the mountaineers value education even though most never went beyond the eighth grade themselves. They want lives for their children that are better than they have had, but they do not know, and cannot know, what a good education is, or the kind of effort it requires. Although eastern Kentucky, with substantial amounts of state aid, has made great progress in education in the past five years, eliminating one-room schools, raising teacher salaries, and increasing the proportion of teachers who are certified with a degree from a college, the education its schools provide is still far behind most of the nation. Perry County has some new elementary schools that are bright and well-equipped, and the Hazard Vocational School, which children from the county high schools can attend, provides training in a number of useful trades. But even the most recent advances have failed to bring education in Appalachia to an effective level. In an age of technical sophistication, most high schools in eastern Kentucky have little laboratory equipment, and sometimes no laboratories at all. A biology student in one school said that his experimental work in biology consisted of "looking through a microscope once." There are few school libraries and few schools with gymnasiums, language laboratories, films, tapes, or records. For many, the most elaborate equipment is the coke machine, and in an area as carbonated as Kentucky, there are many of those. Meanwhile, school authorities confront incredible problems of transportation. Schools open in mid-August because snow in the winter often makes the roads impassable, forcing the schools to close sometimes for several weeks. Perry County, with about 7800 public school children, spends $144,000 a year busing them.

Despite these difficulties, the respectable citizens of the county towns —some of which have separate school systems—remain smug and provincial; many of them deny that there is any poverty in Appalachia, and they resent outside help. Hazard, which is surely one of the ugliest small towns in America, is ringed with signs, sponsored by a local bank, proclaiming "We Like Hazard" and "We Like Perry County." While thousands of tons of coal flow almost untaxed from mechanized mines, and the region's top-soil flows down the muddy rivers, and the ambitious kids move to the north, no one takes much local interest in the problems of education in the county. School officials shrug with a kind of hopelessness about their overcrowded, inadequate buildings, saying they are "bonded to the hilt," but rarely mentioning the incredibly low county tax structure; the town burghers say the schools are fine, that "they're doing a good job," and the women's church groups resent the idea that some of the clothing they gave for the poor was actually returned to the same counties in which it was donated.

Local pride rests in high school football and basketball teams, but few take any active interest in the minds of the kids. In those schools where Parent-Teacher Associations are active, the parents help raise funds for library books and team athletic equipment, without much protest about the fact that the Board of Education provides neither books nor a program in physical education. With the exception of the Hazard *Herald*, which has criticized some of the more flagrant manifestations of school politics, there is not one organization in all Perry County that is critical of the schools. Ever since the coal companies began to exploit eastern Kentucky and its people, outsiders have been suspect, and no one wants their advice now. Thus even those with the best intentions must work carefully and cooperate with the local politicians. To do otherwise is to be ineffective.

Although large amounts of state and federal money are going into public education and welfare programs in eastern Kentucky—90 per cent of the Perry County School budget comes from the state—attempts to achieve educational reform at the state level have been frustrated. Harry Caudill, the Whitesburg attorney who is the author of *Night Comes to the Cumberlands*, was a member of a special legislative committee that proposed, among other things, a strong educational Hatch Act to prohibit teachers from engaging in school politics, and the election of school board members on a countywide basis, rather than from intracounty districts. "A great howl went up," Mr. Caudill said. "We were called agents of the Pope and a whole lot of other things." Since other political issues diverted the attention of those who might have supported them, the committee's proposals were never enacted.

Despite is poverty, Appalachia remains perhaps the most typically American region; its people have not entirely shaken their frontier attitudes about the conservation of resources, about the value of education, and about relations with the outside world. Rivers are polluted with trash and garbage, refuse dumps foul scenic valleys, and the hulks of abandoned cars line many highways. While most of the nation has become more European, more cosmopolitan, Appalachia has changed but little, remaining behind its protective mountains. Thus there remains a suspicion of change, and of anything but the most conservative education.

Nevertheless a few voices have been raised recently to challenge the old isolation, the brightest of them being Harry Caudill's. And even conservatives like Mrs. W. P. Nolan, the editor of the *Herald,* are expressing a new consciousness. Like some of her fellow citizens, she is worried about Communist infiltration and outside interference in Kentucky. But she also concedes that something is drastically wrong with the schools. "Someone should talk about short-changing the kids," she said. "If we'd had good education in this state fifty years ago, we wouldn't be so embarrassed now before the nation and the world. A lot of this welfare money goes down the drain. We really need help on just three things: flood control, highway construction, and education. If we got that, we could take care of ourselves." Indications are that federal support will be forthcoming for the first two items. If it is, then perhaps there is also a chance for the schools.

APPALACHIA:
HUNGER IN THE HOLLOWS

Robert Coles

It all started eight years ago in Appalachia, in West Virginia, where the young Catholic Senator from Massachusetts, with his Boston and Harvard accent, had to demonstrate that thoroughly Protestant Americans, suspicious of Easterners and city people and "Romans" (as I hear it put in the hollows) would take to him—which they did. What came after is painful history. I have been working in the Appalachian mountains since 1962, when John Kennedy was trying to get help for the region out of a reluctant Congress. During that year, I spent time in western North Carolina, in Asheville and in the little town of Burnsville, the capital of Yancey County. I came there because I was studying school desegregation as it took place in city after city of the South, but I lingered because I realized there was something else to see, a whole way of life that was part Southern, part old Anglo-Saxon, part rural, and part nothing but itself. Since then

Reprinted by permission of The New Republic, © *1968, Harrison-Blaine of New Jersey, Inc.*

I worked closely in Kentucky and West Virginia with the Appalachian Volunteers, an impressive and effective group made up of students from within and without the mountain states and, as the students sometimes put it in moments of self-consciousness, "just plain folks," men and women of all ages from say, Floyd County, Kentucky, or Raleigh County, West Virginia, who have joined the Volunteers because they've had enough of—well, enough of everything that shocked and angered John Kennedy "back then."

That is how I hear it put in the hollows today. Like us, they remember, and perhaps they have more reason to do so: "I can recall him coming here, back then. They brought him up the creek, and I thought the next thing he'd be up the hollow, too. He was a fine-looking man, and you know how he won us all over—I'll tell you. We're used to those politicians coming around here just before election day and promising us this, that and everything, usually everything. You can smell them a mile away. But he didn't do that. He was sort of like us, actually. He didn't try to talk too much. He just looked around, and for a while you didn't know what he was thinking. Then he'd say something, not too long, like 'it's real bad here, I can see, and I'm going to do the best I can, the best I can to help you out.' Something like that was what you could trust—you knew the guy meant it. But he got killed, and his brother, too. He came here just last spring, his brother, and I heard him. He was looking into things for the Senate—it was a 'hearing,' I guess they called it. He came all by himself. The rest of the Senators, they had other things to do. He was like his brother, a fine-appearing man. I never saw so many people turn up, not around here, not in the shadow of these mountains. My wife and I, we said he gave us the greatest talk we'd ever heard in our whole lives. He'd be questioning those county officials—and it was as though you could believe in your country again. He told them they weren't doing their jobs, and that they owed it to America that we all lived better, here in Kentucky and all over. It wasn't only the words. It was you knew he meant it. The guy had real honest-to-goodness feelings inside of him and he didn't go on and on trying to persuade you. He said what needed saying—the same thing we say day after day with no one listening but ourselves. But that was back then in the spring, a long time it seems. First you'd hear people talk about 'back then when President Kennedy was here,' and now it's 'back then in April when Robert Kennedy came to see us.' Now I don't know, I don't know who I want. Neither of them two, I know that. I think I'll vote for Wallace. A lot of people say they will. He's fed up and so are we."

By turns angry, sad, wry, ironic, resigned or stubbornly determined, he is glad to speak his mind and let me know that like a lot of people from all over the country, he feels cheated this year. So, we talk, hour after hour, and I hear his disenchantment—in a way like mine, but also less wordy, less abstract, more concrete, more tied to the particulars of everyday life. He is 41, the father of nine children. He was once a mine worker, but lost his job along with many others about 15 years ago. Now strip mines tear away at the beautiful mountains and leave a legacy of polluted streams, recurrent landslides, destroyed homes and farms and wildlife. "But they get the coal they want, with machines and not our broken backs." He says that angrily, and I'm not the first doctor to whom he has recited the story. Nor is he the first hurt and ailing man I've met in West Virginia or Kentucky.

Even before he was laid off there was trouble, the beginning of serious trouble: "I had a bad cough all the time, like you do when you work down in the mines. After a while you stop thinking about it. You cough like you breathe, on and off all day. Then the cough got real bad and I saw a couple of doctors, company doctors. They gave me medicine to keep the cough down, and I stopped worrying. You can't be a coal miner and worry about what it looks like inside, in your lungs. Then I got hurt, my back. That happens a lot, too—and you either can go back to work or not. I wanted to go back, and I was lucky because I could. I'd still have trouble, but like with the cough, I could keep going. I took some pills when it got bad, but most of the time I showed up first thing in the morning and stuck it out to the end. And I miss those days. Time went fast, and there was money around, enough to pay the bills and live real decent-like and feel like a man, like somebody who was doing at least something with his life.

"Then they mechanized, and they started stripmining all over with those machines, and we were through, me and all my friends. And ever since it's been the same. We're lucky to be alive each day, that's how I'd put it all together. I've been trying and trying to get on assistance [relief] but they just won't do it, they won't let me by. The doctors, they say I might have some trouble with my lungs and my back, but I was working when I got fired, and I could work now, so far as they're concerned. Hell, you don't have to be a full-fledged cripple to be on assistance, but it's politics, and if I was on the sheriff's good side, that would be fine—I'd have been collecting a check for years; but I'm not, because I got fresh way back and asked them to send the bus up the hollow to pick up my kids. They freeze in the winter walking those two miles to that bus and standing waiting for it. (They don't have the right clothes. We just can't pay for them.) When the courthouse gang heard that, they decided I was real fresh, a real wiseguy. So they said if I was so ungrateful for all that was being done for me—and me not working—then I'd learn to regret it. And I'll tell you, I have."

But he is a proud man. Like hundreds of thousands all over those lovely Appalachian mountains he can find no work, is refused any relief by the county officials, who have near absolute power in the region, and still somehow survives. He grows vegetables. He has a few chickens, and they lay eggs. He goes up the mountains and finds herbs, which he can sell "because they like to cook with them over in the East." And he is always on the lookout for a job, any job, for any length of time: "I can't stand sitting around and doing nothing. You get to hate it. You get to hate yourself. You get to hate everyone around you. I hate my kids growing up like this, seeing me without work. The oldest one, he wants to go to Ohio or Chicago or someplace like that, and get a job in a factory and make some money and then come back here. If I was in better health I'd have done it a long time ago. That's the only answer these days, go to the city for a while and try to make a few bucks. But you hear it's lousy there, 'lousier than you can ever believe' is the way I hear them say. So, they stay for as long as they have to, and then, believe me, they come back here to die. Yes sir. No one born here wants to leave. The tourists say it's pretty, but we *know* it is."

He may be from the oldest American stock, "here from the beginning," but right now he and his family are in this kind of fix: from odd jobs and an occasional gift sent by a brother (who *did* go to Ohio, to Cincinnati and then Dayton) about $750 a year comes in, and that is all, all the money this family of eleven American citizens receives. They grow some food and they cook and preserve some of it for the winter, but they cannot plant nearly enough (on an acre or two of land up along a steep hill) to keep a supply of tomatoes or beans or cucumbers throughout the long winter and spring. Of course to keep them from literally starving to death the rich and powerful American government offers its food stamps, which require even now, after all the inquiries and hearings and struggles of the last year, an expenditure of $22 at a minimum every month—for a family of eleven that can go for weeks without money. Recently the Congress voted an emergency bill that would allow even that minimum to be waived in cases where there is simply no cash to be had. And here is how it all goes, life and largesse and emergency largesse in the Great Society: "Sometimes we can just raise the money, so we can buy the food stamps, and get about $100 worth of food for the month. But we are eleven of us, and it's as expensive to buy food here as any place else. By the third week we're down to nothing, and I'm desperate. They take up collections at the church, and we go borrowing, and with your kin you don't starve to death, no sir. But it's not very good either, I have to admit. For breakfast there's not much I can give the kids. In the winter I have to warm them up. I just have to. So I given them tea, real piping hot. Sometimes they have oatmeal, if there is some, and some biscuits, hot biscuits. Then for supper it depends—if the chickens have left us a few eggs, and if I have some preserves left. The worst time is around January, thereabouts. There's no work. There's no garden. There's nothing but those stamps, if we can raise the money. Then we'll go without supper sometimes, and breakfast, too. Then it's tea and cornbread and oatmeal if we're lucky."

How about the emergency funds that Congress voted, presumably so that no American would starve? It so happens that this family, and dozens others like it I know, failed to learn about that bit of legislative news. They don't read the Congressional Record or The Washington Post. They don't even read the very fine Louisville Courier-Journal or the not-so-fine Lexington Herald Leader. They don't have a tel-

evision set, and for them a trip to town, unless offered by a neighbor, can cost five dollars. So they remain ignorant of the progress in America: "If it hadn't been for the AV [Appalachian Volunteer] who comes here we'd never have known about the new program, the stamps you're supposed to get if you don't have money to buy them. But it's been more trouble instead of less; it's been a heartache, trying to get them to certify us and tell us we're eligible for the 'emergency provision,' they call it. We would have to pay someone almost as much as the stamps cost to get to their office—they don't know about things like that in Washington—but the AV drove us over to town, and then it was what we know: the same old people in the county courthouse, sending you back and forth, back and forth, and delaying and telling you they have to investigate and things like that. Now either you're going through an emergency or you're not. I have to borrow food at the end of every month, and they know it. I have to go begging at church and with my kinfolk down the creek to pay for those stamps every month, and they know it. I should be on public assistance, and they know it. But they get everything federal that comes through here, every bit, every dollar, no matter what the senators meant to do in Washington. It may say on paper that the money is for us, but the money goes to the county people, the people who get all the money that comes in here. And they don't intend to let anyone in on the gravy who isn't right in their pockets. I remember when I asked them to send that school bus nearer. They told me, 'You'll live to be sorry you ever asked.' Well they were right—though from day to day I wonder if I'll live much more, and be sorry about anything. It can't get much worse than it is."

Their home—one like hundreds I have seen, one like many thousands that stand all over the region—can be tactfully described as extremely modest. It is of wood and tarpaper, and stands on cement blocks. The wind blows right through it. There is no central heating, no plumbing. Water comes from a well several miles away. In winter, in the cold, snowy Appalachian winter, a fireplace provides heat, and eleven bodies leave their five beds to huddle near the burning coals. In summer, flies and mosquitoes are undeterred by screens—and a nearby stream has been badly polluted by a stripmine. Yet they all try hard as a family. They sleep close together, rely on one another impressively, and keep a very neat home. An old picture of John Kennedy is on one wall, and beside it a picture of Robert Kennedy talking with some miners: "After he came here, the teacher gave each child who wanted one a copy of the picture. They got a stack of them from the paper."

The teacher is distant kin of theirs and would like to give them all even more, but cannot: "No sir, none of the children get their lunch at school. No sir, they don't. It's up to the principal, who gets the lunches and who doesn't. The well-off kids from town, they bring their money and so they get fed. It don't mean nothing to their parents, a few dollars here or there. But I can't give each of the kids a quarter every day. I don't have it; I don't have one quarter, never mind six of them. So, they just sit there, while the others eat. And they're not the only ones, at least I know that. Sometimes a kid will offer them something he doesn't want to eat, and sometimes my kids are too proud to accept, but sometimes they swallow their pride to get some of that soup they have."

That is the way it is, not only for that one family but for families up and down hollows in several states of these United States. Respectfully, solemnly one listens, hears the stories, sees evidence of and feels the bravery and courage and honesty and dignity. But one also has to notice the wear and tear on body, mind, on spirit, that goes with hunger and idleness; and one has to notice the illnesses that are never treated, the feet that lack shoes, and most painful of all, the children. On my most recent visit, late this summer, I asked a little girl of seven what she'd wish to be if she were given a wish: "Well, I don't know," she answered. Then she had a thought: "Maybe a beaver." I didn't have the nerve to ask her why, but her mother wanted to know, and asked. " A beaver, child?" For a second or two there was silence, and then the answer came, cheerfully spoken: "Well, they have a good time. They can chew all day long on trees, like they was bubblegum, and they always get to eat, and they can stop by a stream and drink from it anytime they want."

Soon, though, I am heading home. On the plane, from Lexington to New York or from Charlestown to Washington the shame and anger live on for a while. The salesmen are all around, full of plans and ready with cash—which the government allows them to write off as expenses. Often there are some government officials aboard, finished inspecting this or that. In hours I will be safely in the university, where I can remind myself how complicated everything is, and how hard it is to change things, and how much better things go in Appalachia or in migrant camps or in Delano or in George Wallace's Lowndes County then, say, Biafra or certainly North Vietnam.

There are other bits of encouragement, too. I can read that the House Committee on Agriculture, headed by the honorable W. R. Poage, from the great state of Texas, and by its own assertion "always concerned about the ability of all Americans to procure adequate food," has done something called a "hunger study"—by sending a letter to the health officers of 256 counties all over the nation. "Do you have any personal knowledge of any serious hunger in your county occasioned by inability of the individual to either buy food or receive public assistance?" The county officers were asked that—and in a chorus they answered, "no." What is more, a Dr. Pollack from the Institute for Defense Analyses (whose purposes are no doubt patriotic) says that those who have observed hunger and malnutrition among thousands of children in every section of the country have been fooled or mistaken: "What the observers are really declaiming is the failure of people to participate in the food-stamp and commodity programs because of lack of understanding or inadequate educational support of these federal programs." And, of course, after extensive hearings by a Senate subcommittee and in response to strong public pressure, the Congress did vote those emergency funds so that, as Mr. Poage said and Dr. Pollack said, penniless Americans can "procure adequate food." Naturally the funds go to county officials, and naturally those are the people (in

Mississippi, in Kentucky, in Delano, California) who are on the side of the poor—or so I can try hard to believe, provided that I can forget statements like this one, written by the director of the Big Sandy Area Community Action Program, with offices in the Johnson County Courthouse, Paintsville, Kentucky: "As you probably know, Emergency Food and Medical Services Program has a very limited amount of money. As a result of this, we do not want our office deluged with people who have been promised aid and that aid cannot be forthcoming."

So, that is that. The man who wrote those words also noted that he has only one employee "working the entire Floyd County area," but nearby in Pikesville, a city of about 5,000 people, there are over 40 lawyers working day in and day out—for what? For poor people? For the poor land that has been torn apart, then abandoned to itself, to its own ways: to landslides; to trickles of acid into streams; to huge rocks that fall upon and crush houses? The answer is yes—if the preposition is changed from "for" to "with." The lawyers work with the poor all right: "They come up to you and they say their mumbo-jumbo and before you know it, you've got to leave your home or you'll go to jail." The lawyers work with the land, too; they make sure it is surrendered to strip-mining companies that do what they say they do to the land, strip it, make it as poor as the people left behind after the machines are gone. But as I constantly hear some mountain people put it, year in and year out, "next season may be better." They always add a qualification, though: "if the trickery down in the court house stops." Then they laugh bitterly.

YESTERDAY'S PEOPLE

Jack E. Weller

THE PSYCHOLOGY OF FEAR

"Another characteristic outstanding among the mountain people is their fearlessness. Either they do not sense danger, or they are indifferent to it." [1] This is true of mountain people in response to some immediate and recognizable danger—a flash flood, a fire, or an accident. Men have related to me many admirable responses to danger in the mines or in the woods. The history of the area is full of illustrations of brave actions by the freedom-loving mountaineer.

In daily life, however, mountain society is filled with apprehension. Beneath his stoical manner, the slow-moving, apparently peaceful, self-assured mountain man or woman may well be the victim of intense anxieties. It is not uncommon even for young peo-

ple in their early twenties to have bleeding ulcers. The simple request to speak a word or lead a meeting in public will strike debilitating fear into the hearts of most mountain folk.

Children are made to obey through fear: "I'll get the law after you, if you don't mind." When a stranger visits in the home, the children cling closely to their parents or hide behind them. I have heard parents say to their pre-school children, as I called in their homes, "That man'll get you if you aren't good," or "I'll give you away to that man if you don't behave. He'll take you away with him." More adults fear "haunts," or ghosts, and graveyards than will readily admit it.

To the outsider, the mountain family is apparently close knit, which would seem to lend security to mountain life. In some respects, this is true. The members of a family, however, are bound to one another by ties of emotional dependence which tend to increase insecurity. In a sense, the family is not so much a mutually supporting group, in which each member gives himself for the others, as it is a group in which each member demands support from the others. I have known young people who have expressed al-

---

Jack E. Weller, Yesterday's People (Lexington, Ky.: University of Kentucky Press, 1966), pp. 44–49, 61–85. Reprinted by permission.

---

[1] W. D. Weatherford and Earl D. C. Brewer, Life and Religion in Southern Appalachia (New York: Friendship Press, 1962), p. 10.

most a hatred of home but could not be away from "Mommy" and "Daddy" for a weekend without becoming homesick.

Since one's security depends upon the approval of others in the family, there is always a fear of being misunderstood, and hence rejected, by the group upon whom one depends. In consequence, people go to great pains to avoid being misunderstood or creating hard feelings within the family. Of course, when one is expecting misunderstandings and hurt feelings, they very often occur. Chance remarks, made unthinkingly or in jest in the ordinary give-and-take of life, may be understood wrongly and recalled years afterward. There is a curious ambivalence in family relationships. On the one hand, members are dependent upon one another for security; on the other, they are suspicious of each other's intentions. One's rights are jealously guarded from encroachment by any of the others.

The occasion of the funeral is a case in point. I have seen undertakers at the very limit of their wits trying to get the family to decide on details. All the relatives must be consulted, and no one can be called upon to make decisions for the group, since there is a great fear of being misunderstood by the others or of slighting some of them. When the immediate family is willing to come to a decision, it is with an eye to what the larger family, and even the community, thinks. No one must be given cause for complaint or criticism.

Another example of the stresses of uncertainty in mountain families can be seen in the arrangements made about heirship land. In Appalachia great quantities of such land have been left by fathers and grandfathers to their children, who now hold the property jointly. Those who want the land for themselves cannot buy it from the others, who do not want it but don't want to see anybody else in the family have it. Thus it is passed down to each generation's children, the ownership being spread thinner and thinner while the land and buildings stand unused. In one example of such heirship property, a son who had to leave his rented house decided to move into the one-time parental dwelling, which had stood empty for years because the family could not decide who should have it or how it should be used or divided. When the son asked the others in the family whether he could move in, they would tell him neither yes nor no. He decided to move in anyway, and began to clean out the house. Immediately the house was set afire, and it burned to the ground—thus being removed from consideration.

Decision making of any kind is a difficult matter. In meetings, no one wants to state his mind or offer a motion unless he is confident that such action represents the consensus of the group. Opinions must be drawn forth piecemeal, with various members of the group contributing. In this manner stronger and stronger opinions may be expressed. If substantial disagreement should develop, factions immediately form. In any group where people mean to be on their best behavior, no vote can be taken unless the group is in agreement. No one will vote.

Never having been taught to face and overcome difficulties, but instead to retreat and "keep out of it," mountain people often have no confidence in their abilities. "I can't do that" is their common reaction on being asked to do something new, whether it be serving on a committee, being treasurer of a group, or taking part in a meeting. This response is not simply a case of extreme modesty, a man confessing that maybe there are others more able than himself, but expresses a deep fear of failure and consequent inferiority. Even young people often show this fear in fairly trivial matters.

One time the youth of the church planned a fund-raising dinner for the community. The girls were to serve and clear the tables. A brief training session was necessary for them, since none had ever done this kind of thing before, at least not outside of their own homes. As the rudiments of serving were being explained to them, one of the girls, a senior high student, broke down in tears because she was terribly afraid of doing something wrong.

There is great reluctance to speak with any one personally about a matter on which there may be a difference of opinion. Neighbors, at odds over the placement of a fence, will not face each other and talk through the matter, but will call the "law" to settle it for them. Few want to "meddle" in anybody else's business or offer advice.

As a newcomer to the area, I felt that the dirt road leading to the church property could be greatly improved by filling it in with slate, a mine refuse which the coal company would gladly haul for us and dump on the road. Presenting this to a committee, I met with no response beyond vaguely evasive mumbles. I went ahead with the project, only to find that at the first rain the slate crumbled into a greasy mess that made driving or walking hazardous. We had to hire a bulldozer to scrape it off. Only at the point of my realizing the error did the committee come forward with the fact that

they had known all along what would happen. They had said nothing because they were afraid I would think they were opposing me.

Mountain people are indeed reared in a society of the "known," a rural environment providing little stimulation or opportunity, and thus acquire neither the attitude of mind nor the few skills needed for meeting new and different situations. There are few broadening experiences available to them—few simple experiences, like sitting with people you don't know on a bus, asking for change from a busdriver, doing business with strangers in stores or supermarkets, meeting and playing with strange children in the park. Though these are not usually thought of as social learning experiences, they actually are, for they teach people to be more competent and secure in new situations and more able to take in stride whatever comes along. Because mountain youths are surrounded by a culture that contains only what is known, they are often extremely reluctant and afraid to attempt any unfamiliar experience.

For example, a group of men from our area were being housed in a YMCA in a city where the church was seeking to relocate them. One night a member of the group stopped in the lobby for a candy bar while the others went on up to their rooms. Following along afterwards, he entered the automatic elevator, which had always been operated by someone else in the group. Finding himself alone with the doors closed, he panicked. He yelled and screamed and beat on the sides of the elevator until someone on the outside punched the button, opening the doors for him. He was so shaken by this experience that the next day he boarded a bus for home. There are no doubt many people who are still suspicious of these automatic devices; yet here was a young man in his early thirties who was so overwhelmed in this new situation that he could not handle his fear.

Such fear is not surprising, for mountain life has traditionally been insecure. This is true economically, for the mountaineer has never been financially secure either on his small farm or in the mines. This is true medically, for the mountaineer has not often shared the advantages of modern medicine. This is true religiously, for even his faith has been a fear-motivated one.

The very permissive and indulgent child-rearing practices of the mountain family also create insecurity, for children are trained to believe that their desires are paramount. Yet every child knows he is not capable of making decisions for himself, and he needs to find a security in parents who do know. The mountain child is made to depend upon his own choices very early in his life, thus building an insecurity into him almost from the start.

Because the mountaineer's security is dependent upon his relationships with those in his family and reference group (see Chapter 4), he must always rely on someone else. His security is not based within himself, on his own abilities and talents. Thus he can never be sure of himself as a person in his own right.

It is difficult and useless, perhaps, to try to name all the fears of the mountaineer, for apprehension pervades his whole life. One does not have to live long in the mountains to see that this anxiety affects persons of all ages, eating away at the relationships of person with person, even within families, at self-confidence, happiness, and health. The mountaineer lacks a confident sense of who he is and where he is going; instead, one finds a reluctant and anxious person who seems to ask for defeat by his very reluctance and uncertainty. Everybody who works in the mountains should be aware of this anxiety and its ramifications, for it determines in great measure the working of the group process as well as the kind and quality of response that can be expected from mountain people.

Babies have a unique place in the mountain family. Though the mountain man often pays little attention to the larger children, he will make a great deal of fuss over babies, playing with them, fondling them, and carrying them about. Even older boys are this way. I have seen teenage boys take a crying infant from its mother's arms during church, amusing it for the rest of the service with an interest and tenderness which is almost unbelievable in the light of the usual male role.

Each child is welcomed happily into the family, no matter how many there already are or how poor the family is. Large families are considered a blessing; for many years past, the more children there were, the more help there was in making a living. Eight or more children are not at all uncommon. Until very recently, death rates were very high among children, and there is hardly an older family that does not keep a small hillside grave plot where sons and daughters are buried. In the past few years, families have become smaller, yet the highest birth rates in the nation are still in the mountains (Leslie County, Kentucky, has the highest.) Methods of family planning are generally unknown, although we have not found great opposition to them. For generations, circumstances have fostered a "live for today" philosophy. The difficulty and uncertainty of life have led most mountain people to accept whatever comes along, including children. Children are highly valued because they give meaning to the parents' lives. One mother expressed it, "If I didn't have my children, I wouldn't have nothin'." Another, speaking of her nine-year-old son, her only child, said, "Yes, I dress him and tie his shoes. It's my pleasure to do it as long as he's at home." I am confident that one reason for the high rate of illegitimate births in the mountains is that the arrival of a child gives a young girl a new sense of her own purpose and worth: her child needs her. I know of few cases where such children are given up for adoption. Many times a married daughter will give a newborn child to her mother to keep; the mother did not have any little ones to care for, while the daughter already had several. Many mountain children are brought up by grandparents. These tangled relationships are so common that school nurses have learned to say, "What name do you go by?" instead of "What is your name?" in filling out immunization cards. In the space marked "Father's name" they quickly accept the response, "My mother's name is ———."

The fact that babies are not planned affects not only the way in which parents relate to them but also the methods by which they are reared. American society today is characterized by three types of families: the *adult-centered*—prevalent in the mountain and working class groups, run by adults, where the children are expected to behave as much like adults as possible; the *child-centered*—found among middle class families, in which children are planned for and in which the parents subordinate their wishes and pleasures to give the child what they think he needs; and the *adult-directed*—an upper middle class pattern, in which parents also place lower priorities on their own needs, in order to guide their children toward the goals planned.[2]

In the middle classes, where children are planned for and the husband and wife share a great deal in their common life, the presence of the children reinforces the relationship between husband and wife. Parents find themselves communicating with each other through the rearing of their children. Parents sacrifice for their children, play with them, carry on many activities with them. Much of the parental concern is to provide for the children—good environment, good schools, wholesome recreation. Participating in Scouts, church, or Little League with the children helps achieve these goals. When children are appearing in special programs at school or church or club, parents make an effort to be present. Their goals for the children may include a college education, or having a happier childhood than they themselves had, or a happier home, or more comforts. These families may be said to be child-centered.

In the professional or upper middle class, the parents are usually college-educated and have arrived at a station in life in which they feel secure. Because the wife is often educated, her interests may well extend beyond the home. These parents know more plainly what they want for their children than

[2] Herbert J. Gans, *The Urban Villagers* (New York: Free Press of Glencoe, 1962), pp. 54 ff.

does the child-centered family. Their relationship may be said to be adult-directed. The child's desires are less important than his goals. Much time and effort will be spent to assure the child's success in school in order that he may be a proper adult, achieving his goals. His parents will exert considerable pressure on him to excel in whatever he undertakes.

The mountain family is adult-centered. Since children are not planned, their arrival does not put them at the family center. They are born into a family that for generations has built its life around making a living from the hard environment of the steep hillsides and the narrow valleys. Making a living (for the male) and making a home (for the female) have been the consuming pursuits of mountain life. Children are expected to fit into this life pattern as soon as they are able.

THE TRAINING OF CHILDREN

While the child is still a baby and does not object to being an adult's toy, he is part of the world of his parents. As he begins to have a mind of his own and to challenge the authority of his parents, adult ego satisfaction diminishes and the process of separation begins. As children grow, they are more and more allowed to form their own reference groups, and parents cease to play with them as soon as they mature beyond infancy. There is a curiously unchildlike quality about mountain children; one sees and hears little spontaneous laughter and enthusiasm and few group games. Children are not allowed play that interferes with adult life. Girls are expected to become little

mothers, and boys are given a great deal of freedom, just as their fathers are. When someone calls on the family, the children will either be shooed off to another room while the grown-ups talk or else be required to sit quietly. Seldom are the children present introduced as part of the family or allowed to participate in the conversation; almost never are they brought from other parts of the house to be introduced, and they are most certainly not allowed to dominate the scene even for a moment.

At community gatherings or family reunions, parents will abandon the younger children to the care of their older sisters while the adults talk or participate in the program. They will notice the children only when discipline is clearly called for. And children gravitate to their reference groups quickly in any gathering. The family pew is unheard of in the mountains. Girls and young boys may sit with their mothers, older boys never. Their group gathers outside or sits together in the back. Church is an adult activity, and adults actually seem oblivious to the misbehavior of their children on the back rows. Parents reprimand their children for misbehavior but seldom offer specific, positive teaching.

Mountain children are reared impulsively, with relatively little of the conscious training found in middle class families. Discipline is meted out with no concern about how the child will react as a child. In such an adult-centered society, children's feelings are not given great weight. When they misbehave, they are punished—and it is always physical punishment, not just a scolding or being sent to their rooms. The ubiquitous apple tree switch is always handy, and its use is quickly threatened for the least offense. Many a slight mountain mother can still use that switch with effect on a teenage son who may be larger than she, and he figures that she has the right to do it. In situations calling for ordinary punishment, she administers the switch herself. If the misdeed is thought to be bad enough, she will wait for her husband to come home. Then, however, if she feels he is punishing too severely, she will intercede for her child. There are times when she may even enter into a conspiracy with the child to prevent the father from finding out about something that would surely bring down his wrath. Punishment is not given in order to press toward a desired result, it is simply to keep the child in line. Because the father tends to be unreasonable in his administering of punishment, and the mother can often be counted on to be overly lenient or can be talked into leniency, the child's strong emotional attachment to "Mommy" is encouraged.

This training, based as it is on the fear of punishment, builds into the child either a resentment toward or a fear of authority of any kind. Rewards are given or promised if children behave or do something which the parents desire them to do. "If you pass your grade, I'll give you a dollar"; likewise, "If you fail your grade, you'll get a whipping."

Child rearing in mountain families is not only impulsive but permissive and indulgent as well. Children are seldom required to do what they do not want to do. I have even known of sick children who, on finding their medicine distasteful, were allowed not to take it, even though their welfare depended upon their doing so. If a child wants candy or pop he can have it, even though his teeth may be rotting out

because of it. If a child does not particularly want to have a new experience (going to camp, for example), parents seldom urge him to go for the good it might do him. They let the child make the decision. Kephart, many years ago, noted this aspect of child rearing: "Most mountaineers are indulgent, super-indulgent parents. . . . The boys, especially, grow up with little restraint beyond their own natural sense of filial duty. Little children are allowed to eat or drink anything they want. . . ."[3] There is little in the mountain child's training that would help him develop self-control, discipline, resolution, or steadfastness. Thus the way is prepared for future difficulties in the army or at work. In his adult life he tends to be capricious, vacillating, and volatile. His feelings are easily hurt; he will quit groups when things don't go his way, and otherwise demonstrate immature behavior.

Mothers tell their children what they expect of them, yet often do not insist on the command's being carried out. I have seen mothers keep up a constant stream of commands and suggestions which the children ignored completely, appearing not even to hear. The command of the father, however, is more likely to be heeded. Children soon learn that words do not count as much as action. They learn that their mother's torrents of words do not mean as much as the impulsive paddling they receive on occasion. They quickly catch on to the technique of appearing to obey for a moment, in order to go right back to whatever they were about without fear of further interference for a time. Because of this

[3] Horace Kephart, Our Southern Highlanders (New York: Outing Publishing Co., 1913), p. 82.

training, young people are not taught to listen to what words mean, but only to what emotion the speaker is conveying. Hence it is extremely difficult for teachers, social workers, ministers, and others to communicate with mountain people. The workers believe that the words themselves, their meaning and arrangement, convey the message. Mountain people "hear" the feeling behind the words. This type of child rearing is basically a conservative one, as one might imagine, being limited by what is already done rather than being pointed toward a goal that might be attained or an ideal that could be reached.

While middle class families tend to have a clear image of the future educational achievement, social status, or kind of life they hope their children will have, and so work toward that end, the mountaineer has no such aims in view. Often the mountaineer's goals for his children are couched in negative terms—what he does not want them to be. Coal miners usually do not want their sons to mine coal, nor do small farmers want their sons to follow in their footsteps. All that mountain people know is that they do want their children to "make good," to get enough education (although they are not sure how much is necessary) and to have a more secure life than they have had. Few know how to go about achieving these goals. If children go wrong, parents often blame the reference group and do not assume the same responsibility or sense of guilt that middle class families would.

MOUNTAIN YOUTH

As children grow, the gulf between them and their parents increases. Adult reference groups have little relationship to either child or youth reference groups. Adult society, accordingly, has little constructive influence in young lives. The adults seem utterly baffled by the young people, not knowing what to do to help them and being almost afraid to try anything. It becomes very difficult, therefore, to find adults who have much interest or success in leading either church or community youth groups. The training of mountain youth consists largely of imitation of their peers as they in turn imitate adults.

These youth reference groups largely operate outside the home, which tends to be small and crowded and adult-dominated. Unlike his city counterpart, the mountain youth still has some home chores. He brings in coal or water and cuts kindling wood. In the more rural areas, youths are kept fairly close to home to help in the garden or with the animals. Once finished with the required chores, the boys, especially, are free to join their friends. It is common to see groups of them gathered on the porch of a country store or under a large tree where the river forks, or perched on a culvert railing. In these groups the boys find their social outlet. I have known boys who were sullen and uncommunicative at home to become talkative and ebullient when they were with a group of particular friends. The boys plan and carry out contests of strength and physical prowess, teach one another about sex (few mountain parents will talk about it to their children), and generally exert a very conservative influence on each other. For example, any boy in the group who does well in school, or who studies hard, or who sets goals for his life which he tells the group about, becomes the object of ridicule; he either succumbs to the pressure or else is dropped from the group altogether. By this means is group solidarity maintained. It is nothing short of tragedy that these reference groups can exert such pressure on the individual boy without being countered by any adult influence. The youth's life is so involved with these groups, his security so bound up with them, that few are strong enough to go their own way outside them. Adults do not know and seem hardly to care what goes on in these groups, so long as there is no community trouble resulting from the boys' activities. Adolescent society, in short, is very much unguided by experienced adults. Boys teach boys and girls teach girls. It is no wonder that mountain culture tends to perpetuate itself in traditional ways.

The girls are far less likely to belong to such separate reference groups than are the boys. Girls have far less freedom, partly because they have more home chores and partly because families feel more protective toward them. Girls are often found in groups of two or three and are more likely to be in someone's home. Boys are expected to "protect" their sisters. There is a close feeling between the brothers and sisters in the families, and the boys are taught that they have a responsibility to look after their sisters. Fairly small boys will walk quite a distance to escort a sister to a neighbor's house, then walk back again to escort her home.

Dating begins about the junior-high age. The nature of mountain society invites troubles immediately: there is nothing to do. For teenagers, life is incredibly dull. They are filled with vague restlessness and longings, and there are neither intellectual nor recreational outlets for them. Little money is available to them, further cutting down their ability to do things. Allowances on a regular basis, either for work done or simply because a certain amount is needed regularly for school, are not at all common. When a young person needs money, he asks his father (usually) for it each time—even if he needs it every day, as for school lunches. This is another aspect of the person-centeredness of the society. Getting or not getting the money is dependent upon the whim of the father at the time. Thus young people soon learn how to "soap up the old man" in order to get what they want. It may be they enlist their mother in the process of getting money out of the father. Few arrangements are made in the family on the basis of impersonal justice or need. What is done is dependent upon the feeling of the giver at the moment of asking or upon the persuasive skill of the requester.

"What do you do on a date?" I have asked young people. "There ain't nothin' to do. You can go over to her house and watch television if they have one, but chances are her folks are sittin' right there with you and hardly even talk to you." And there is no other place to go. A boy and girl dating seldom join with other couples. In all kinds of weather you see young couples out walking along the roads. They have no adult guidance and nothing to do. Is it any wonder that the illegitimate birth rate of the mountain area has always been high?

Illegitimacy is common and is more accepted than it is in middle class society. Adult society seems to say, "We had nothing to do with the situation, and we can't do anything about it. Might just as well accept it." Sometimes the boy is required to marry the girl; often he is not. The girl will keep her baby; she may quit school to tend it, or perhaps she will give it to her mother to keep and bring up. Because babies are so highly regarded in mountain families, illegitimate children are welcomed gladly and spoiled with the rest. The baby's mother quickly takes her place in society again, sometimes even in her old reference group, as if nothing had happened. Even though she has had one or more children, a girl is still very eligible for marriage. Either the grandparents will add the illegitimate children to their family or the husband will accept them as if they were his own. Putting these children up for adoption is not only practically unheard of in the mountains, it is thought to be a cruel practice. How could the unwed mother, or the grandparents, even think of giving up their own child to a stranger!

There is actually very little delinquency in the mountains. The gangs of boys will get into various kinds of devilment just for amusement; a group in one valley may have fights with groups from adjacent valleys or develop intense rivalries with them. Mailboxes may be removed, windows in old buildings broken out, apples stolen, outhouses dismantled and moved, or chickens stolen for a feast. Occasionally tires and gas will be stolen from cars to provide for a vehicle that the boys will use. But few premeditated, vicious acts are ever done. Senseless mugging, or destruction of school property, or molesting of older people is almost unheard of. This is partly because the rural nature of the area provides plenty of room to work off pent-up emotions. A good hike in the mountains, exploring caves or rolling boulders down a hill just to hear them crash, going hunting or fishing—this kind of activity is readily available and provides physical and emotional outlets for the boys. A second reason for the low rate of delinquency is the person-centeredness of the society. When we asked some of the boys why they don't act in the delinquent ways that some city youths do, they replied, "Why, these are our own people, our friends and neighbors. We couldn't do things like that to them!" It wouldn't be easy to get away with it unrecognized, either.

In any society, young people often utter remarks like "I hate school" or "I wish school would get out sooner." In other cultures, these feelings, which are fairly common, are not allowed to gain much influence. Parents quickly squelch such statements, and the overall pressure of society is directed toward making good in school. But among the reference groups of mountain youth, where adult influence is almost nonexistent, this feeling is allowed to grow and predominate. Many young people either put forth just enough effort in school to be kept on the ball team, or drop out early and thereby gain status in the reference group.

Church activities are regarded in the same way. As long as the church can provide some excitement for their dull lives, young people will be found at church. Few can make any serious commitment to the church, because the pressure of the reference group is against it—unless, as occasionally happens, a whole group can be enlisted together.

MARRIAGE

While childhood seems to be only a waiting period until adulthood is attained, adolescence is in many ways the high point of life—especially the courting period, and especially for girls. At this time, for once in their lives, girls have a significance and honor and have some attention paid to them. It is a brief moment, remembered with nostalgia, for marriage comes early for many. Family life for the adolescent is often very unhappy. Marriage presents the promise, as least, of some escape. Parents have no insight into youthful feelings and do not try to understand. Since neither educational nor vocational plans stand in the way, parents feel they can do no other than let young people marry when they wish. Many marry in order to get away from home, succeeding only in setting up another household where the same problems are perpetuated. Even in this rebellious breaking away, the youths are still tied emotionally to their parents, hating them yet needing them. The bridal glow very soon disappears, and the slow, dull pace of life sets in with added responsibilities and frustrations. After marriage, mountain women seem to age quickly, becoming passive and less conscious of themselves as being attractive than are middle class women. The men, while going through a somewhat similar pattern, are freer in their choices and activities, and do not seem to age so quickly.

Though mountain young people are romantic to a degree, the wedding is often thought of as "doing what's necessary" rather than being an experience that is planned for, savored, and remembered. Often the young couple will just "decide to get married" one weekend, going to the courthouse for the tests and license and then going to find any "preacher" who will perform the service right away—with neither parents nor friends sharing the experiences. No honeymoon is planned, and the bride and groom may return to one of their families immediately after the service to begin living together while they plan where and how they will live permanently. Sometimes they live for some weeks or months with either parent, apparently experiencing little conflict with them. Often the boy has no job.

Very soon after the marriage, the romantic side disappears and each spouse takes up again with the reference-group friends of the same sex. Family life patterns are largely molded by this pull and the resulting lack of communication, as husband and wife lead almost separate existences side by side. Elizabeth Bott describes this relationship between husband and wife as "segregated," in contrast to the "joint" relationship of the middle class couple, and notes that it results in a separation of tasks, friends, leisure-time pursuits, interests, and activities.[4] The fact of marriage, moreover, does not mean that the basic emotional dependence of the couple is changed. Dependence on "Mommy" and "Daddy" is preserved intact. Thus, if either spouse needs to be hospitalized, and a decision must be made by the family in consultation with the doctors, the other spouse is not the one consulted; it is the parents of the sick one that are called in to decide.

Once my wife and I invited a group of young couples to a New Year's Eve party; children were left at home. Several couples remarked that it was the first time in many years (for one couple it was twelve years) that they had done anything together as

[4] *Family and Social Network* (London: Tavistock Publications, 1957), pp. 53–54.

husbands and wives. In counseling couples who are having marital troubles, I have often found that they have nothing in common. He resents her wasting time gossiping with her friends all day long, and she resents his going off every evening to play cards or talk with his friends, leaving her alone. Middle class persons often find it difficult to accept what seems to them a total unconcern of husband and wife for each other, yet this pattern has been common for people of the mountains for generations. The husband was often taken by death in the mines or through the hardness and hazards of frontier life, and the wife would be forced to carry on by herself to keep the family together. Likewise, illness or death in childbirth might remove the woman before her time. This lack of closeness has made it easier for the remaining parent to maintain the household, along with the help of the extended family. It is remarkable how many such broken-by-death families exist in the mountains.

The fact that a reference group is either all men or all women means that there is a distinct separation of the male and female roles. The males are less adept in a heterosexual relationship than are the females. When people get together, the men gather in one group, the women in another. Only during the adolescent courting period is this pattern broken to any extent or for any length of time. Sunday school classes are often divided in this way, and it is even common in church worship services to have the men sitting on one side or in one section and the women and children in another. Though this pattern of separation of the sexes is common in many societies, in mountain society it is extreme.

In middle class society the tasks connected with the home are also partly the man's duty. He expects to clean the garage or the basement or to relieve his wife of the care of the children for a time, will help with the dishes or laundry, and may even enjoy cooking. In mountain culture, however, the lines of duty are drawn much more rigidly, and seldom are the tasks assigned to one spouse shared by the other. When the husband comes home from work, no wife asks him to help in the house or with the children. Many a coal miner, on getting home from work, finds his wife almost his obedient slave, having the water hot for his bath (sometimes heated in pans on top of a stove in the wash house out back), with clean clothes all laid out and supper ready. Few wives would dare to be absent when their husbands come home. The husband's task is to earn the living. The wife's duty is to care for the house and family; often she even tends the garden or the yard and does the inside painting. Gardening, however, is acceptable male work.

The sexes tend to be uncomfortable with each other, and few words pass between them. The man's inability to converse with women is part of a traditional pattern. In the hard life of the frontier the father and boys had to work outdoors; few social contacts were made or were necessary, and few social skills were developed. The pursuits of farming, logging, and mining, or of hunting and fishing, actually prevent the learning of social skills. Often, too, the mountain male has less education than the female, and he will not place himself in a position where a "smarter" woman can show him up. He functions best when he is with his own reference group.

Girls, on the other hand, are brought up in a more social environment. While learning sewing and cooking and housekeeping, they also learn social skills as a byproduct. In a society which has exalted male dominance in the form of authority and strength, these have been her defense. The mountain male often retreats to cover in the face of a "good talkin' " woman, wholly inadequate to compete. This, in a sense, has been the mountain woman's main weapon against her husband. She may not be able to command, but she can talk her way to what she wants.

The mountaineer is always wary of heterosexual encounters and deliberately shuns them. In making home visits for the church on a financial or evangelistic canvass, for example, men go with men and women with women. Pastors indigenous to the area often take either their wives or some male member calling with them, since it would not be considered proper for a man to go visiting where a woman might be present alone.

THE CHANGING ROLE OF THE SEXES

Gradually, under the force of economic circumstance, the male role has been changing. The mountain man who is no longer able to be the breadwinner, no longer able to make his own independent way, has lost his traditional reason for living. No one wants his strength. In the mines, machines have replaced the pick and shovel and the strong arm. Frustrated at every turn, the mountaineer has suffered a loss of self, of worth. Once the dominant member of the family, he is now its burden. Forced to sit at home, unemployed,

while his family suffers or becomes the object of various forms of relief, he becomes discouraged and beaten. Because this has happened not just to individual men but to the entire society, the whole image of maleness has suffered.

The mountain man has found, on moving to the cities, that his better-educated wife can more easily get and keep a job, while he must stay at home to keep the house and children. Even if he stays in the mountains, his wife is more likely to find a job than he—doing housework, keeping a store, or serving in a nearby clinic or hospital. He has come to see that the education he never got (or wanted) is the very thing that the society holds up to him as necessary. One by one the symbols of his maleness have fallen.

The mountain woman, however, has not been subjected to this kind of humiliating need for changes in her role. Her place in the family as wife and mother has remained intact. If the family has had to move, her ability to socialize has stood her in good stead in the outside world. Thus, bit by bit, as her husband's role has decreased and as his life has lost its meaning, her life has taken on new meaning in the community or at work. This situation is leading to a reversal of the roles of the sexes in mountain life. The woman is becoming the strong one, able to make decisions and cope with the increasingly complex world that is reaching in. A matriarchal society is developing; as it does, the male becomes all the more baffled in his existence and a burden to his family—with tremendous effects on family, church, and community life.

Before some of the present government aid programs went into effect, the epitome of irony was found in the situation where the family could get no relief as long as an employable male was at home. In order to enable his wife and children to be provided for, even in a minimal way, the husband had to abandon them. Then his wife could apply for relief assistance for the family. The father might still live close by, but he always had to be careful not to be found by the welfare worker. Thus, in order to have his family provided for, he was forced to make himself invisible. Few schemes more destructive of the mountaineer's sense of his own worth could have been devised. It is devastating enough for the middle class man to lose his job and place as breadwinner for his family; such a loss of position destroys the mountain man's inmost self.

ADULT REFERENCE GROUP LIFE

In working class or folk society, as has been noted, social life revolves around the reference group. This is not to say that this social life is comparable to the middle class round of parties, friends to dinner, or evenings out. Rather, it takes the form of more casual, almost daily encounters to exchange gossip and news and to compare ideas. The more limited the outlook of the persons involved, the more likely is the reference group to be confined to family members, and the less comfortable the person will be in outside contacts. The more upwardly mobile persons, those exhibiting more nearly middle class tendencies, will belong to one or more groups composed of like-minded friends, who will most often be close neighbors. The women are often found talking over the back fence or having coffee in the kitchen. The men can be found on the porch, or on the steps of a nearby store, chatting away about the latest rumors regarding work, or relishing stories of the mines or mountains which they tell with great skill.

Herbert Gans describes the reference-group society as being held together by rubber, alternately stretching and contracting as the various members of the group vie and jockey with each other for recognition or acceptance.[5] It is within this group that one is able to express one's individuality. Though some are looked to as natural leaders and do more of the talking, practically everybody in the group is able to relate what he knows, tell a story, or give an opinion. Considerable joking and teasing go on as the members test each other out. Outside the group, mountain people are often uncommunicative, almost sullen, but within it they take on new life and expression. If a man's "turn" is unusually quiet, even in the group, he is accepted in this role. It may thus be said that one's personality is whole only in interaction with this particular group of persons.

Subjects that might engender conflict are not discussed. For people so dependent on relationships, any kind of slight or hurt is devastating to both happiness and security. And since new ideas are hard for the mountaineer to handle, persons who differ with him are at least suspect and may become enemies. A give-and-take discussion where differing opinions, honestly held, are expressed is not common to reference-group conversations. When splits do occur, they are deep and lasting, and

5 Gans, p. 81.

the techniques for healing them are unknown. In counseling couples before marriage, I have often tried to find out how the bride and groom express their anger, in an effort to point to ways of settling differences within their marriage relationship. Time and again comes the statement, "I never get angry with anybody in the family," which means "We all agree to stay away from controversial subjects" or "I bottle it up inside myself."

The closeness of this interrelated reference group means that there are always strong tensions which are not at all visible to the outsider. They are generally kept under control, for everyone in the group knows how far he can safely go. But when someone does go too far, the blowup appears much too large to the outsider, because he cannot feel the tremendous undercurrent which has been present all along. Such blow-ups affect large segments of the community; clubs, PTA, churches and other ongoing activities inherit reference-group troubles.

Relations in the reference group are equalitarian, and there seems to be an almost total disregard for the kind of status represented by the "keeping up with the Joneses" attitude. The fickleness of the economic situation through the years has reduced the possibility of this kind of behavior to a minimum. No family could depend from day to day on having any material security, and so status based on possessions was never structured into the culture. There is a great deal of extravagant impulse buying of furniture and appliances, but seldom, if ever, are such acquisitions used for rising above the neighbors or the reference group. New cars are a status symbol only to the young boys, who are quickly disabused

of such thoughts after marriage or a few years of poverty living. The stratification that does exist seems to be based on external morality. People "look down on" drunks, adulterers, and people who don't pay debts, and the more stable look down on those who can't keep a job or don't keep clean.

Since one of the main functions of the reference group is to provide a means of individual expression, the members are not really interested in the achievement of goals or in joint activities. The group is unable to function to achieve desired goals unless all share them. If group tasks are presented, there is always the fear that dissension will occur over decisions that need to be made or that the group will be manipulated or used by the leaders to gain power over the rest. Hence it is always difficult to find those within the society who will dare to risk the danger of separation from the group in order to undertake leadership responsibilities or even to take a stand on any issue. A classic example of this reluctance to make a stand on anything for fear of cutting oneself off from the group or causing hard feeling was an incident in which a new postmaster wished to move the post office to a building closer to his home. He began circulating a petition among the citizens to support his request to the Post Office Department. Another man in the community, at that point, began also to circulate a petition opposing the move, since he wished the post office to remain close to *his* home. When the petitions were in, it was found that almost all of the citizens involved had signed both petitions.

Outside of the reference group, the mountaineer is uneasy, even suspicious. When he is sufficiently motivated to go beyond the group—to the PTA for instance—he is often unwilling to enter into any discussion and refuses to vote when a possibly controversial issue must be decided. There are usually upwardly mobile people present who will do the talking and say what they think. Then naturally, they are accused of "running things." The fear of criticism (which may never be uttered but often imagined) is the weapon the reference group holds over its members. Thus it acts as a conservative force, molding its members quite effectively and keeping the society in a state of near stagnation. It would take a strong person, indeed, to go counter to the reference group, for he would not only be ostracized from his social life but would lose his source of security and individuality as well. County judges recognize this fact and sometimes sentence habitual troublemakers to complete separation from their reference groups by banning them from the county where they get into trouble.

LEAVING THE FAMILY

Loyalty to the family and the reference group is built into the cultural structure of the mountains. Persons who leave the family find life very difficult. In fact, the middle class axiom that the task of the parent is to bring up his child so that the child won't need him any more but can be independent is simply not at all true of mountain culture. Almost the opposite is true. No mountain parent would dream of bringing up a child in such a way. A child is brought up to become part of the family and reference group.

Families that migrate to the city often move into the same neighborhood (or even the same house) as other mountain families, to the consternation of landlords. City officials and ordinary citizens frown on the formation of such new ghettos; yet this is part of the pattern one would expect. When uprooted, these families seek to recreate their mountain culture as nearly as possible.

The mountaineer does not join in with the neighborhood groups or the larger organizations of the city, which are often operated on very impersonal bases. Partly through fear of impersonal social contacts, and partly from the traditional pull of the family group to center in itself, he does not enter fully into city life. This reluctance increases his alienation. When middle class persons move from one city to another, as often happens in our mobile culture, they find substitutes for their friends and peers. "People are much the same wherever you go" is a common phrase. But mountain families do not often say this when they are forced to move, because no one can replace the family in the security pattern. Nor does distance in miles break the psychological dependency ties. Many mountain families who have been living in the city for years would move back to the mountains in a minute if they could be assured of jobs there. The fierce loyalty of mountain people to home is mostly a loyalty to the only culture in which they feel secure and which operates in ways they know and appreciate. This is one reason, at least, why armchair economists who say that the only answer to the Southern Appalachian unemployment problem is migration, answer too simply. From the vantage point of middle or upper class culture, moving is easy. For the mountaineer, moving is a kind of death to his way of life. It cuts him off from his sustaining roots.

THE REFERENCE GROUP AND THE SELF

Since every part of the mountain man's life is aimed toward person-to-person encounter, he finds it difficult to react to situations in other than personal ways. He relates almost every new possibility or every new plan to himself. This attitude could well lead an outsider to believe that the mountaineer is a very selfish person. Actually, to those within his reference group he is more than generous, and he is even so to others in the area. I know one man who is working, for example, to assist as many as five other families whose breadwinners are out of work; he gives them food and money for utilities. And yet, his individualism does make the mountaineer "look out for himself."

Because the mountain man finds his self-identification mainly in his relationship with others, he has never developed a satisfactory self-image as a single individual. He is only somebody in relation to his peers. Thus he finds it difficult to accept a particular "role" either in his family or in another group —as teacher of others or leader of a meeting. He tries, but he always slips back into the personal, nonreflective role of reference-group participant. In contrast, the middle class person can present to a group a particular cause or position that perhaps does not even involve him personally. He may even present a position he does not share, in order to have both sides heard. When he becomes chairman, he can separate himself from the group, and

because he has object goals toward which he seeks to guide the group, he can function as an effective leader. The mountaineer, because he has no image of himself as a person, can involve himself only impulsively, directly, and personally in such situations. He can enter in only without reflection. Because object goals are not primary in his life, as a leader he may be very ineffective; the meetings he leads are directed more toward satisfactory interpersonal relationships and feeling than toward any goal which the group might have. This fact makes the task of finding and training leaders for groups within the mountains extremely difficult. In short, when the mountaineer can act impulsively within the security of the reference group, he feels at home. Outside this group, when he must act in thought-out ways he feels himself at a disadvantage. He is unsure of himself, tends to depreciate himself and his abilities, will lapse into shyness or even fear. This combination of forces makes it very difficult to get volunteers to take on particular jobs. Within the reference-group, to volunteer would mean to step out unduly from the rest, while outside the reference group to volunteer would be to make a frightening move into the unknown.

This inability to relate to persons on other than a personal basis, which the impulsive child-rearing practices of the mountain family no doubt help to foster, also tends to make the mountaineer suspicious of the outsider. "If you want to be friendly, that is one thing, but if you want to do something for me or to me, that is another," is almost the attitude. Indeed, the mountaineer, by the lessons of his past if by nothing else, has every right to be suspicious of anybody's doing anything for him. His history has been one of being "done out of" by fast-talking outsiders who have often stripped him of his very means of livelihood. He therefore tends to play it safe, to be ultraconservative, to be reluctant to accept any changes (for they will probably be for the worse), to reject what the world tries to thrust upon him.

It has always been interesting to me to listen to politicians or business- men or clergymen who have come out of this reference-group background, as they speak to persons still within the reference-group society. They invariably say, somewhere near the beginning of their talk, something like, "Now I'm just a country boy myself," and then go on to use two or three local idioms that would tend to bear them out. It is as though they were saying, "You can trust me, you see. I'm just like you."

Excerpt from

IN THE MIDST OF PLENTY:
THE POOR IN AMERICA
But $40 Don't Pay for a
House, a Kid, and a Car

Ben H. Bagdikian

"You mean you want to take a look at a hillbilly!"

Homer Burleigh, thirty-three; from Anniston, Alabama, hefty, freckle-faced and sandy-haired, dressed in T-shirt, dark slacks, loafers, and for the moment immobile with resentment, blocked the doorway to his flat. Like 20,000 other Southern whites living in the two and one-half square miles on Chicago's Uptown, he had his pride, his problems, and an innate suspicion of the Eastern city slicker.

Homer Burleigh finds it hard to stay angry for long and he led the way inside. Four of his five children, ages two, three, five, and seven (a ten-year-old boy was still in school), ran about in bare feet, dressed only in underpants. Mrs. Burleigh, a wan, hard, very pregnant woman, also was barefooted.

The five-year-old boy chanted to the visitor, "You got on a necktie. You got on a necktie."

He walked into a small kitchen, sat down, rubbed a large hand over his face and sighed. He was in trouble and he knew it and he was, after the first resentment, anxious to talk about it. His trouble was not just the meagreness whose clues lay about: the drab four rooms, a living room with two pieces of furniture—television set and, opposite, old sofa; two bedrooms with four beds for seven people; the "extra room," a horrid chamber painted throughout—ceiling, walls, closet, doors —in a mottled grey and black; and a back room with a good kitchen table and four chairs, refrigerator, and kitchenette. Homer Burleigh was penniless, about to be evicted, maybe even jailed. Much of this was his own fault, the panicked response to crises. But basically he was living through the recurring ritual of the poor in which they are reminded that theirs are fragile, leaky vessels in the sea of life, barely able to keep afloat with the best of

brink of poverty

luck and in danger of sinking with the slightest storm. Homer Burleigh made mistakes when the margin of safety with which he had to live permitted no mistakes whatever.

On one side there was the Burleigh family, which had not done so badly. A complete country boy who hadn't finished the fourth grade had gone to the city and from nothing made himself a skilled industrial worker with respectable wages. On the other side was the turbulent social sea from which they tried constantly to escape—the Uptown world of Chicago, reminder of the probability of poverty. This was the urban world of the Southern white and the refugee from Appalachia.

A walk through it shows the transient desperation. Families of four live in one room at $25 a week. A single man can rent a room for $1 a night if he wears plain slacks and sport shirt or $1.75 if he has on a suit, $7 if he has a girl. A broken down building bears a sign, *Old Age Welfare Pensioners Welcome—Will Move You In Free.* Some of the buildings are locally famous. One had a fire that killed five people, including three children. Another on Winthrop Avenue for a time had a tenant who was a Hatfield of the Hatfields-and-McCoys and when he was visited by a local city worker Mr. Hatfield said coldly, *"I don't want nothing to do with no smooth-shaven Northerner."* One three-story tenement had a fire in which nobody was killed, somehow, but which resulted in the discovery that eighty-two children lived there. A city youth worker checked on a boy in a playground team and found him a member of a family of thirteen living in a basement apartment with a constantly flooded floor, feces and garbage, the smell of sewer gases, charred walls

from a number of aborted fires from bad electrical wiring—$130 a month.

Sixty per cent of the people in the rooming houses have been at their address for less than a year. One landlord complained that he was losing money on the building he had owned and tended all his life; a curious outsider checked the real estate records and found the building had been constructed in 1925 with apartments for six families, that it was long since paid for, and he found that there were now twenty-eight mailboxes in the hallway. Children don't go out much because they are relatively new to the neighborhood and to the city or their parents are fearful. Underneath the nearby elevated train platform are strings of abandoned automobiles where police are supposed to keep out street walkers and amateur sex parties. The kids in the neighborhood are no better or worse to begin with but the odds are against them, as they are against their parents. A city youth worker thinks he has known about five hundred families in Uptown during the three years he has worked there but he has never known a child to go on to college. From this fearsome sea Homer Burleigh shrank, but it seemed ready to draw him and his family into the depths.

Homer Burleigh has an engaging charm and it is easy to see him shrugging off life's blows. They began early.

To begin with, he was born in a poor region into a poor family in a dying occupation. His father was a sharecropper in Alabama. His mother died when he was three. He did not get along with his stepmother; he quit school before he finished the fourth grade. When he was seventeen he left his father's house, which was dominated by his stepmother and her three daughters, and went to live with an uncle in town who worked in a small industrial plant. Then his uncle lost his job and went looking for work in Detroit, so young Homer went with him.

In Detroit, Homer stood in line for work at the Budd plant and when finally the man barked, "What kind of work?" Homer remembered a sign that had said, "Punch press operators needed," so he said.

"Punch press."

The man looked up, perhaps because of the Alabama drawl. "You ever work a punch press before?"

Homer said, "No, Sir, I never did."

"Then how come you're asking for a job doing it?"

"Well, I want a job." Homer is a man easy to like. He got the job.

For a year he took to his boarding house room between $80 and $120 a week, fabulous pay for a country boy. At least half of it went every week on gay parties with girl friends and weekend gambling. When the work week was cut down and take-home pay was only $70 he went looking for a new job. Homer was never the type to wither on the vine. He was a go-getter, the way a man is supposed to be when he is climbing upward. Having faked his way into a punch press job, he now pretended to be an experienced cook and took over a bording house at $300 pay a month plus free room and meals. Homer thinks his meals were quite good; it is not possible to obtain a more objective judgment. This time he cut down on the fun and games until he had $3000 saved in a sock in his dresser drawer. When he had an even $3000, about a year later, he bought a 1940 Chevrolet and headed back for Anniston where he cut a mighty swath. "Between me and the car and a few good-looking women, the $3000 didn't last ten months."

He was back living with his father again, doing odd jobs around town. But there were too many fights. One morning he washed his best chinos in well water, laid them in the sun, and when they were dry put them on, got out a clean sports shirt and told his stepmother, "Tell Dad it might be a year or two before I come back."

In Pontiac, Michigan he stood in line for five hours and at closing time still hadn't reached the hiring window. The next day he appeared at 3 a.m. "There were already six men ahead of me." He got a punch press job where he made $1.80 an hour with about $85 a week take-home pay.

The Horatio Alger instinct was irrepressible. One day he saw a notice on the bulletin board that they were hiring buffers at $2.21. He told his foreman he was going to apply. "What makes you think you're a buffer?" the foreman asked.

"Two dollars and twenty-one cents," said Homer in his slow, nasal drawl.

The plant was producing the 1955 Pontiac and Homer was given the job of smoothing the raw front fender on a buffing wheel, requiring careful abrasion of the curved surface but not too long in one place because the heat would make the metal buckle. The foreman dubiously turned Homer over to an experienced buffer, a Negro from Meridian, Mississippi. Homer jauntily took up his first fender and burned a hole right through the metal. He looked curtly at the hole in the metal, chucked the fender back in a box, and started walking away. "Where you going?" the Negro asked.

"I'm quitting before they fire me,"

Homer said. Homer put his arms up on his kitchen table as he recalled the day in the Pontiac plant.

"That colored boy he said to me, 'You come on back here and do what I say. Now pick up another fender and hold it just like this'—he took one and made me take one and grab it the way he did—'and you hold it just like a baby, and rock it back and forth, back and forth, gentle but fast, just like a baby.' Well, I began doing all right. I spoiled a couple after that but the colored guy fixed them up for me."

So the white man from Anniston, Alabama, with the help of a fellow immigrant from Meridian, Mississippi, learned to be a buffer and took home well over $100 a week. When the Pontiac plant shut down for change of models, the Negro, typically, waited workless in Michigan; he felt he had no place to go back to. But Homer, typically for the Southern white man, headed back to Anniston.

Back in Alabama Homer was driving a dump truck for $40 a week when he met Millicent, a waitress with a two-year-old son from a previous marriage. *"I decided I wanted her and the kid. But $40 don't pay for a house, a kid, and a car."*

It is significant that everywhere in Homer's plan there was a car. This is normal for almost any American male. It was more intense for the wandering man on the way up, for a car represents not only social status, but in a mobile society it means freedom, privacy, pursuit of work, and the ability to go home if there is no work. There has quietly evolved a generation of Americans who feel self-consciously exposed in a railroad coach or a bus and for whom the only self-respecting transportation is in one's own private vehicle.

And, indeed, so much of the country has adapted itself to this—factories as well as stores and apartments—that by now the car represents the only practical way to get to many jobs and homes.

The trip North with Millicent—her mother would care for her son for a short time—was in a 1951 sky-blue Studebaker with a new black top, financed with the help of $100 borrowed from Homer's uncle. They were headed for Detroit but in a Nashville gasoline station Homer noticed a car at a neighboring pump. It was an impressive Oldsmobile with Illinois plates. *"How things in Illinois?"* he asked the man.

"Oh, pretty good," the Oldsmobile owner said. *"What you looking for?"*

"My wife and me are going up looking for work," Homer told him.

The man had a Chicago *Tribune* on the front seat and offered it to him. *"Look at the want ads if you want to."* And that's how the Burleighs happened to become Chicagoans. Four days after they arrived in Chicago Homer was making $110 a week doing piecework on a punch press.

Life was good in Chicago, or as good as he expected it to be. Millicent was confused by much of the city, but she was resourceful in getting meals and making do in furnished flats. Homer was a good worker and on piecework he turned out profitable quantities.

Neither one of them can remember just when or how the change occurred but sometime between that first week seven years before and the day Homer sat at the kitchen table and told about it, their lives took a downturn. For one thing, they had four children, which with Millicent's son, made a household of seven. Expenses began to climb, in lurches with each child. They needed a bigger apartment than the neat three-room flat they had the first year and this meant more furniture. As their needs went up for more bedrooms, they were pushed into a category of apartment that is in short supply, which meant that they began drifting downward in quality of neighborhood and of building. Medical bills, which they never had considered a normal running expense, somehow became a constant drain, at first just for the deliveries and then for baby illnesses.

There was no single period when these problems emerged into their consciousness. But it bore down on them in the late 1950's when business took a turn for the worse. Homer felt it in the machine shop where he worked.

The men were cut back on hours a week, Homer being among the first to suffer because it was a relatively small shop with men of more seniority in it. When he was cut back to three days a week he couldn't pay for his rent and food and everlasting car payments.

So despite the urging of his boss to stay on a little longer until business improved, Homer struck out for another job that would pay a full week's work. He found one at once. Again he did well because he is a hard worker and an engaging fellow with initiative and a certain brassy friendliness. But when the new shop cut down on the workweek, Homer was among the first to feel the reduction because he was the most recently hired. He left for another shop to get a full week's work. In each place his lack of seniority made him the first hit by reduced time. A home economist could have told Homer that he simply didn't earn enough money to support a family of seven properly and an ingenious one might even have drawn a curve to show precisely when the Burleigh fertility outran the Burleigh income. All Homer knew was that no matter what he did, he didn't have enough money. Yet he was trying as hard as ever.

He was working in a machine shop making $85 a week, when the sores began. These were strange running sores, first under his arm and then in his groin. Even before this he knew he was facing a financial crisis of some sort. His take-home pay was about $300 a month. Rent took $110 of this. The car, by now a 1954 Pontiac, took $60 a month. This left $130 for everything else, which for a family of seven is not enough for the most economical complete diet. Yet he also had to extract from this amount clothes, gasoline and oil, medical care.

He shifted to a plastic molding plant where, for a time, the take-home pay was higher, but it, too, sagged down to about $300 a month. He began falling behind on his car payments. Then he claims he lost his car-payment booklet with his receipts, showing he had paid $400 of the total of $1200, and when the finance company reissued a new book it showed him owing the full $1200. The finance company threatened to attach his pay. His sores gave him more and more trouble and got infected from the dust in the plastic factory. A doctor told him he'd have to stop that kind of work. At this point he committed folly. He applied for a new Social Security number under which to get his pay, thus, he thought, escaping the clutches of the finance company. He says the finance company then seized the car on the street but told Homer he still owed them $1200.

It is difficult to be sure what did happen. Homer is a hard worker but he is not a creature of cold rationality. He is not too hard on himself in the car episode and he may have been all wrong. But car dealers and finance companies have perpetrated documented frauds on the innocent immigrants and on some not so innocent. Welfare workers, for example, confirmed the case of a Mexican-American from Texas who bought a six-year-old car that had a true value of about $400. The dealer charged him $800 for it, plus a flat $240 carrying charge, plus ordinary finance company interest on the whole amount, including the carrying charge and $120 insurance that they took out for him. He had made four monthly payments of $75 each and had paid $200 for a set of four new tires when he had an accident, rolled over, and ruined another car. He was in the hospital when he learned that the finance company had claimed the wreck, declared it a total loss (although the new tires presumably were usable), and threatened court action to recover all the money the man allegedly owed. At the same time lawyers for the man whose car the Mexican-American had ruined, brought suit because the $120 for insurance was for collision only, not for liability. The finance company protected their interest in the car but not the owner's.

Homer Burleigh, car gone, job almost gone, finally turned to welfare, for the first time after seven years in the city. The welfare worker told him it would be two weeks before the payments would start, so Homer worked out the two weeks. His welfare came to $261 a month and this would not pay the rent and food for them all, so from time to time toward the end of the month, Millicent would go to a nearby Presbyterian Church for free food.

The wheels of bureaucracy turned. Six months after the welfare payments started Homer was notified that he would lose his payments and would be charged with fraud. He thought they had caught up with his new Social Security number. But they had not. He was charged with having received unreported pay while getting welfare. He had. It was the pay for the last two weeks of work, after he had applied for aid to dependent children but before the payments began. The day he talked at the kitchen table, the last of the final welfare payment had been spent and in four days he was to be evicted from his flat for non-payment of rent.

"If the arm continues this way, and if they don't give me assistance, I'm going to have to put the kids in a home." His eyes filled. "These kids are young. They don't know all these problems. But that older boy, he's pretty bright. You can't keep things from him forever. Anyway, we haven't been able to pay the rent and Monday is the end. When they move us onto the sidewalk, the kids will know, all right."

And so the lines of failure seemed to converge for Homer Burleigh: a motherless home full of contention, almost no formal education, an impoverished landscape to grow in with no hope for a young man, a pattern of wandering to where there was money without making a permanent commitment, a drifting of life without heed for the consequences of more children. But he was not an evil man, nor a lazy one. His was simply the fragile vessel of endemic poverty, never strong enough to withstand a prolonged storm.

And his children seemed doomed to go forth in a similarly brittle craft.

The plight of the Burleighs seemed ultimate, an emergency that needed immediate attention. A few blocks away, in a city office of the Youth Commission, a cigar-smoking worker who had seen several hundred emergencies agreed. But time had taught him that as one got increasingly desperate, one tolerated a smaller margin of safety.

"*Middle class people think they've got an emergency if they can't pay the grocer,*" he said. "*Poor people don't think they've got an emergency until they've got no groceries.*"

By chance a confirming telephone call came in. He leaned back in his chair, listening, his cigar still. He covered the mouthpiece of the phone with his palm and told his partner in the office, "*It's the Mayfields. They don't have any food for the weekend. Not a thing, they say.*" He turned back to the telephone and said to the Mayfields:

"*Try Goudy School. They had some food for distribution earlier this week.*"

His partner waved his hand violently and said, "*Goudy's all out.*"

The cigar smoker said to the telephone, "*No. No. I'm told Goudy's all out of food. How about the church down on the avenue, the Protestant church? They don't have any, either? Well, I'll tell you what to do. You try Father Maguire at the big Catholic Church on the other side of your block. Remember now, Father Maguire, not Father Landers. Father Maguire may have some. If he hasn't call me back. Yeh, okay. Good luck.*"

He put the phone down, and lit his cigar.

"*I'm not too worried about them. His mother's on welfare so I know she's got some dough and he's got a married sister on ADC so they'll have some food. It isn't as though they had no place to go.*"

BLACK YOUTH

Excerpt from

MANCHILD IN THE PROMISED LAND

Claude Brown

The first thing I did when I got into the show that day was to yell out, "Forty thieves!" to see if any of my friends in the gang were there. That afternoon I got a loud "Yo!" from one of the front rows. It was Bucky. He hadn't been to school that day and had sneaked into the show about one o'clock. He had already seen the movie, but it was good, so he was seeing it over. "Goldie was in here a little while ago, but he hadn't been home for the past few nights, so he had to go and steal something to eat," he said. Bucky told me that he hadn't seen any of the other fellows all day. They must have been downtown stealing.

Bucky was about my age, had curly hair, was always dirty, like most of us, and had buck teeth. Of all the dirty kids on the block, Bucky was the dirtiest. He had just moved to our neighborhood around the first of the year.

Reprinted with permission of The Macmillan Company from Manchild In The Promised Land by Claude Brown. Copyright © 1965 by Claude Brown.

Bucky had lots of sisters and brothers, and his mother was still having more sisters and brothers for him. He also had some sisters and brothers who, he said, lived with their aunts. These I had never seen. Bucky didn't have a father, and his mother was on relief. All the kids in Bucky's family knew when the relief check came. On that day, they would all follow Miss Jamie around until she cashed it. Then they would beg her to buy some food before she started drinking up the money. Every month when check day rolled around, Bucky and his brothers and sisters would always be arguing with their mother. Miss Jamie was forever telling them to wait someplace until she cashed the check, that she would come back and buy some food. But they all knew that if they ever let her out of their sight with that check, they wouldn't see her for days. When she did show up, she would tell them how she got robbed or how her pocket was picked or how she lost the money. So she would spend half of the day trying to duck the kids, and they would stick with her. If there was only one kid around, or even two she could easily get away. She would usually go into a bar, where she knew the kids couldn't follow her, and she would leave the bar by another exit. When the kids got wise to this, one of them would start looking for the other exit as soon as she entered the bar. But even then she could get away if there was only one at the exit she used. She would give him fifty cents as a bribe and jump into a cab.

Bucky was the only guy I knew who could stay out all night and not be missed. Sometimes he would go out and stay for days and still get home before his mother. Sometimes Bucky would go home and there would be nobody there. The lady next door always had the lowdown. The usual reason for the house being empty was that the welfare investigator had come by and had taken all the kids to the Children's Shelter. Whenever this happened while Bucky was away from home, he would go to the police station and tell them what had happened. After the policemen had gotten to know Bucky and were familiar with his home situation, he only had to walk in and they would send him to the Shelter without asking him anything. The Shelter was a second home to Bucky. He liked it more than his first home. At the Shelter, he always got three meals a day, and three meals beats none any way you look at it. Whenever I missed Bucky from around the block, I had a pretty good idea where he was, but he would always say that he was staying with his aunt in Brooklyn. That aunt was the great mystery in Bucky's life.

When Bucky moved into the neighborhood, I sort of adopted him. He had his first fight in the neighborhood with me, and since he was pretty good with

his hands, we became friends after three fights. I used to take him home with me and feed him. After a while Bucky got to know what time we usually ate supper, and if he didn't see me on the street, he would come to my house looking for me. If I wasn't in, he would ask if he could come in and wait for me. He knew that somebody would offer him something to eat if he was there at suppertime. Dad started complaining about Bucky coming up to the house for supper every night. So Mama would tell Bucky to go downstairs and look for me if I wasn't there when he came by. When I brought him home with me, sometimes the family would slip into the kitchen one at a time to eat without his knowing it, or they would try to wait until he left. Bucky would never leave as long as he thought that we had not eaten supper. When Bucky was finally gone, Dad would start telling me how stupid I was and threatening to give my supper to Bucky the next time I brought him home with me. Dad said that Bucky had a roguish look about him and that he didn't trust him. Some of the fellows didn't like him either. They said he looked too pitiful.

That day after we saw the show, I went up to Bucky's house to show him a homemade that I had found a week before. I didn't have any bullets for it yet, but that wasn't important—I knew somebody I could steal them from. As I walked through the door—which was always open because the lock had been broken and Miss Jamie never bothered to have it fixed—I saw Bucky on the floor with his arm around his little sister's throat. He was choking her. Meanwhile, his big sister was bopping him on the head with a broom handle and they were all screaming. After I had watched the three-way fight for a minute or less, I started toward Dixie to grab the broom. Before I could get close enough to grab the broom handle, everything stopped. For a whole second, everything was real quiet. Dixie threw down the broom and started crying. Debbie was already crying, but I couldn't hear her because Bucky was still choking her. He let her go and started cursing. When Debbie got up, I saw what she and Dixie were crying over and what Bucky was cursing about. The three of them had been fighting over one egg, and the egg was broken in the scuffle.

Bucky had run out of the house cursing, and I was standing where he had left me. Dixie and Debbie were facing me on the other side of the room. They were staring at the broken egg on the floor, and their crying was getting louder all the time. I was staring at them and wondering why they were making so much fuss over one broken egg. They sure looked funny standing there with their mouths wide open and tears rolling down their dirty faces and into their mouths. I began to laugh and mimic them. Dixie threw the broom at me and missed. Knowing what they were going to do as soon as I left, I decided to get even with Dixie for throwing the broom at me. Before either of them realized what I was doing, I had stepped on the egg and was smearing it all over the floor. Debbie began to cry louder, and Dixie was all over me, scratching, biting, and hitting me with what seemed like ten hands. Without thinking, I started swinging. I didn't stop swinging until I heard Dixie crying again. She went over to what was left of that old ragged couch they had in the living room, threw herself

down on it, and went on crying into the cushions. I went over and touched her on the shoulder and told her I was sorry. She only raised her head enough to scream as loud as she could and tell me to let her alone. I told her to wait there while I went to steal her some eggs. She yelled that she didn't want any eggs and that when her older brother got out of jail, she was going to get him to kick my ass.

Less than ten minutes after I had left Dixie crying on the couch, I walked in the house with a dozen eggs and a loaf of bread. Dixie was sitting up on the couch now. Her eyes were red, but she wasn't crying; her face still had tearstains on it, and her mouth was stuck out as if she were mad at somebody. Not saying anything. I walked over to her and offered her the eggs and the loaf of bread. I was standing in front of her holding out the eggs and bread. She just sat there staring at me as if she didn't believe it or as if she wondered how I had come by these things. Seeing that she needed a little encouragement, I pushed the eggs and bread against her chest saying, "Here, take it." She took them and started walking slowly toward the kitchen. It seemed as though she still didn't believe it was really happening, that if she should make a fast or sudden move, the eggs and bread would be gone. She carried the food to the kitchen like somebody carrying a large basin of water that was filled to the brim. When I heard Dixie moving about in the kitchen, I went in, feeling that everything was all right now and that she knew I hadn't played a joke on her.

Dixie was running some water into a small pot. She asked me if I wanted a boiled egg. I told her that I liked my eggs scrambled. She said the only grease in the house was some fish grease and if she scrambled the eggs in it, they would taste like fish. After she had put six eggs on the stove to boil, Dixie said she was sorry for scratching me and didn't mean what she had said about telling her brother to beat me up when he came home. I told her that I was sorry for laughing at her and that I hadn't meant to hit her so hard. I asked her if she wanted to make friends, and she said all right. We shook hands and started talking about the things we disliked in each other. She said I just thought I was too bad and was always messing with somebody. I told her that she was all right, but she should stop licking the snot off her lip when her nose was running. Also, I thought she looked crazy always pulling her bloomers up through her skirt.

While Dixie and I were testing out our new friendship, Debbie had come in and sat down. She just sat quietly and kept watching the pot. When Dixie got up and went over to the stove to turn the fire off beneath the pot, Debbie's eyes followed her. Dixie started cutting up eggs to make sandwiches, but I told her to just give me an egg and some salt. She made two sandwiches, one for herself and one for Debbie.

NIGHTMARE

Excerpt from
The Autobiography of
Malcolm X

Malcolm X/Alex Haley

When my mother was pregnant with me, she told me later, a party of hooded Ku Klux Klan riders galloped up to our home in Omaha, Nebraska, one night. Surrounding the house, brandishing their shotguns and rifles, they shouted for my father to come out. My mother went to the front door and opened it. Standing where they could see her pregnant condition, she told them that she was alone with her three small children, and that my father was away, preaching, in Milwaukee. The Klansmen shouted threats and warnings at her that we had better get out of town because "the good Christian white people" were not going to stand for my father's "spreading trouble" among the "good" Negroes of Omaha with the "back to Africa" preachings of Marcus Garvey.

My father, the Reverend Earl Little, was a Baptist minister, a dedicated

Reprinted by permission of Grove Press, Inc. Copyright © 1964 by Alex Haley and Malcolm X; 1965 by Alex Haley and Betty Shabazz.

organizer for Marcus Aurelius Garvey's U.N.I.A. (Universal Negro Improvement Association). With the help of such disciples as my father, Garvey, from his headquarters in New York City's Harlem, was raising the banner of black-race purity and exhorting the Negro masses to return to their ancestral African homeland—a cause which had made Garvey the most controversial black man on earth.

Still shouting threats, the Klansmen finally spurred their horses and galloped around the house, shattering every window pane with their gun butts. Then they rode off into the night, their torches flaring, as suddenly as they had come.

My father was enraged when he returned. He decided to wait until I was born—which would be soon—and then the family would move. I am not sure why he made this decision, for he was not a frightened Negro, as most then were, and many still are today. My father was a big, six-foot-four, very black man. He had only one eye. How he had lost the other one I have never known. He was from Reynolds, Georgia, where he had left school after the third or maybe fourth grade. He believed, as did Marcus Garvey, that freedom, independence and self-respect could never be achieved by the Negro in America, and that therefore the Negro should leave America to the white man and return to his African land of origin. Among the reasons my father had decided to risk and dedicate his life to help disseminate this philosophy among his people was that he had seen four of his brothers die by violence, three of them killed by white men, including one by lynching. What my father could not know then was that of the remaining three, including himself, only one, my Uncle Jim, would die in bed, of natural causes. Northern white police were later to shoot my Uncle Oscar. And my father was finally himself to die by the white man's hands.

It has always been my belief that I, too, will die by violence. I have done all that I can to be prepared.

I was my father's seventh child. He had three children by a previous marriage—Ella, Earl, and Mary, who lived in Boston. He had met and married my mother in Philadelphia, where their first child, my oldest full brother, Wilfred, was born. They moved from Philadelphia to Omaha, where Hilda and then Philbert were born.

I was next in line. My mother was twenty-eight when I was born on May 19, 1925, in an Omaha hospital. Then we moved to Milwaukee, where Reginald was born. From infancy, he had some kind of hernia condition which was to handicap him physically for the rest of his life.

Louise Little, my mother, who was born in Grenada, in the British West Indies, looked like a white woman. Her father was white. She had straight black hair, and her accent did not sound like a Negro's. Of this white father of hers, I know nothing except her shame about it. I remember hearing her say she was glad that she had never seen him. It was, of course, because of him that I got my reddish-brown "mariny" color of skin, and my hair of the same color. I was the lightest child in our family. (Out in the world later on, in Boston and New York, I was among the millions of Negroes who were insane enough to feel that it was some kind of status symbol to be light-complexioned—that one was actually fortunate to be born thus. But, still later, I learned to hate every drop of that white rapist's blood that is in me.)

Our family stayed only briefly in Milwaukee, for my father wanted to find a place where he could raise our own food and perhaps build a business. The teaching of Marcus Garvey stressed becoming independent of the white man. We went next, for some reason, to Lansing, Michigan. My father bought a house and soon, as had been his pattern, he was doing free-lance Christian preaching in local Negro Baptist churches, and during the week he was roaming about spreading word of Marcus Garvey.

He had begun to lay away savings for the store he had always wanted to own when, as always, some stupid local Uncle Tom Negroes began to funnel stories about his revolutionary beliefs to the local white people. This time, the get-out-of-town threats came from a local hate society called The Black Legion. They wore black robes instead of white. Soon, nearly everywhere my father went, Black Legionnaires were reviling him as an "uppity nigger" for wanting to own a store, for living outside the Lansing Negro district, for spreading unrest and dissension among "the good niggers."

As in Omaha, my mother was pregnant again, this time with my youngest sister. Shortly after Yvonne was born came the nightmare night in 1929, my earliest vivid memory. I remember being suddenly snatched awake into a frightening confusion of pistol shots and shouting and smoke and flames. My father had shouted and shot at the two white men who had set the fire and were running away. Our home was burning down around us. We were lunging and bumping and tumbling all over each other trying to escape. My mother, with the baby in her arms, just made it into the yard before the house crashed in, showering sparks. I remember we were outside in the night in our underwear, crying and yelling our heads off. The white police and firemen came and stood around watching as the house burned down to the ground.

My father prevailed on some friends to clothe and house us temporarily; then he moved us into another house on the outskirts of East Lansing. In those days Negroes weren't allowed after dark in East Lansing proper. There's where Michigan State University is located; I related all of this to an audience of students when I spoke there in January, 1963 (and had the first reunion in a long while with my younger brother, Robert, who was there doing postgraduate studies in psychology). I told them how East Lansing harassed us so much that we had to move again, this time two miles out of town, into the country. This was where my father built for us with his own hands a four-room house. This is where I really begin to remember things —this home where I started to grow up.

After the fire, I remember that my father was called in and questioned about a permit for the pistol with which he had shot at the white men who set the fire. I remember that the police were always dropping by our house, shoving things around, "just checking" or "looking for a gun." The pistol they were looking for—which they never found, and for which they wouldn't issue a permit—was sewed up inside a pillow. My father's .22 rifle and his shotgun, though, were right out in the open; everyone had them for hunting birds and rabbits and other game.

After that, my memories are of the friction between my father and mother. They seemed to be nearly always at odds. Sometimes my father would beat her. It might have had something to do with the fact that my mother had a pretty good education. Where she got it I don't know. But an educated woman, I suppose, can't resist the temptation to correct an uneducated man. Every now and then, when she put those smooth words on him, he would grab her.

My father was also belligerent toward all of the children, except me. The older ones he would beat almost savagely if they broke any of his rules —and he had so many rules it was hard to know them all. Nearly all my whippings came from my mother. I've thought a lot about why. I actually believe that as anti-white as my father was, he was subconsciously so afflicted with the white man's brainwashing of Negroes that he inclined to favor the light ones, and I was his lightest child. Most Negro parents in those days would almost instinctively treat any lighter children better than they did the darker ones. It came directly from the slavery tradition that the "mulatto," because he was visibly nearer to white, was therefore "better."

My two other images of my father are both outside the home. One was his role as a Baptist preacher. He never pastored in any regular church of his own; he was always a "visiting preacher." I remember especially his favorite sermon: "That little *black* train is a-comin' . . . an' you better get all your business right!" I guess this also fit his association with the back-to-Africa movement, with Marcus Garvey's "Black Train Homeward." My brother Philbert, the one just older than me, loved church, but it confused and amazed me. I would sit goggle-eyed at my father jumping and shouting as he preached, with the congregation jumping and shouting behind him, their souls and bodies devoted to singing and praying. Even at that young age, I just couldn't believe in the Christian concept of Jesus as someone divine. And no religious person, until I was a man in my twenties—and then in prison—could tell me anything. I had very little respect for most people who represented religion.

It was in his role as a preacher that my father had most contact with the Negroes of Lansing. Believe me when I tell you that those Negroes were in bad shape then. They are still in bad shape—though in a different way. By that I mean that I don't know a town with a higher percentage of complacent and misguided so-called "middle-class" Negroes—the typical status-symbol-oriented, integration-seeking type of Negroes. Just recently, I was standing in a lobby at the United Nations talking with an African ambassador and his wife, when a Negro came up to me and said, "You know me?" I was a little embarrassed because I thought he was someone I should remember. It turned out that he was one of those bragging, self-satisfied, "middle-class" Lansing Negroes. I wasn't ingratiated. He was the type who would never have been associated with Africa, until the fad of having African friends became a status-symbol for "middle-class" Negroes.

Back when I was growing up, the "successful" Lansing Negroes were such as waiters and bootblacks. To be a janitor at some downtown store was to be highly respected. The real "elite," the "big shots," the "voices of the race," were the waiters at the Lansing Country Club and the shoeshine boys at the state capitol. The only Negroes who really had any money were the ones in the numbers racket, or who ran the gambling houses, or who in some other way lived parasitically off the poorest ones, who were the masses. No Negroes were hired then by Lansing's big Oldsmobile plant, or the Reo plant. (Do you remember the Reo? It was manufactured in Lansing, and R. E. Olds, the man after whom it was named, also lived in Lansing. When the war came along, they hired some Negro janitors.) The bulk of the Negroes were either on Welfare, or W.P.A., or they starved.

The day was to come when our family was so poor that we would eat the hole out of a doughnut; but at that time we were much better off than most town Negroes. The reason was we raised much of our own food out there in the country where we were. We were much better off than the town Negroes who would shout, as my father preached, for the pie-in-the-sky and their heaven in the hereafter while the white man had his here on earth.

I knew that the collections my father got for his preaching were mainly what fed and clothed us, and he also did other odd jobs, but still the image of him that made me proudest was his crusading and militant campaigning with the words of Marcus Garvey. As young as I was then, I knew from what I overheard that my father was saying something that made him a "tough" man. I remember an old lady, grinning and saying to my father, "You're scaring these white folks to death!"

One of the reasons I've always felt that my father favored me was that to the best of my remembrance, it was only me that he sometimes took with him to the Garvey U.N.I.A. meetings which he held quietly in different people's homes. There were never more than a few people at any one time—twenty at most. But that was a lot, packed into someone's living room. I noticed how differently they all acted, although sometimes they were the same people who jumped and shouted in church. But in these meetings both they and my father were more intense, more intelligent and down to earth. It made me feel the same way.

I can remember hearing of "Adam driven out of the garden into the caves of Europe," "Africa for the Africans," "Ethiopians, Awake!" And my father would talk about how it would not be much longer before Africa would be completely run by Negroes—"by black men," was the phrase he always used. "No one knows when the hour of Africa's redemption cometh. It is in the wind. It is coming. One day, like a storm, it will be here."

I remember seeing the big, shiny photographs of Marcus Garvey that were passed from hand to hand. My father had a big envelope of them that he always took to these meetings. The pictures showed what seemed to me millions of Negroes thronged in parade behind Garvey riding in a fine car, a big black man dressed in dazzling uniform with gold braid on it, and he was wearing a thrilling hat with tall plumes. I remember hearing that he had black followers not only in the United States but all around the world, and I remember how the meetings always closed with my father saying, several times, and the people chanting after him, "Up, you mighty race, you can accomplish what you will!"

I have never understood why, after hearing as much as I did of these kinds of things, I somehow never thought, then, of the black people in Africa. My image of Africa, at that time, was of naked savages, cannibals, monkeys and tigers and steaming jungles.

My father would drive in his old black touring car, sometimes taking me, to meeting places all around the Lansing area. I remember one daytime meeting (most were at night) in the town of Owosso, forty miles from Lansing, which the Negroes called "White City." (Owosso's greatest claim to fame is that it is the home town of Thomas E. Dewey.) As in East Lansing, no Negroes were allowed on the streets there after dark—hence the daytime meeting. In point of fact, in those days lots of Michigan towns were like that. Every town had a few "home" Negroes who lived there. Sometimes it would be just one family, as in the nearby county seat, Mason, which had a single Negro family named Lyons. Mr. Lyons had been a famous football star at Mason High School, was highly thought of in Mason, and consequently he now worked around that town in menial jobs.

My mother at this time seemed to be always working—cooking, washing, ironing, cleaning, and fussing over us eight children. And she was usually either arguing with or not speaking to my father. One cause of friction was that she had strong ideas about what she wouldn't eat—and didn't want us to eat—including pork and rabbit, both of which my father loved dearly. He was a real Georgia Negro, and he believed in eating plenty of what we in Harlem today call "soul food."

I've said that my mother was the one who whipped me—at least she did whenever she wasn't ashamed to let the neighbors think she was killing me. For if she even acted as though she was about to raise her hand to me, I would open my mouth and let the world know about it. If anybody was passing by out on the road, she would either change her mind or just give me a few licks.

Thinking about it now, I feel definitely that just as my father favored me for being lighter than the other children, my mother gave me more hell for the same reason. She was very light herself but she favored the ones who were darker. Wilfred, I know, was particularly her angel. I remember that she would tell me to get out of the house and "Let the sun shine on you so you can get some color." She went out of her way never to let me become afflicted with a sense of color-superiority. I am sure that she treated me this way partly because of how she came to be light herself.

I learned early that crying out in protest could accomplish things. My older brothers and sister had started to school when, sometimes, they would come in and ask for a buttered biscuit or something and my mother, impatiently, would tell them no. But I would cry out and make a fuss until I got what I wanted. I remember well how my mother asked me why I couldn't be a nice boy like Wilfred; but I would think to myself that Wilfred, for being so nice and quiet, often stayed hungry. So early in life, I had learned that it you want something, you had better make some noise.

Not only did we have our big garden, but we raised chickens. My father would buy some baby chicks and my mother would raise them. We all loved chicken. That was one dish there was no argument with my father about. One thing in particular that I remember made me feel grateful toward my mother was that one day I went and asked her for my own garden, and she did let me have my own little plot. I loved it and took care of it well. I loved especially to grow peas. I was proud when we had them on our table. I would pull out the grass in my garden by hand when the first little blades came up. I would patrol the rows on my hands and knees for any worms and bugs, and I would kill and bury them. And sometimes when I had everything straight and clean for my things to grow, I would lie down on my back between two rows, and I would gaze up in the blue sky at the clouds moving and think all kinds of things.

At five, I, too, began to go to school, leaving home in the morning along with Wilfred, Hilda, and Philbert. It was the Pleasant Grove School that went from kindergarten through the eighth grade. It was two miles outside the city limits, and I guess there was no problem about our attending because we were the only Negroes in the area. In those days white people in the North usually would "adopt" just a few Negroes; they didn't see them as any threat. The white kids didn't make any great thing about us, either. They called us "nigger" and "darkie" and "Rastus" so much that we thought those were our natural names. But they didn't think of it as an insult; it was just the way they thought about us.

One afternoon in 1931 when Wilfred, Hilda, Philbert, and I came home, my mother and father were having one of their arguments. There had lately been a lot of tension around the house because of Black Legion threats. Anyway, my father had taken one of the rabbits which we were raising, and ordered my mother to cook it. We raised rabbits, but sold them to whites. My father had taken a rabbit from the rabbit pen. He had pulled off the rabbit's head. He was so strong, he needed no knife to behead chickens or rabbits. With one twist of his big black hands he simply twisted off the head and threw the bleeding-necked thing back at my mother's feet.

My mother was crying. She started to skin the rabbit, preparatory to cooking it. But my father was so angry he slammed on out of the front door and started walking up the road toward town.

It was then that my mother had this vision. She had always been a strange woman in this sense, and had always had a strong intuition of things about to happen. And most of her children are the same way, I think. When something is about to happen, I can feel something, sense something. I never have known something to happen that has caught me completely off guard—except once. And that was

when, years later, I discovered facts I couldn't believe about a man who, up until that discovery, I would gladly have given my life for.

My father was well up the road when my mother ran screaming out onto the porch. *"Early! Early!"* She screamed his name. She clutched up her apron in one hand, and ran down across the yard and into the road. My father turned around. He saw her. For some reason, considering how angry he had been when he left, he waved at her. But he kept on going.

She told me later, my mother did, that she had a vision of my father's end. All the rest of the afternoon, she was not herself, crying and nervous and upset. She finished cooking the rabbit and put the whole thing in the warmer part of the black stove. When my father was not back home by our bedtime, my mother hugged and clutched us, and we felt strange, not knowing what to do, because she had never acted like that.

I remember waking up to the sound of my mother's screaming again. When I scrambled out, I saw the police in the living room; they were trying to calm her down. She had snatched on her clothes to go with them. And all of us children who were staring knew without anyone having to say it that something terrible had happened to our father.

My mother was taken by the police to the hospital, and to a room where a sheet was over my father in a bed, and she wouldn't look, she was afraid to look. Probably it was wise that she didn't. My father's skull, on one side, was crushed in, I was told later. Negroes in Lansing have always whispered that he was attacked, and then laid across some tracks for a streetcar to run over him. His body was cut almost in half.

He lived two and a half hours in that condition. Negroes then were stronger than they are now, especially Georgia Negroes. Negroes born in Georgia had to be strong simply to survive.

It was morning when we children at home got the word that he was dead. I was six. I can remember a vague commotion, the house filled up with people crying, saying bitterly that the white Black Legion had finally gotten him. My mother was hysterical. In the bedroom, women were holding smelling salts under her nose. She was still hysterical at the funeral.

I don't have a very clear memory of the funeral, either. Oddly, the main thing I remember is that it wasn't in a church, and that surprised me, since my father was a preacher, and I had been where he preached people's funerals in churches. But his was in a funeral home.

And I remember that during the service a big black fly came down and landed on my father's face, and Wilfred sprang up from his chair and he shooed the fly away, and he came groping back to his chair—there were folding chairs for us to sit on—and the tears were streaming down his face. When we went by the casket, I remember that I thought that it looked as if my father's strong black face had been dusted with flour, and I wished they hadn't put on such a lot of it.

Back in the big four-room house, there were many visitors for another week or so. They were good friends of the family, such as the Lyons from Mason, twelve miles away, and the Walkers, McGuires, Liscoes, the Greens, Randolphs, and the Turners, and others from Lansing, and a lot of people from other towns, whom I had seen at the Garvey meetings.

We children adjusted more easily than our mother did. We couldn't see, as clearly as she did, the trials that lay ahead. As the visitors tapered off, she became very concerned about collecting the two insurance policies that my father had always been proud he carried. He had always said that families should be protected in case of death. One policy apparently paid off without any problem—the smaller one. I don't know the amount of it. I would imagine it was not more than a thousand dollars, and maybe half of that.

But after that money came, and my mother had paid out a lot of it for the funeral and expenses, she began going into town and returning very upset. The company that had issued the bigger policy was balking at paying off. They were claiming that my father had committed suicide. Visitors came again, and there was bitter talk about white people: how could my father bash himself in the head, then get down across the streetcar tracks to be run over?

So there we were. My mother was thirty-four years old now, with no husband, no provider or protector to take care of her eight children. But some kind of a family routine got going again. And for as long as the first insurance money lasted, we did all right.

Wilfred, who was a pretty stable fellow, began to act older than his age. I think he had the sense to see, when the rest of us didn't, what was in the wind for us. He quietly quit school and went to town in search of work. He took any kind of job he could find and he would come home, dog-tired, in the evenings, and give whatever he had made to my mother.

Hilda, who always had been quiet, too, attended to the babies. Philbert and I didn't contribute anything. We just fought all the time—each other at home, and then at school we would team up and fight white kids. Sometimes the fights would be racial in nature, but they might be about anything.

Reginald came under my wing. Since he had grown out of the toddling stage, he and I had become very close. I suppose I enjoyed the fact that he was the little one, under me, who looked up to me.

My mother began to buy on credit. My father had always been very strongly against credit. "Credit is the first step into debt and back into slavery," he had always said. And then she went to work herself. She would go into Lansing and find different jobs—in housework, or sewing—for white people. They didn't realize, usually, that she was a Negro. A lot of white people around there didn't want Negroes in their houses.

She would do fine until in some way or other it got to people who she was, whose widow she was. And then she would be let go. I remember how she used to come home crying, but trying to hide it, becuase she had lost a job that she needed so much.

Once when one of us—I cannot remember which—had to go for something to where she was working, and the people saw us, and realized she was actually a Negro, she was fired on the spot, and she came home crying, this time not hiding it.

When the state Welfare people began coming to our house, we would come from school sometimes and find them talking with our mother, asking a thousand questions. They acted and looked at her, and at us, and around in our house, in a way that had about it the feeling—at least for me—that we were not people. In their eyesight we were just *things*, that was all.

My mother began to receive two checks—a Welfare check and, I believe, a widow's pension. The checks helped. But they weren't enough, as many of us as there were. When they came, about the first of the month, one always was already owed in full, if not more, to the man at the grocery store. And, after that, the other one didn't last long.

We began to go swiftly downhill. The physical downhill wasn't as quick as the psychological. My mother was, above everything else, a proud woman, and it took its toll on her that she was accepting charity. And her feelings were communicated to us.

She would speak sharply to the man at the grocery store for padding the bill, telling him that she wasn't ignorant and he didn't like that. She would talk back sharply to the state Welfare people, telling them that she was a grown woman, able to raise her children, that it wasn't necessary for them to keep coming around so much, meddling in our lives. And they didn't like that.

But the monthly Welfare check was their pass. They acted as if they owned us, as if we were their private property. As much as my mother would have liked to, she couldn't keep them out. She would get particularly incensed when they began insisting upon drawing us older children aside, one at a time, out on the porch or somewhere, and asking us questions, or telling us things—against our mother and against each other.

We couldn't understand why, if the state was willing to give us packages of meat, sacks of potatoes and fruit, and cans of all kinds of things, our mother obviously hated to accept. We really couldn't understand. What I later understood was that my mother was making a desperate effort to preserve her pride—and ours.

Pride was just about all we had to preserve, for by 1934, we really began to suffer. This was about the worst depression year, and no one we knew had enough to eat or live on. Some old family friends visited us now and then. At first they brought food. Though it was charity, my mother took it.

Wilfred was working to help. My mother was working, when she could find any kind of job. In Lansing, there was a bakery where, for a nickel, a couple of us children would buy a tall flour sack of day-old bread and cookies, and then walk the two miles back out into the country to our house. Our mother knew, I guess, dozens of ways to cook things with bread and out of bread. Stewed tomatoes with bread, maybe that would be a meal. Something like French toast, if we had any eggs. Bread pudding, sometimes with raisins in it. If we got hold of some hamburger, it came to the table more bread than meat. The cookies that were always in the sack with the bread, we just gobbled down straight.

But there were times when there wasn't even a nickel and we would be so hungry we were dizzy. My mother would boil a big pot of dandelion greens, and we would eat that. I remember that some small-minded neighbor put it out, and children would tease us, that we ate "fried grass." Sometimes, if we were lucky, we would have oatmeal or cornmeal mush three times a day. Or mush in the morning and cornbread at night.

Philbert and I were grown up enough to quit fighting long enough to take the .22 caliber rifle that had been our father's, and shoot rabbits that some white neighbors up or down the road would buy. I know now that they just did it to help us, because they, like everyone, shot their own rabbits. Sometimes, I remember, Philbert and I would take little Reginald along with us. He wasn't very strong, but he was always so proud to be along. We would trap muskrats out in the little creek in back of our house. And we would lie quiet until unsuspecting bullfrogs appeared, and we would spear them, cut off their legs, and sell them for a nickel a pair to people who lived up and down the road. The whites seemed less restricted in their dietary tastes.

Then, about in late 1934, I would guess, something began to happen. Some kind of psychological deterioration hit our family circle and began to eat away our pride. Perhaps it was the constant tangible evidence that we were destitute. We had known other families who had gone on relief. We had known without anyone in our home ever expressing it that we had felt prouder not to be at the depot where the free food was passed out. And, now, we were among them. At school, the "on relief" finger suddenly was pointed at us, too, and sometimes it was said aloud.

It seemed that everything to eat in our house was stamped Not To Be Sold. All Welfare food bore this stamp to keep the recipients from selling. It's a wonder we didn't come to think of Not To Be Sold as a brand name.

Sometimes, instead of going home from school, I walked the two miles up the road into Lansing. I began drifting from store to store, hanging around outside where things like apples were displayed in boxes and barrels and basket, and I would watch my chance and steal me a treat. You know what a treat was to me? Anything!

Or I began to drop in about dinnertime at the home of some family that we knew. I knew that they knew exactly why I was there, but they never embarrassed me by letting on. They would invite me to stay for supper, and I would stuff myself.

Especially, I liked to drop in and visit at the Gohannas' home. They were nice, older people, and great churchgoers. I had watched them lead the jumping and shouting when my father preached. They had, living with them—they were raising him—a nephew whom everyone called "Big Boy," and he and I got along fine. Also living with the Gohannas was old Mrs. Adcock, who went with them to church. She was always trying to help anybody she could, visiting anyone she heard was sick, carrying them something. She was the one who, years later, would tell me something that I remembered a long time: "Malcolm, there's one thing I like about you. You're no good, but you don't try to hide it. You are not a hypocrite."

The more I began to stay away from home and visit people and steal from the stores, the more aggressive I became in my inclinations. I never wanted to wait for anything.

I was growing up fast, physically more so than mentally. As I began to be recognized more around the town, I started to become aware of the peculiar attitude of white poeple toward me. I sensed that it had to do with my father. It was an adult version of what several white children had said at school, in

hints, or sometimes in the open, which really expressed what their parents had said—that the Black Legion or the Klan had killed my father, and the insurance company had pulled a fast one in refusing to pay my mother the policy money.

When I began to get caught stealing now and then, the state Welfare people began to focus on me when they came to our house. I can't remember how I first became aware that they were talking of taking me away. What I first remember along that line was my mother raising a storm about being able to bring up her own children. She would whip me for stealing, and I would try to alarm the neighborhood with my yelling. One thing I have always been proud of is that I never raised my hand against my mother.

In the summertime, at night, in addition to all the other things we did, some of us boys would slip out down the road, or across the pastures, and go "cooning" watermelons. White people always associated watermelons with Negroes, and they sometimes called Negroes "coons" among all the other names, and so stealing watermelons became "cooning" them. If white boys were doing it, it implied that they were only acting like Negroes. Whites have always hidden or justified all of the guilts they could by ridiculing or blaming Negroes.

One Halloween night, I remember that a bunch of us were out tipping over those old country outhouses, and one old farmer—I guess he had tipped over enough in his day—had set a trap for us. Always, you sneak up from behind the outhouse, then you gang together and push it, to tip it over. This farmer had taken his outhouse off the hole, and set it just in *front* of the hole.

Well, we came sneaking up in single file, in the darkness, and the two white boys in the lead fell down into the outhouse hole neck deep. They smelled so bad it was all we could stand to get them out, and that finished us all for that Halloween. I had just missed falling in myself. The whites were so used to taking the lead, this time it had really gotten them in the hole.

Thus, in various ways, I learned various things. I picked strawberries, and though I can't recall what I got per crate for picking, I remember that after working hard all one day, I wound up with about a dollar, which was a whole lot of money in those times. I was so hungry, I didn't know what to do. I was walking away toward town with visions of buying something good to eat, and this older white boy I knew, Richard Dixon, came up and asked me if I wanted to match nickels. He had plenty of change for my dollar. In about a half hour, he had all the change back, including my dollar, and instead of going to town to buy something, I went home with nothing, and I was bitter. But that was nothing compared to what I felt when I found out later that he had cheated. There is a way that you can catch and hold the nickel and make it come up the way you want. This was my first lesson about gambling: if you see somebody winning all the time, he isn't gambling, he's cheating. Later on in life, if I were continuously losing in any gambling situation, I would watch very closely. It's like the Negro in America seeing the white man win all the time. He's a professional gambler; he has all the cards and the odds stacked on his side, and he has always dealt to our people from the bottom of the deck.

About this time, my mother began

to be visited by some Seventh Day Adventists who had moved into a house not too far down the road from us. They would talk to her for hours at a time, and leave booklets and leaflets and magazines for her to read. She read them, and Wilfred, who had started back to school after we had begun to get the relief food supplies, also read a lot. His head was forever in some book.

Before long, my mother spent much time with the Adventists. It's my belief that what mostly influenced her was that they had even more diet restrictions than she always had taught and practiced with us. Like us, they were against eating rabbit and pork; they followed the Mosaic dietary laws. They ate nothing of the flesh without a split hoof, or that didn't chew a cud. We began to go with my mother to the Adventist meetings that were held further out in the country. For us children, I know that the major attraction was the good food they served. But we listened, too. There were a handful of Negroes, from small towns in the area, but I would say that it was ninety-nine percent white people. The Adventists felt that we were living at the end of time, that the world soon was coming to an end. But they were the friendliest white people I had ever seen. In some ways, though, we children noticed, and, when we were back at home, discussed, that they were different from us—such as the lack of enough seasoning in their food, and the different way that white people smelled.

Meanwhile, the state Welfare people kept after my mother. By now, she didn't make it any secret that she hated them, and didn't want them in her house. But they exerted their right to come, and I have many, many times reflected upon how, talking to us children, they began to plant the seeds of division in our minds. They would ask such things as who was smarter than the other. And they would ask me why I was "so different."

I think they felt that getting children into foster homes was a legitimate part of their function, and the result would be less troublesome, however they went about it.

And when my mother fought them, they went after her—first, through me. I was the first target. I stole; that implied that I wasn't being taken care of by my mother.

All of us were mischievous at some time or another, I more so than any of the rest. Philbert and I kept a battle going. And this was just one of a dozen things that kept building up the pressure on my mother.

I'm not sure just how or when the idea was first dropped by the Welfare workers that our mother was losing her mind.

But I can distinctly remember hearing "crazy" applied to her by them when they learned that the Negro farmer who was in the next house down the road from us had offered to give us some butchered pork—a whole pig, maybe even two of them—and she had refused. We all heard them call my mother "crazy" to her face for refusing good meat. It meant nothing to them even when she explained that we had never eaten pork, that it was against her religion as a Seventh Day Adventist.

They were as vicious as vultures. They had no feelings, understanding, compassion, or respect for my mother. They told us, "She's crazy for refusing food." Right then was when our home, our unity, began to disintegrate. We

were having a hard time, and I wasn't helping. But we could have made it, we could have stayed together. As bad as I was, as much trouble and worry as I caused my mother, I loved her.

The state people, we found out, had interviewed the Gohannas family, and the Gohannas' had said that they would take me into their home. My mother threw a fit, though, when she heard that—and the home wreckers took cover for a while.

It was about this time that the large, dark man from Lansing began visiting. I don't remember how or where he and my mother met. It may have been through some mutual friends. I don't remember what the man's profession was. In 1935, in Lansing, Negroes didn't have anything you could call a profession. But the man, big and black, looked something like my father. I can remember his name, but there's no need to mention it. He was a single man, and my mother was a widow only thirty-six years old. The man was independent; naturally she admired that. She was having a hard time disciplining us, and a big man's presence alone would help. And if she had a man to provide, it would send the state people away forever.

We all understood without ever saying much about it. Or at least we had no objection. We took it in stride, even with some amusement among us, that when the man came, our mother would be all dressed up in the best that she had—she still was a good-looking woman—and she would act differently, lighthearted and laughing, as we hadn't seen her act in years.

It went on for about a year, I guess. And then, about 1936, or 1937, the man from Lansing jilted my mother suddenly. He just stopped coming to see her. From what I later understood, he finally backed away from taking on the responsibility of those eight mouths to feed. He was afraid of so many of us. To this day, I can see the trap that Mother was in, saddled with all of us. And I can also understand why he would shun taking on such a tremendous responsibility.

But it was a terrible shock to her. It was the beginning of the end of reality for my mother. When she began to sit around and walk around talking to herself—almost as though she was unaware that we were there—it became increasingly terrifying.

The state people saw her weakening. That was when they began the definite steps to take me away from home. They began to tell me how nice it was going to be at the Gohannas' home, where the Gohannas' and Big Boy and Mrs. Adcock had all said how much they liked me, and would like to have me live with them.

I liked all of them, too. But I didn't want to leave Wilfred. I looked up to and admired my big brother. I didn't want to leave Hilda, who was like my second mother. Or Philbert; even in our fighting, there was a feeling of brotherly union. Or Reginald, especially, who was weak with his hernia condition, and who looked up to me as his big brother who looked out for him, as I looked up to Wilfred. And I had nothing, either, against the babies, Yvonne, Wesley, and Robert.

As my mother talked to herself more and more, she gradually became less responsive to us. And less responsible. The house became less tidy. We began to be more unkempt. And usually, now, Hilda cooked.

We children watched our anchor giving way. It was something terrible that you couldn't get your hands on, yet you couldn't get away from. It was a sensing that something bad was going to happen. We younger ones leaned more and more heavily on the relative strength of Wilfred and Hilda, who were the oldest.

When finally I was sent to the Gohannas' home, at least in a surface way I was glad. I remember that when I left home with the state man, my mother said one thing: "Don't let them feed him any pig."

It was better, in a lot of ways, at the Gohannas'. Big Boy and I shared his room together, and we hit it off nicely. He just wasn't the same as my blood brothers. The Gohannas' were very religious people. Big Boy and I attended church with them. They were sanctified Holy Rollers now. The preachers and congregations jumped even higher and shouted even louder than the Baptists I had known. They sang at the top of their lungs, and swayed back and forth and cried and moaned and beat on tambourines and chanted. It was spooky, with ghosts and spirituals and "ha'nts" seeming to be in the very atmosphere when finally we all came out of the church, going back home.

The Gohannas' and Mrs. Adcock loved to go fishing, and some Saturdays Big Boy and I would go along. I had changed schools now, to Lansing's West Junior High School. It was right in the heart of the Negro community, and a few white kids were there, but Big Boy didn't mix much with any of our schoolmates, and I didn't either. And when we went fishing, neither he nor I liked the idea of just sitting and waiting for the fish to jerk the cork under the water—or make the tight line quiver, when we fished that way. I figured there should be some smarter way to get the fish—though we never discovered what it might be.

Mr. Gohannas was close cronies with some other men who, some Saturdays, would take me and Big Boy with them hunting rabbits. I had my father's .22 caliber rifle; my mother had said it was all right for me to take it with me. The old men had a set rabbit-hunting strategy that they had always used. Usually when a dog jumps a rabbit, and the rabbit gets away, that rabbit will always somehow instinctively run in a circle and return sooner or later past the very spot where he originally was jumped. Well, the old men would just sit and wait in hiding somewhere for the rabbit to come back, then get their shots at him. I got to thinking about it, and finally I thought of a plan. I would separate from them and Big Boy and I would go to a point where I figured that the rabbit, returning, would have to pass me first.

It worked like magic. I began to get three and four rabbits before they got one. The astonishing thing was that none of the old men ever figured out why. They outdid themselves exclaiming what a sure shot I was. I was about twelve, then. All I had done was to improve on their strategy, and it was the beginning of a very important lesson in life—that anytime you find someone more successful than you are, especially when you're both engaged in the same business—you know they're doing something that you aren't.

I would return home to visit fairly often. Sometimes Big Boy and one or another, or both, of the Gohannas' would go with me—sometimes not. I would be glad when some of them did go, because it made the ordeal easier.

Soon the state people were making plans to take over all of my mother's children. She talked to herself nearly all of the time now, and there was a crowd of new white people entering the picture—always asking questions. They would even visit me at the Gohannas'. They would ask me questions out on the porch, or sitting out in their cars.

Eventually my mother suffered a complete breakdown, and the court orders were finally signed. They took her to the State Mental Hospital at Kalamazoo.

It was seventy-some miles from Lansing, about an hour and a half on the bus. A Judge McClellan in Lansing had authority over me and all of my brothers and sisters. We were "state children," court wards; he had the full say-so over us. A white man in charge of a black man's children! Nothing but legal, modern slavery—however kindly intentioned.

My mother remained in the same hospital at Kalamazoo for about twenty-six years. Later, when I was still growing up in Michigan, I would go to visit her every so often. Nothing that I can imagine could have moved me as deeply as seeing her pitiful state. In 1963, we got my mother out of the hospital, and she now lives there in Lansing with Philbert and his family.

It was so much worse than if it had been a physical sickness, for which a cause might be known, medicine given, a cure effected. Every time I visited her, when finally they led her—a case, a number—back inside from where we had been sitting together, I felt worse.

My last visit, when I knew I would never come to see her again—there—was in 1952. I was twenty-seven. My brother Philbert had told me that on his last visit, she had recognized him somewhat. "In spots," he said.

But she didn't recognize me at all. She stared at me. She didn't know who I was.

Her mind, when I tried to talk, to reach her, was somewhere else. I asked, "Mama, do you know what day it is?"

She said, staring, "All the people have gone."

I can't describe how I felt. The woman who had brought me into the world, and nursed me, and advised me, and chastised me, and loved me, didn't know me. It was as if I was trying to walk up the side of a hill of feathers. I looked at her. I listened to her "talk." But there was nothing I could do.

I truly believe that if ever a state social agency destroyed a family, it destroyed ours. We wanted and tried to stay together. Our home didn't have to be destroyed. But the Welfare, the courts, and their doctor, gave us the one-two-three punch. And ours was not the only case of this kind.

I knew I wouldn't be back to see my mother again because it could make me a very vicious and dangerous person—knowing how they had looked at us as numbers and as a case in their book, not as human beings. And knowing that my mother in there was a statistic that didn't have to be, that existed because of a society's failure, hypocrisy, greed, and lack of mercy and compassion. Hence I have no mercy or compassion in me for a society that will crush people, and then penalize them for not being able to stand up under the weight.

I have rarely talked to anyone about my mother, for I believe that I am capable of killing a person, without hesitation, who happened to make the wrong kind of remark about my mother. So I purposely don't make any opening for some fool to step into.

Back then when our family was destroyed, in 1937, Wilfred and Hilda were old enough so that the state let them stay on their own in the big four-room house that my father had built. Philbert was placed with another family in Lansing, a Mrs. Hackett, while Reginald and Wesley went to live with a family called Williams, who were friends of my mother's. And Yvonne and Robert went to live with a West Indian family named McGuire.

Separated though we were, all of us maintained fairly close touch around Lansing—in school and out—whenever we could get together. Despite the artificially created separation and distance between us, we still remained very close in our feelings toward each other.

Excerpt from

COMING UP BLACK:
PATTERNS OF
GHETTO SOCIALIZATION

David A. Schulz

THE HIGH SCHOOL YEARS

The most common dilemma faced by the high school girl is poised by the conflict over "career" versus motherhood. In the ghetto, however, this has much more of an ominous overtone than in the world of the middle class. The problem is accentuated by the fact that many girls have had sexual relations by the time they enter high school. It is considered the normal thing to do to "please" your boyfriend. They are, however, largely ignorant of effective contraceptive techniques, fearful of using them, or conduct their sexual activities in situations where several contraceptive devices would be useless because they require that lovemaking be planned in advance. In the case of seven out of ten of the mothers and five of the fifteen teenage daughters

David A. Schulz, Coming Up Black: Patterns of Ghetto Socialization (Englewood Cliffs, N.J.: Prentice-Hall, Inc. 1969 , pp. 48–58. Reprinted by permission.

in these families, children out of wedlock resulted from this "natural" lovemaking.

An Extreme Case of a Common Choice

The problems faced in handling sexuality and the boyfriend are dramatically potrayed in the following account given by Madeline Patterson who, at the age of twenty-three, has given birth to five illegitimate children, four of whom are still alive. She had her first child, Bootsie, when she was fourteen while still going to school:

> Bootsie's father Donnie [nineteen] wasn't going to school when I met him. Him and some other fellows used to be down by the school when school let out. Every afternoon he would chase me home and then he started coming over to the school during recess when we would be outside taking exercises. One night Louis R. gave a dance. He lived two flights over us on the sixth floor. Donnie was there. L. R. introduced me to Donnie. Donnie would come down to see me. Sometimes I would be downstairs with

one of my sisters and he would come and sit on the bench with me. We'd talk and everything. After that we started going together. He gave me his ring. *I didn't know anything about sex or where babies came from because didn't nobody tell me.* We had been going together for about nine months. This lady I used to baby-sit for she didn't mind me having company or nothing like that as long as they leave at a reasonable time if she wasn't home. Donnie'd come down there and sometimes my sister or my brother would come down. This particular night he asked me and I refused and one thing led to another. He wanted to know "Why?" *I told him I was scared.* He said it wasn't going to hurt. I told him I didn't know and I didn't want to find out. We got to wrestling and—this is sort of embarrassing—he just kept on pestering me. He told me I didn't care anything for him and things like that. He said he wouldn't let anything happen to me or something similar to that. This went on for about an hour and a half. I said "Okay" and that was that.

Madeline was in the eighth grade at the time and the school nurse finally had to send her home. "I just kept getting bigger and I had to leave my skirt unfastened and I slept a lot." The principal called her mother, her mother called Donnie's mother. The juvenile officer came to talk to Madeline: "He explained that I could have Donnie locked up for statutory rape. But he said if I had pressed charges against him that I had to go to jail too or something for overnight. I told him no." At the time they were planning on getting married—that is, they talked about it in an offhand manner:

At the time Donnie was running around with a rowdy crowd and they was forever into fights and things . . . and he stayed in jail more than he did out at that time.

So I just told mother that I didn't want to marry him.

Her mother consented to her wishes, but her father felt she ought to marry. After she became pregnant, she saw Donnie only on the street:

Before I had my baby I couldn't stand Donnie. I guess because he was the cause of my being pregnant. I could see him walking down the street and I'd get angry and want to cry.

Her parents discussed the matter of her pregnancy out of her hearing and concluded that they would look into the matter of sending her to a special home where she could give birth to the child. This was apparently her father's alternative to marrying. "I believe he was more hurt and disappointed than she was." However, after a visit to the home convinced her mother that she could not send her daughter to such a place, it was decided that Madeline should not go. Her mother mostly took care of her first child.

Madeline began going out with boys again shortly after she gave birth: "It wasn't as if the baby was holding me down or anything because if I wanted to go any place my mother she would usually watch the baby for me." The kids at the dances she went to, however, "looked like my little sisters and brothers." She preferred Dave (nineteen) who didn't like to go out. Dave gave her her second child, Carol, when she was fifteen. She does not know how she became pregnant:

I don't remember. To tell the truth I actually don't remember. I think maybe the reason I can't remember is because when I found out I was pregnant, I was so hurt and disappointed and everything else and I didn't know just what to do. I thought about giving the baby away when

I had it. But my mother talked me out of that. And I just tried to forget everything about Carol's father and Carol and how it happened, because Dave and I we was going to get married, but I found out that he was already married and I didn't know this. He hadn't never gotten a divorce from his first wife. . . . His aunt told me [this].

She did not think about abortions:

One of the girls I used to go to school with was telling me something that I could take or something, but I was scared. . . . I thought of other things such as leaving home and things like that and leaving my first child with Donnie's mother since she wanted her from the beginning.

Her mother again interceded for the child: "She said that she raised us and she never had gave a child of hers away." Since Madeline was herself born before wedlock when her mother was nineteen, this argument had some weight.

Madeline's second child, Carol, came after only seven months of pregnancy, and Madeline became very sick after the delivery. Her mother took care of this child also. "I was afraid I would drop her or something." She never saw Dave again until Carol was ten months old. After Carol was born Madeline left home and has been living on her own with her children for about seven years now.

When she was sixteen she met Jay (twenty-three). Jay was the first boyfriend to regularly support her, giving her about fifteen or twenty dollars every week, usually on Friday or Saturday. Jay left suspecting, unjustifiably, that she was pregnant:

He asked me if I was pregnant and I told him "No." Then he told me a friend of mine told him I was going to the doctor to get rid of his baby. I told him that was a lie, because I wasn't pregnant, and if I was I wouldn't do anything like that. I would rather have it and give it away than do anything like that.

Q: Were you in love with Jay?

I think so. The reason I say that is after that I just didn't trust men. I mean I don't really trust them now, but it seems like he destroyed something in me. I don't know.

About a year afterward she met her next boyfriend, Raymond, the father of Val, born when Madeline was nearly eighteen. Until she met Raymond she stayed around the house moping. Raymond is a friend of the family and a constant drinker, even though he suffers from bleeding ulcers. "We all have to go sometime." He is divorced and in his late twenties. Raymond still visits with Madeline's parents and drinks quite often with her father. He had proposed marriage seriously, gotten her to the license bureau, but she backed out:

. . . I think it was more or less the idea of getting married. I was thinking about the *types of marriages they had on television and in the books.*[1] I know it's not like that. I always said I would never get married because lots of men do their wives so bad. I wanted to, but when the time come, I just didn't want to.

At about this time in her life her father left her mother for the second or third time since the family had moved

---

[1] Characteristically, women in the project watch television a good part of the day and prefer "soap operas" and programs with plots related to domestic intrigues. Many will say they like these because it lets them think about someone else's problems for a change or because the shows are so much like real life that they can readily identify with the characters.

to the city, and her mother was stuck with a very sick daughter and no food in the house. Madeline, once the favorite of her father, now despises him for what he has done to her mother.

Since Carol, Madeline has had three more children. John was born when she was twenty and Willie shortly thereafter. Willie died in infancy. Mark's father left before Madeline knew she was pregnant. Willie's father —like Carol's—was already married. She remembers that Willie's father, Cal, used to get confused and call her by his wife's name, Sally:

> Some nights he would be asleep and he would get to talking in his sleep. He said, "Sally, Madeline has a little girl named Carol also and she's just as big as our girl." . . . He said, "Sally, I don't want to hurt Madeline. . . . Sally, I'm not going to see you any more because Madeline is nice and I don't want to hurt her because she's good to me."

Cal was twenty-six when he first met Madeline. He talked of marriage, as is the appropriate thing to do when "making out," but Madeline thought she was in love with him. "Val and Willie were the only two babies I really wanted," but Cal got sent up to the federal penitentiary for three years, and that more or less ended the affair.

At the present time Madeline is going with Stan, twenty-four. He is single but has two children by a girl he had been going with. He has been going with Madeline for about three years. He gets paid every two weeks and gives her twenty-five to thirty dollars, maybe more. Most of their enjoyment is in the context of her home where his concern extends to the children as well. She muses: "They seem warmer towards him than they do perhaps to their own

father." Marriage is something that she is still looking for, but she is not certain if Stan is the man to marry:

> Marriage don't necessarily have to be perfect. The only thing I'm looking for and the only thing I ask is that they respect my kids and me and do whatever they can for us.

An Alternative Pattern

With examples such as Madeline's always before them, and the awareness that men are not dependable, a minority—but an interesting minority—of girls attempt to put off engaging in sexual intercourse with boys until they are out of high school. Madeline's younger sister Glennora, eighteen, has this to say:

> I had my first boyfriend when I started in high school. That was in 1964. He was really a boyfriend. The others weren't really boyfriends.
>
> Q: Well, when you really become boyfriend and girlfriend what does that mean?
>
> I don't know. Things change so much in years. It seems like sometimes if a boy asks you to be his woman, well, you say "Yeah," and you all go together. I guess because you all like each other. Then again some boys, like if they be talking to you . . . just keep talking to you, well you all just take it for granted that you all go together instead of him asking you and he'll treat you like you're his girlfriend or somebody he likes. But then again some people just go with people for to be doing something. You know, they might not really like them and they just go with them. Like the pimps. The boy pimps be calling their girlfriends and they don't really like them . . . they just be going with them to get some money. So people take it in different ways.
>
> Q: Well, how do you take it?
>
> When I call somebody my boyfriend, it

would be somebody that I like. I might not like them a great deal, but I do care for them. . . .

Q: Have you done it with a boy?

No I haven't . . . because I really haven't liked anybody enough to really go through those changes and when I do I want it to be with someone I really like and who really likes me. And furthermore that's my pride. *When I give that away I haven't got anything else to offer a boy.* . . . I'm not ready for that type of thing. . . .

Q: What about Harris [her boyfriend]? Does he understand?

Yes he do. Because he understands that I'm trying to get out of school and I guess he knows I want the better things in life and I guess he wants to see that I try to get it. . . . We have been going together for two years and nothing has happened.

For Glennora the notion of being in love—really in love—is mixed with a concern to get through school and establish her own earning power. She is well aware of the fact that "love is an everyday word" in her neighborhood, and she sees "how boys are doing these girls today . . . getting them pregnant and going on to somebody else." This awareness is reinforced by her sister's experience and her own concern about marriage stemming from the very disappointing experience of her parent's marriage.

Dora Buchanan (fifteen) has also the example of her older sister Della to consider, but her concern about not having relations with a boy is more a matter of propriety:

I don't think it's right, not yet anyway, because it's too many boys these days going with girls and you know they'll go out and talk about everything they do with this girl. And it's really not no right

place to do it. I mean some people might just go out and do it in the storage room and then they don't care if you catch them or nothing like that.

Dora is young and one has the feeling that if the right time and place presented themselves, she would have no objections to doing it.

Friends

In these years friends are very important to both boys and girls, but a close friend is hard to cultivate in such a manipulative community, and very few girls keep the same close friends through high school.[2] Friends change schools, get pregnant, and/or get married, break your confidence, or start running with another crowd, and you drift apart from them. This happens with great regularity so that only one of the teenagers has managed to keep the same close friends through the teens —Christine Wards, who is still "tight" with Rosie Henry after over ten years. Glennora Patterson complains:

Yeah, I had several friends, mostly girls. All of us was really tight. Three of them was older than I. You know, they graduated before I did and graduated out of high school before I did too. One girl, me and her, we started grade school together. Now we're in the same grade. We stayed together. We went to the same school.

Q: She's your close friend, is she?

She used to be. . . . She can't help

[2] Seventy-four per cent of the persons with whom our respondents interacted most frequently were known less than eleven years, 49 per cent less than seven years, 24 per cent less than three years. In contrast, 9 per cent were non-relatives known since childhood. Stromberg, "A Preliminary Report . . . ," p. 74.

herself. She lies a great deal on people, you know.

Girlfriends do a lot of things together, mostly recreation after school: volleyball, dancing, joining various groups like singing groups. Double dating is not popular, parties are. One expects a great deal of one's close friends:

> They're my friends. . . . If I'm in need
> . . . if I really need something and they
> have it, I expect to be able to go to them
> and get it: And if they're my close friends,
> they wouldn't lie or nothing like that to
> me. . . . I wouldn't expect [them] to go
> with my boyfriend either.

Most of the time friends just get together and talk or listen to records. The conversation is mostly about boys, but strangely enough, "tight" friends are not likely to hear about such matters as a first pregnancy; such news is more frequently reported to a less well-known acquaintance. When a girl becomes pregnant, her old friends tend to drop away and she enters another circle—she is no longer a "school girl."

A lot of girls have boyfriends who are brothers of their girlfriends. Indeed, this is a common way in which couples meet. They are introduced by a sibling and, since many of these relationships result in children, families are interlocked by illegitimate children. This constitutes a kind of pseudo-kinship network that binds families together and offers some modicum of support.

In this community the word "girl" is a term of endearment when used between women, indicating a bond of solidarity and affection. It denotes "femininity" in a way for which there is no masculine counterpart. Quite often it is used in place of a first name. Thus, Mary tells of a conversation with a friend, "I said, 'You know if Karen wasn't a girl I'd go with her.' She said, 'Girl, you watch what you sayin', hear?' " When a mother scolds her daughter quite often it will be "Girl, don't you do that." She does not follow a comparable pattern for her sons. Likewise, the use of the term "man" among men is too much associated with the reaction to Whitey's derogatory "boy" to be comparably used as a term of endearment among men. Furthermore, grown women in the project use the term "girl" in the same manner when referring to one another. "Woman" is rarely used. When it is, it generally means to be "somebody's woman." The term "man" is not extended downward to boys, and so a woman is a "girl" all of her life in a common bond of identity, but a boy becomes a man after he has proven himself—often by his sexual conquests.

THE GIRL'S VIEW OF MEN

The feminine attitude toward men is composed of a number of strands. A dominant element is disgust at their not being able to provide for their women.

Young Woman: What's wrong with these men today anyhow? They lazy. They don't wanna work. They get families, marry these girls . . . then they want to lay around.

Young Man: You know why . . . because they know if they try to get a job they couldn't get one.

Young Woman: I don't understand that. . . . I don't understand why it should be that way. I don't think it's actually that way, but most of the men are just like that.

Another element in their sentiment toward males is to be derived from their mother's account of her experience. Alliena Billit's mother gave her this advice:

"Alliena, let me tell you, *if you don't think you can just lay down and let that man walk all over you, don't you marry him.*" I thought that was so silly. I said, "Is that why you let daddy walk all over you?" She said, "I loved your daddy," as if I couldn't understand her saying that to me, but I do now. When her love was gone that was just it. She didn't take nothing off of him. I mean he would come in and say "Dee!" [Her father's nickname was "Bango."] She would say, "Call me by my name, right. Don't holler at me!" I can remember when this change came about and I would think, heck, maybe she's going to stand up for what's hers. By him beating on her so much, I swore I would never let a man beat me. And I don't.

Also among the attitudes that women have toward men is the notion that they think they are "too good" or too "uppity." Tilly, thirty-three exclaims:

It seems like the men are wiser,[3] more intelligent, they think they know more. They think they do more and everything is just going too fast. . . . He probably knows more but probably thinks he knows double more and it just swells him and after a while that's a problem.

What is being said here is that the man knows more of the world of hard knocks, the street, and the world of wanderers. In Tilly's case, she was a high school dropout and, therefore, "average" in educational achievement.

[3] Stromberg, *ibid.,* p. 20, indicates that men in the project have a slightly better median of years of education than the women (9.6 years to 8.7 years).

The experience of boys "coming up" is the subject of the next chapter.

CONCLUSIONS

The data suggest the following generalizations:

1. Many lower-class Negro women who are first born daughters feel "overrun" with children both because of the extensive amount of time spent in their childhood caring for "her" (their mother's) children, and because of the large families of their own. They thus suppress an anger toward children that makes it difficult to discipline them because of the fear of "going too far." Indulgence toward children can be seen as one response to his inner anger.

2. Most ghetto adults, particularly women, admit to having more children than they desired.

3. Children pass out of the center of parental concern for a significant period in their grade school years. Formerly they were the center of attention and affection as the baby of the house, now they are comparatively ignored. Later they are once again much more central to their parents' concern, but then it is more likely to be as sources of trouble (pregnancy, delinquency, etc.).

4. Sex is "natural" in the ghetto and girls generally "do it" to please their boyfriends. From an early age there is much experience in sexual play, but little understanding of the possible consequences. Some girls sometimes confess that they "did it" before they knew where babies came from.

5. For girls in their teens a choice must be made between planning a career (as typist, secretary, or nurse, for example) or "doing it" with their boyfriends. The decision to "do it" almost inevitably means pregnancy and the termination of their education. Not to "do it," however, means cutting oneself off from a central aspect of teenage life and an immediate mark of maturity (should a baby be born). The majority choose to "do it."

Excerpt from

DEATH AT AN EARLY AGE

Jonathon Kozol

All books used in a school system, merely by the law of averages, are not going to be blatantly and consistently bad. A larger number of the books we had in Boston were either quietly and subtly bad, or else just devastatingly bad only in one part. One such book, not used in my school but at the discipline school, was entitled *Our World Today*. It seems useful to speak about it here because it exemplifies to perfection the book which might be remarkably accurate or even inspired in its good intentions in one section and then brutally clumsy, wrong and stupid in another. Right and wrong, good and bad, alternate in this book from sentence to sentence and from page to page:

"The people of the British Isles are, like our own, a mixed people. Their ancestors were the sturdy races of northern Europe, such as Celts, Angles, Saxons, Danes, and Normans, whose energy and abilities still appear in their descendants. With such a splendid in-

heritance what could be more natural than that the British should explore and settle many parts of the world, and, in time, build up the world's greatest colonial empire?"

"The people of South Africa have one of the most democratic governments now in existence in any country."

"Africa needs more capitalists. . . . White managers are needed . . . to show the Negroes how to work and to manage the plantations . . ."

"In our study of the nations of the world, we should try to understand the people and their problems from their point of view. We ought to have a sympathetic attitude toward them, rather than condemn them through ignorance because they do not happen always to have our ways."

"The Negro is very quick to imitate and follow the white man's way of living . . ."

". . . The white man may remain for short periods and direct the work, but he cannot . . . do the work himself. He must depend upon the natives to do the work."

"The white men who have entered Africa are teaching the natives how to live."

Something similar to this, though

it was not in a printed textbook, was a mimeographed test about American history that the Fourh Grade teachers at my school had been using for several years. The test listed a number of attributes and qualities that were supposed to have been associated with George Washington: "courageous, rich, intelligent, wise, handsome, kind, good in sports, patient, believed in God, sense of humor, dressed in style, rode a horse well." From these the class were asked to underline the things that made George Washington "a great leader." The answers that would get points were only the noble virtues. "Rich," handsome," "dressed in style," "rode a horse well" and "good in sports" were wrong. It was, I felt, not really a lesson on George Washington but a force-feeding of a particular kind of morality:

These are good qualities.

George Washington got someplace.

These must be the things that made him great.

What had happened, very clearly, was that the right answers had never been derived from a real study of George Washington but rather they were taken from somebody's cupboard of good qualities ("moral builders") and then *applied* to George Washington exactly like plaster or paint. All the things listed were assumed to be true of him, but only the moral uplifters could be considered to be the things that helped him to be great. I thought this wrong for several reasons. One reason simply was a matter of accuracy: George Washington was not really a very handsome man so it seemed unwise and dumbly chauvinistic to say he was. Another mistake,

though it is a small one, was that he did not really have much of a sense of humor and people have even said that he was rather short-tempered. On the subject of his religion, it seemed presumptuous to me, and rather risky, to make any statements at all in regard to a belief in God about which, if it was really so, only George Washington himself could have known. On the opposite side, we do know well that good looks and lots of money have helped many men and do not even necessarily diminish them but have formed romantic parts of their greatness. This was true, for example, of President Kennedy, and it does him no dishonor to say so. What does do a man dishonor is to paint him up in false colors which we either do not know about or which we do know about and know that he did not have. I spoke to the Reading Teacher about this and I pointed out to her that it seemed to me Washington's wealth would not be at all a bad answer. The matter of his belief in God seemed questionable. The Reading Teacher did not often get openly angry with me, but she did on this occasion.

"That's out of the question! We are not going to start teaching cynicism here in the Fourth Grade."

I found myself equally angry. I said that I did not think that it would be teaching cynicism at all, but quite the reverse. I said I thought children should learn now, and the sooner the better, that money frequently, and more often than not, counted for more than religious intensity in the political world. I also said that I thought it was a far greater kind of cynicism to dish out to them at this age a fatuous and lyrical idealism which was going to get smashed down to the ground the first time that any one of them went out into the City of Boston and just tried to get himself a decent job, let alone try to follow George Washington on the strength of such qualities as "patience," "sense of humor," "belief in God," and hope to become President of the United States with the kind of education they were getting here. I said I thought the highest cynicism of all was not to let the people in a running-race have any knowledge of the odds. I said that the only way in which one of these children ever *could* be President was if he understood absolutely and as soon as possible how many fewer advantages he had than had been the fortune of George Washington. With that knowledge first, not cynical in the least but having a true connection with the world, then those admired qualities might perhaps be the attributes of greatness, but not without a prior sense of the real odds.

When I began to talk about some of these things more openly, as I did now more frequently with the Reading Teacher, she would tell me sometimes that, temperamentally, she agreed with my ideas and did not believe that in themselves they were wrong but that to teach such things to the children "at this level and at this stage" was something that she could not allow because this was "not the proper age at which to start to break things down." The Fourth Grade, she told me in some real awkwardness and verbal confusion (which made me feel guilty for having brought the subject up), was the age "in which a teacher ought to be building up things and ideas." Later on, she seemed to be saying, there would be time to knock the same things down. I thought this a little like a theory of urban renewal, but it seemed a kind

of renewal program that was going to cost somebody dearly. It was to erect first the old rotten building (pollyanna voyages, a nation without Negroes, suburban fairy tales, pictures in pastel shades), let it all stand a year or two until it began to sway and totter, then tear it down and, if the wreckage could be blasted, put up a new, more honest building in its spot. If a city planner ever came up with a theory like that, I should think he would be laughed out of business. Yet this was not very different from the Reading Teacher's view of children and of education. There was a lot in the Boston curriculum, furthermore, to support her.

I've said something about the social studies books and teacher attitudes already. One thing I've scarcely mentioned is the curriculum material in literature and reading. Probably this would be the best place to make some reference to it, for nothing could better typify the image of the crumbling school structure than the dry and deadly basic reading textbooks that were in use within my school. Most of these books were published by Scott Foresman. The volume aimed at Third Graders, used for slow Fourth Graders at my school, was called *New Streets and Roads*. No title could have been farther from the mark. Every cliché of bad American children's literature seemed to have been contained within this book. The names of the characters describe the flavor of the stories: Betty Jane Burns and Sarah Best and Miss Molly and Fluffy Tail and Miss Valentine of Maple Grove School. . . . The children in my class had been hearing already for several years about Birmingham and Selma and tear-gas and cattle-prods and night-courts and slumlords—and jazz. To expect these children to care about books which even very comfortable suburban children would probably have found irrelevant and boring seemed to me futile. Yet there were no other books around. These were the only ones we had. I wondered if it was thought that the proper way to teach reading to slow Fourth Graders was by foisting upon them a pablum out of nursery land. Possibly it was a benevolent school-lady's most dearly held belief that she could shut out the actual world in this manner and could make the world of these growing Negro children as neat and aseptic as her own. It may have been another belief that a few dozen similarly inclined white ladies in a few dozen Negro classrooms with a few hundred pure white texts would be able to overcome taste and appetite, sight and sound. I didn't think so. The books seemed so overwhelmingly boring. Wouldn't the children find them boring too? The look of boredom seemed always so apparent in the faces of those children. The books did not refer to them. What did refer to them was obvious.

Once I asked a class to think of a sentence using both the word "glass" and the word "house." The first answer I received told me that "there is a lot of glass out back of my house."

To a boy in the reading group: "Do you know an antonym for dry?"

"Mr. Kozol—isn't there something called a dry martini?"

The Reading Teacher's reactions to these kind of student responses, when I related them to her, were generally pretty much the same:

"We cannot use books that are sordid."

"Children do not like gloomy stories."

"I haven't seen any evidence that children like to read especially about things that are real."

I suppose it is true that the children she took for reading generally were attentive, at least on a temporary basis, to the texts that she was using with them, but I think there were two special reasons for this. One reason was that she could "sell" almost anything to anyone if she wanted, being such a very experienced and such an intensely persuading teacher. The other was that the children, in reading with docility and in writing without their own imagination, were always more than willing to confirm a white teacher's idea of them and to put forward in their writings and conversations not what they really felt or dreamed but what they had good reason by now to know that she wanted to believe about them. I was not asking for children's books to be sordid, either, but the Reading Teacher was pretty much suggesting an identity between *sordid* and *real*. I had the idea that to build upon some of the things the children already knew would be more fruitful than to deny them. I also had a suspicious, ungenerous feeling about the reluctance of the white teachers to make use of more realistic books. Their argument, stated one way or another, was that such books might be bad for the children but I thought that that was not what they really believed. I thought the denial came not from a fear that such things might be bad for the child but rather from a certainty that they would be bad for the teacher. I thought that the Reading Teacher and the Deputy Superintendent and many others like them would have been confused to be told that the world of those Negro children was in a great many cases a good deal more interesting and more vital than their own. It seemed to me that what they were trying ineffectively to do was to replace a very substantial and by no means barren lower-class culture with a concoction of pretty shopworn middle-class ideas. The ideas they introduced, moreover, did not even have the joy of being exuberant, for they were mainly the values of a parched and parochial and rather grim and beaten lower middle-class and were, I felt, inferior by many times to that which the children and their parents already had. More succinctly, what I mean is that the real trouble with perpetrating such colorless materials upon very colorful children was not only that the weak culture they purveyed was out of kilter with the one the children already had, but that it also was mediocre by comparison.

There was another problem in the basic readers. This was the old and obvious one of inherited tales of time-worn prejudice:

"Once upon a time there was a woman who had two daughters. One of them was beautiful, but the other one was ugly."

When you read this, you may look up at the illustration on the top of the page but you know, even before you look, which daughter is going to have yellow hair and which one will have dark hair. The dark-skinned girl, the bad one, also has pimples or some kind of coal-smudge beneath her nose, along her cheek and on her jaw. In the story each of these daughters goes for a visit under the ground to stay with a mysterious lady. Each behaves according to her kind. The good daughter behaves nicely, works hard, and receives as her reward a rain of gold coins. The other daughter behaves poorly, refuses to do any work, is selfish, wants something for nothing, and receives as her punishment a shower of black tar. "The tar did not come off the girl until she stopped being lazy," the author tells us. "And it was a long time before she learned that lesson."

In such a way as this, a point perhaps dear to generations of white school-ladies and moralistic educators is gotten across, but it must be obvious that such a point as this no longer can be either dear or acceptable to Negro people. Yet nothing or next to nothing had been done at the time of my teaching to get rid of these kinds of books. Again, as with the social studies books, when the editor of one of these readers went out of his way to find something that would have to do with Negroes, it tended to be embarrassing and awkward. One instance of this was a story called "You Never Can Tell." The story seems memorable because, so far as I can recall, it is the only story in any storybook on any shelf that I ever saw within my school in which an American Negro child was described. The problem about the story was that it could not present the child in anything but a slavelike, superstitious and pathetic-comic light. The Negroes were described not with malice but with condescension as the funny, sad and sweet little wandering attendants to a supercilious, incredibly distant but also unexpectedly generous white lord.

"Mister Colonel, [said one of the little boys] your horse is mighty dusty from rolling. Peas and I will be proud to brush him up for you."

"Very well," said the Colonel.

The boys borrowed brushes from Big Hand and they brushed the Colonel's horse until he shone like satin in the sunshine.

"I could use two boys like you," the Colonel said, "come to my barn tomorrow and I'll put you to work."

Beans turned to Peas. "Man! We got a job," he said, and he grinned at Peas.

It was not an evil story. If there were others of a different nature also, I know that this one would not have stood out as especially bad. It was only when this stood as the sole literary treatment of an American Negro that it led to the unattractive assumption that the Negro it described was characteristic. In the same way, it was not always a poor African chapter which would be so disturbing in the geography textbook as it was the fact that no counterbalance of any kind existed in an honest treatment of the Negro as an American living in the same land in which the Negro children who were reading the book also lived. There are of course plenty of books that show these things and many of them have been available now for some time and were available at the time that I was teaching. The tutorial programs in Boston were using them and so were many of the more enlightened private schools. I had myself had access to some of these books when I was working as a tutor during the summer before I had come into the schools. The striking thing—the thing that was really revealing and unmistakable—was the force and the lightning-like rate of the resistance that cropped up as soon as I made the first mild offer to bring in a few of these new books to try with my Fourth Grade.

One of these was a book called Mary Jane. It had been given to me by one of my summer reading pupils, and told a story about the first Negro

girl in a Southern town to attend an all-white school. The child who gave it to me was not a particularly good reader. Yet she had read this book with much involvement and she told me that it made her cry every time she read it again. Another child in the class, no better reader than the first, borrowed the book and read it through in a couple of days. It was 218 pages long. Remembering this now, and confronted every day in school by the monotony and tedium of textbooks, I dug up a few copies of Mary Jane and brought them to class with me. They were gone from my table the next day. I got hold of a half-dozen more and they also immediately began to be read. Finally, I ordered from New York about two dozen extra copies so that there were now enough of them for almost every child in my room. I felt the excitement and anticipation that a teacher knows when he recognizes that something unexpected and self-generating is beginning to develop in the classroom. Then it all came to a halt.

The Reading Teacher had gotten wind that the book was in the building and she came up into my room and put her foot down. Her excuse, I remember, was, first, that it would be an excellent book for enrichment for "the very brightest children"—a very few—but that it was infinitely too difficult, too advanced and too sophisticated for use as a regular book. Now it happened to be a fact that one of the slowest readers in my class not only asked me to sell her one of my copies but then took it home and read it every night in bed before going to sleep for an entire week until she was finished. She said, when I asked her, that it was the first book she had ever owned in her life. The same sort of thing happened when I brought in half a dozen copies of a children's biography of Martin Luther King. Not only did several children read it with excitement but, when Christmas came, a number of their mothers asked if they could obtain copies from me to give as Christmas gifts. If this curiosity and motivation were so real (and I couldn't think what better proof was needed), then I did not see why we could not allow the larger number of children in the class to read these books too. They were not particularly radical in tone or content. They were not hot-headed and fiery. They were just timely and richly textured books. The Reading Teacher's answer, as I have shown, was first that they were too difficult for most of the pupils (this was not the truth), and then, only latterly, that they were about people who were Negro.

"I wouldn't mind using them," was the way she finally said it to me, "if these were all Negro children in your room. But it would not be fair to the white children in the class to force such books on them too. We do not have all Negroes. If we did, it would be different. I could see using them if this were a segregated school. But it isn't. We have white children. As matters stand it simply would not be right or fair." Whether it was right or fair to the large majority of Negroes to use all white books for their regular work was a question which this otherwise observant lady teacher was not willing to ask. Only whether it would be fair to white children, for once in their lives, to encounter the reverse.

"Things are changing," the Reading Teacher sometimes would say to me as epilogue to these conversations. "I am changing too," she would say. "But everything cannot happen just like

that." Yet she had been teaching these children in Roxbury already for a good many years and nothing very much had happened up to now. The schedule for correction of grievances was plotted so slowly. Is there any reason to think it will be different in the future? Next year some integrated readers in a few schools, maybe. And then, with luck, some day later on, they may even use the same kind of racially honest readers in public schools all over town. And some day in those books perhaps it will be a matter not of photographic integration only but of honest inward content too. And then one day possibly not merely the texts but the real children in the real schools also will be integrated and will no longer go to school separately but will be sitting within the same classrooms side by side. In that day, five years, twenty years hence, possibly the teachers as well will begin to think of things differently and will no longer assume that Negro children are poor material because they will not read books that deny them and because they will not work out of their hearts for white teachers who despise them. Perhaps, by the time another generation comes around, the great majority of these things will be corrected. But if I were the parent of a Negro child in school today I know that I would not be able to accept a calendar of improvements that was scaled so slow.

If poison were not spreading at this moment I might agree with the people who say that Negroes ought to sit and wait a little and let some of these things change at their own pace. But when time is destroying the present lives of your own children I do not believe that anyone should wait. No child in the ruined Fourth Grade at my school can ever have that terrible year returned to him. No boy once whipped for society's, not his, wrong is ever again likely to have his whole sense of dignity returned. No young man made to lie and apologize for something he did not do in order to avoid a greater punishment can ever be graced again with the gift of belief in a world or society in which authorities are just. And who in the slow calendar of days in which "things are changing" will find a way, after that change, to give back to the boys at that discipline school the lives that have been taken from them by the Boston Public Schools?

So when a serious woman like the Reading Teacher said to me that things were changing, I thought that it was taking much too long and that things had been changing for one hundred years yet there was still slavery of the deepest kind within these rooms. The slowness of change is always respectable and reasonable in the eyes of the ones who are only watching; it is a different matter for the ones who are in pain. The anger of the Negro mother whose child's years in elementary school have been wasted may seem inexplicable to a person like the Reading Teacher. To me, to that mother, perhaps to some readers also, it is the complacence and the gradualism and the hypocrisy of a woman like the Reading Teacher that seem unjust and strange. It is the comfortable people, by and large—those like the Reading Teacher—who make the decisions in our society. It is only the people that those decisions are going to affect who are expected to stand quietly, and watch patiently, and wait.

Excerpt from

IN THE MIDST OF PLENTY:
THE POOR IN AMERICA
I have these debts I never
had before. Never

Ben H. Bagdikian

The farmer has always been the folk image of The Perfect American: hard-working, self-reliant, his own boss, prospering from his own labor and beholden to no man.

It is an image promulgated by well-fed orators, not just for farmers but for urban Americans as well. They preach the gospel that given his bare hands there is no excuse for a man of character to fail, because each man is master of his own economic fate. Since it is the individual alone who determines his own success or failure, government and society have no responsibility for what happens to a man's livelihood except to let nature take its course. This particular myth is believed most fervently by its hero, the small farmer, which makes all the more poignant his contemporary tragedy.

Farmers and farm workers are

Reprinted by permission of the Beacon Press, copyright © 1964 by Ben H. Bagdikian.

among the poorest people in the United States. They aren't very healthy. They do not prosper. And they are so beholden to others that they are among the most desperately debt-ridden citizens in the land.

The fallacy that the Good American has total control over his own income is disbelieved by the industrial worker and small businessman who see that while hard work, thrift, and skill are important they can be swept away by impersonal forces of technology and economics. Yet it seems to come as a terrible shock to farmers that they, like the factory worker, are caught in social change over which they have little influence.

The brutal fact is that most farmers aren't really needed any more. The classic figure, the man with the plow, is still a hero in political oratory but in cold economics he is ridiculous. Forty acres and a mule no longer will support a family. It takes at least 325 acres for an average American standard of living, plus good credit at the bank and heavy investment in fertilizers, weed killers and complicated machinery. Fifty years ago one farmer grew enough food and fibre for seven people; today he provides for twenty-four. There are 312,000 big farms in the United States that produce half of all agricultural sales. The 1,600,000 at the poor end, each earning less than $1000 a year, produce only 5 per cent of sales. At this moment there are over 1,500,000 young men between the ages of ten and nineteen growing up on farms but in the next ten years there will be only 150,000 openings for farm operators. It is a chilling thing when a basic activity of man has room for only one in ten of its children. It is not surprising that in the last ten years 8,000,000 Americans left farms for the cities. By 1973 another 10,000,000 will have left. This has been a revolution come not with trumpet call or clap of doom, but by silent, relentless change that puzzles rather than shocks. Against it most farmers still resist with the compulsive instinct to make things grow and a continuing bitter love for the land.

Columbus Cooper is fifty-seven years old. He inherited his land from his father and cleared it by his own hand, starting when he was sixteen years old. He built his house himself. Four years ago, for the first time, he had to mortgage his home and farm.

On a rainy spring day he stood on the porch of his unpainted clapboard cottage, a rough hand grasping the slender-smooth weather-bleached pine trunk that supported the porch roof. He looked out on his land in Sumter County, South Carolina, at the dull enameled sky, the sagging tobacco shed, the drizzle glistening on the small tractor and moistening the rust on his six-year-old Ford under the big magnolia tree. For him, too, the revolution was a perpetual puzzle.

"Things are kind of standing still. That's what's worrying me. I'd like to redeem myself, but the expenses are growing. Things could break bad for me if I can't stop this expense and pay back my indebtedness. And if the older boys go off on their own, I don't think I could do it all by myself. I'm getting old now."

It is generally agreed that a farmer in the United States, if he wants to live at an ordinary standard of living, needs to gross at least $10,000 a year cash income. Columbus Cooper, with a family of twelve, grosses $1500.

He is no rarity in American farming. There are 350,000 fulltime family farms that average $438 a year in sales. Because he is a Negro, Columbus Cooper is worse off than most. Over 40 per cent of all Negroes in rural areas have less than $1000 a year income. The average white-operated commercial farm in the South has 382 acres, the Negro, fifty-six acres (Cooper has twenty-six acres of his own plus fifteen he rents). The gap between Negro and white farmer increases constantly. In 1950 the median income of colored farm families was 52 per cent of white Southern farm families; in 1960 it had dropped to 45 per cent. Most Southern farm counties are eligible for Federal agricultural aid because of their impoverished Negroes, but most of the aid goes to white families. In nine counties around Cooper's where Negro farmers are a majority, only one of the county committees that decide whether a farmer will get a Farmers Home Administration government loan has a Negro on it. A friend of Cooper's who had farmed twenty-one years and had good credit with the Federal government was turned down by such a county committee and immediately thereafter one of the white members of the committee offered him $10,000 for his 100 acres. Cooper's friend had to borrow $5400 at 25 per cent interest to keep his farm.

Yet white farmers are not much better off. Half earn less than $3000 a year and 20 per cent less than $1000. All farmers are feeling the crush and, while it is easier if one is white, the worst circumstance is to be a *small* farmer, white or black. In 1950 there were 139,000 farms in South Carolina; today there are fewer than 75,000. Against this the Coopers struggle with courage.

Mr. Cooper, a thoughtful man who dresses neatly and looks out steadily through shell-rimmed glasses, can't quote national statistics. But he feels the revolution. *"I built this house myself forty years ago and I had no mortgage on it until four years ago."* His $2000 mortagage is at 7 per cent, lucky and low for a small farmer. *"I don't get to pay as much on the principal as I'd like,"* he says, but he has reduced it to $1500, some of it with bales of cotton. But each year he seems to have less cash to start the next crop and has to borrow for seed, fertilizer, and fuel to cure his tobacco.

He is not ignorant of the economics of size. His gross income is $1500 a year, $800 of it from his official allocation of 0.81 of an acre of tobacco and $700 from his allocation of 4.7 acres of cotton. He knows he needs to enlarge his operation to enlarge his income. He applied for an FHA loan to clear twenty more acres for planting, which would bring in perhaps two or three times his present income. But the all-white committee turned him down. This does not necessarily reflect race. There is a decent relationship between the Cooper farm and white businessmen. But Cooper sees what this means in the years to come: as the government reduces acreage to prevent surpluses from the growing yields per acre, all farms are cut proportionately. The farm operator who grosses $100,000 from his tobacco and cotton acreage is cut the same percentage as Mr. Cooper with his 0.81 of an acre of tobacco and his 4.7 of cotton. The big farmer can survive on a cut of 10 per cent in his acreage; Columbus Cooper can't stand a cut of 10 per cent in his $1500 yearly income. Of course, should he and others like him go out of business, their acreage then becomes divided proportionately among the survivors, and many small farmers wonder whether big operators on county committees turn down loan applications with that in mind.

How do you support a family of twelve on $1500 a year?

He grows most of the vegetables they eat—cabbage, collards, turnips, peas, beans. He raises his own pork, selling the better cuts and keeping the fatty ones. If the cow is milking, the children get milk. In summer he and the boys may catch pike and bream and catfish. In winter and fall they hunt for squirrel which Mrs. Cooper boils and then fries. Or they may catch raccoon which she boils and hashes with onions.

They spend about $600 a year for store food—rice, flour, sugar, and occasionally stew meat. He pays $400 a year on his tractor, $200 for fertilizer, $150 for clothes, $85 for kerosene to cure his tobacco, and $200 for life insurance. This provides nothing for the $300 he still owes on his car, nothing on the mortgage, and no provision for medical or dental bills. And it already adds up to more than $1500. The slight additions to the $1500 income are contributions made by the older boys when they get an occasional odd job in the summer, or the sale of pork, or a gift now and then from his eldest son working in the North. The surplus does not go over $200 in the best of years.

Mrs. Cooper is fifteen years younger than her husband but her round, pleasant face looks sad and tired. She thinks she works harder than her mother did. For years both husband and wife have promised themselves they would pipe water into the six-room house but now they speak of the pump in the back yard with weary resignation. They both get up at 5 a.m. and go to bed about 10 in the evening. The youngest child is one year old, the oldest at home is nineteen. The girls' ages are three, five, seven, eleven, and fifteen. *"I do a lot of mending and altering hand-me-downs,"* Mrs. Cooper said and then with eyes closed added, *"but they're getting on to their teens and you know girls that age in school and what they feel about clothes."*

The living room was neat (*"the roof leaks in two or three places but not bad"*), with clean yellow curtains on the windows, an old scrubbed yellow-and-orange linoleum on the floor, two sofas used for sleeping in the summer (there are seven beds for twelve people), and a piano with instruction books on the rack.

"Jo Earl, she's fifteen, takes lessons. They cost 60 cents a week. It's quite a lot for us, but I think the girls ought to have something like that," Mr. Cooper said.

An aunt in North Carolina gave them the piano. Five years ago an uncle in Miami gave them an old TV set. They have a deep freezer they paid $300 for when they got the mortgage money four years ago, using it to preserve summer food. Their farm vegetables, hunting, fishing, and the deep freezer give them a better diet than most $1500-a-year families (and this diet an imponderable support for their obvious strength of spirit).

Their breakfasts include bacon and eggs, "bacon," of course, meaning "soft" bacon or fatback. At noon there are boiled vegetables. For supper there are vegetables, two or three times a week some chicken, canned peaches, or pears in homemade cane syrup, and, if the cow is lactating, milk for the children.

The children's clothing comes partly from the family income, partly from the boys' odd jobs in summer on other farms. Mrs. Cooper bought a dress two years ago. Mr. Cooper bought a suit four years ago. They have not been to a movie since they were married.

Doctors and dentists are visited in desperation. Though seven of the children are less than nine years old, a doctor was last in the house four years ago when an older boy had pneumonia. When toothaches become unbearable a child visits a dentist in town at $3 a visit. It has worked out to about one visit to the dentist a year for some members of the family. Some of the children have never been in a dentist's office and at the rate so far the probabilities are for one visit every twelve years for each child.

Christmas is still an important day for the Coopers and the parents try to spend $2 per child, getting dolls for the girls and a toy for each young boy. Birthdays are observed, but not with presents. "We always do something special on a birthday," Mrs. Cooper said, "like have chicken or a sweetbread for supper."

Though they operate on the lowest income-per-healthy-person imaginable in the United States (less than $2.50 each a week) the Coopers have a strong sense of family, of ambition, and of productivity. Mr. Cooper finished the tenth grade; Mrs. Cooper the ninth. Their oldest son finished the twelfth grade and wanted to go further, but could not because the younger children were in school. A nineteen-year-old boy finished high school and a seventeen-year-old plans to graduate.

One reason for this remarkable family cohesion is, obviously, the strong character of Mr. Cooper and the gentle perseverance of his wife. Another is the persistence of older values of affluence while their family economy gradually deteriorates, though "affluence" is not a good description of the high point of the Cooper fortunes.

"The most I ever made in a year was $2000 in 1947–48," Mr. Cooper said with evident nostalgia. "But I didn't have the headaches and overhead I have now. Right now if everything turned out the best it possibly could I might make $2000 a year but I wouldn't be anywhere near so well off as I was back in '48."

One reason $2000 now would be less comforting than fifteen years ago is the increased cost of living and farming. Another is that in the lean intervening years, Mr. Cooper acquired debts which now soak up some of every dollar. But the main reason is that in 1948 he had only three children and the five Coopers each had $400 to spend that year; if they had the same gross income, the twelve Coopers would have only $167 each.

"Only time I used to do pretty good farming I didn't have all the children. I'm standing still but the expenses are growing. I hope when my children go on their own they won't have as big a family as I have. But that's in the Lord's hands, not ours."

The assignment of family size to the Deity is common among the poor, especially the rural, Bible-belt poor, but whatever its cause it is the explanation for the continuing tide to the cities. Millions have left the South and the farms for the cities but the balance between numbers of people and the ability of the land to support them has not been struck, partly because large rural families are repopulating the farms.

Mr. Cooper does not complain. He looks steadily at his plight and recognizes it.

"I used to farm with mules but they could up and die in the middle of the season. I'm lots better off with my tractor because it does more work than the mule and operating expenses aren't as bad. A good mule would cost $275, $300. But of course a tractor costs maybe $1200. That's the worst of it. I know I'm better off with the tractor and with the modern fertilizer and seed. But no matter how much better they are, they cost a lot of money and sometimes I can't sleep nights trying to solve my problems.

"I have these debts I never had before. Never. In forty years of farming. The worst one is that $1500 still on the farm, but I farmed thirty-six years before I had to have a mortgage. Right now I got to worry about the $85, $100 for fuel to cook the tobacco. Miz Cooper says the worst months are

August for school clothes and December and Easter, but I have my own. It's April. April you've got to start the year with the farm, credit for fertilizer, credit for seed, credit for fuel. I used to pay cash for these things but now it seems I have to have credit. But if you don't solve that April money trouble, you're dead for the year."

Mr. Cooper longs for the ability to pay cash instead of going into debt. He wishes he could get his government loan to clear twenty more acres. He wishes he could be a little bit ahead instead of falling ever further behind.

He was the kind of man an official spoke of in Washington:

"Down on our small farms we've got a hard core of people who are occupationally set in their life pattern. They may or may not have low I.Q. but they possess enough native shrewdness to operate well in their native environment except that they are now shocked and dulled by the loss of their jobs or debts on their farms. There is very little hope for them. I hate to say this, but we've got just so much money to work with in our programs and if we have to decide where to spend it, then we are going to spend it on the young people. We're just not going to be able to do much with the older folk. But maybe we can catch the young people

before it is too late and discouragement becomes permanent and we have a whole generation of lifetime welfare cases."

Mr. Cooper has ideas about his children, too.

"Mostly I hope my kids do better than I'm doing. They'll have to achieve something on their own and they'll have to study for that, learn modern farming, or a trade like brickmasonry. Everyone can't do farming. But I hope they won't have to leave home. Oh, I hope they won't. But I want them to do better than I have. I'm thankful to be living, to be healthy, and to be able to do the best in me. But I'm not happy enough of the time. I'm not happy now."

The Coopers are in the best tradition of the small American farmer—they are hard-working, sober courageous, and a fine family. But they are poor, they are getting poorer, and their best hopes are doomed.

As we drove through the spring rain, through the splashing roads that parted the fertile fields, an expert on farming in South Carolina looked out over the land and the lowering sky and said, "In ten or fifteen years there'll be no small farms to speak of in South Carolina . . . the farmers are going to go to the cities, most of them, or else they're going to starve."

THE HUNGRY WORLD OF
TERESA PILGRIM

William Hedgepeth

Teresa Pilgrim, age 6, lives with her family in Yazoo City in the Mississippi Delta, on a nameless street in a house with no number, no water and no food.

"I like the s'ghetti one with cheese best cause it's goooood!" She pointed up to the spaghetti steaming away in the torn-out ad on the kitchen wall, then tipped her six-year-old head sideways and squinted at it. Alongside—papering over more cracks in the planks—was another one from some women's section, dated May 20, 1958, and headlined: "Two Fresh New Designs in Needlepoint." Through the window came the soft stare of cold cotton plants, spaced in rows wide enough for the picking machines. The plants grew so close they almost came in the kitchen. Teresa didn't know why they called it a "kitchen." There was no stove, no refrigerator—just flies, trash and old jars. Up in the front room,

Courtesy of the editors. From the December 26, 1967 issue of Look Magazine. Copyright 1967 by Cowles Communications, Inc.

where the Pilgrim family slept and just sat, little Dometa Jo broke into a breakfast-cereal jingle, "It's gonna be a *nice day*. . . ." The frail, black frame of a boy called "Pig," age five, danced a few steps. "That be an advertise-ment on TV," Teresa explained. Nathan, her father, got the TV from a burnt-out house. Its knobs were melted out of shape. Near the TV, a bric-a-brac shelf held the food supply: flour, a quarter jar of instant coffee and an inch of rice in a cellophane bag. Cardboard and newspaper scraps covered gaps in the wall over Teresa's head. The headline of one yellowed recipe asked: "Chicken, Everyone?" "I had me some bologna las' week. Ain't had nair milk. Naw," she slowly shook her head, "we don't get much of th' won'erful things folks eats." We jus' stays 'roun here," said Teresa, swinging her legs from the edge of the porch. (Dometa Jo played near the porch in the tub of a broken wringer washer. "Daniel Boone was a maaan . . . yes, a maaan . . . oh, maaan," she sang, twitching her shoulders.) Teresa raised her eyebrows, "My father, he take me to the sto' once. Hooo, that sto' got everything. They got food there. They got chicken an flour an lard an balls an things. Got balloons, too—an shoes an neckties an matches an macaroni an 'nanas an beans an horanges. I likes the fish too. Fish. Fish," the child said—squintingly feeling the sound—"Fish."

Inside, little Lerlene remained asleep in the single bed that all four children slept on, crossways. Nathan had gone to wait with a crowd of others in front of Woo Hor Grocery, where Yazoo City whites come if they needed a day laborer. Teresa's mother, big Lerlene, stared defeatedly at the TV. ("My husban' los' his job when the ce-ment plant went out of bus'ness. They say he's 'able-bodied,' an lessn' he leaves me we don' get no kinda welfare.")

"They some chur'un down yonder," Teresa pointed to some shacks, "but they too ol'. I seen white chur'un downtown. Some of 'em lick their tongues at me." She stuck out her tongue. "I think they have mo' than th' coloreds. I don' know about white people." Pig, licking rice grease off his fingers, came out, and Teresa hopped to her feet "Come on, Pig, les' run," and they struck off around the house. (The house stands frozen in the act of collapse, on a dirt road a half mile off U.S. 49W, with no mailbox—they get no mail—no phone, water, flush toilet or glass in most of the windows, and no warmth except from the tiny wood burner in the front room. It is raised off the ground so that, through holes rotted in the floor, you can see earth and daylight and, on occasional hot days, a snake keeping cool, coiled. The bricks that propped the left-rear corner have crumbled, and the house twists slouchways and droops as if it were going to sink like a ship, stern first into the ground.)

Teresa wandered inside and pretended to iron a shredded sweater. She wants to "wash an iron" when she grows up—or else "hoe in the fiel' " or "go to New Yo'k an get me a job an a 'frigerator an a stove an then eat all th' food." The only thing that takes her from the house is school—"But they makes fun of me 'cause I cain't learn nothin'." She liked the time she went to church and wants to go again. ("She ain't fixed up 'nuff to go to church," said big Lerlene. "Got no shoes.") "I believes in God," Teresa nodded, "cause He do things. He bring you food." Sometimes, Nathan brings home $2 worth of starchy, filling food. Then the Pilgrims gorge themselves silently, sit listless in front of the TV amid the whine of flies, and drop to sleep on reeking sheets—if, that is, he has found work that day. If not, they just go to sleep a little earlier.

DOES IT HURT TO GO HUNGRY HERE?

—"I lay . . . with my head muffled . . . to keep from hearing the bellowing of that ox, which the hungry nomads were leaping on from all sides, tearing morsels out of its living flesh with their teeth."

—Five small children ripped apart a live, shrieking hen and devoured it uncooked, feathers, blood and all. It was the first meat they had eaten in three months.

The first of these scenes took place in the Gothic starkness of a Franz Kafka fable. The second, no less Kafkaesque, actually took place this year near the Virginia-Tennessee border. It's obvious that Kafka's nomads are starving. But would we think the same of American children? Says Dr. Leslie Dunbar, cochairman of the Citizen's Board of Inquiry into Hunger and Malnutrition, "It would take some degree of embarrassment before the Government would admit to hunger approaching starvation in this country."

Yet such hunger exists. "We do not want to quibble over words . . . ," a six-man medical team reported last summer to a Senate subcommittee, upon returning from the Mississippi Delta. "The boys and girls we saw were hungry—weak, in pain, sick; their lives are being shortened; they are, in fact, visibly and predictably losing their health, their energy, their spirits. They are suffering from hunger and disease and directly or indirectly they are dying from them—which is exactly what 'starvation' means."

Though it can be a matter of semantics, the issue comes clearer when defined not in words but children. Sunken eyes, spindly legs, running sores, rampant mental retardation, skin eruptions, lethargic unawareness and hideously bloated bellies are harder to argue with. One Negro mother in Yazoo City, having neither milk nor food nor hopes of getting any, fed her baby a lethal dose of lye.

"The salient thing about the hungry," says Dr. Dunbar, "is the monotony of their story." When human existence is reduced to the endless, animal—often unsuccessful—fight for food, a petrified sameness sets in. It becomes nontransferable destitution. Nathan Pilgrim, third-grade educated and earning perhaps $600 a year, says, "If'n I had enough money, we'd leave here tonight. Chicago's a nice little town.

But any kind of money I get got to be eat off of." Through the food-stamp program, 50 cents worth of stamps can buy $12 in groceries for a needy family. But this program is locally administered, and in the case of some Delta towns, that often means arbitrarily or racially administered. Says one Negro, "Lessn' you got some big white man to fill out the stamp-verification form, they jus' looks at it"—he unfolds his hands like a book cover—"an pass it back to you."

At no point does the Federal bureaucracy touch the lives of the Pilgrims. And as for local help: "The mo'jority of white folks here, you ain't workin' fo' em, they don' help you." So, without understanding where they went wrong or how it could have been otherwise, the Pilgrims plod along as if they realize they had been condemned on the day they were born. They have no decent food, no money to buy food, no prospects for money in Yazoo City, no means of getting out of town—and absolutely no hope of being able to assure their children a future life any less primitive. Malnutrition becomes the hub in a circle of self-perpetuating poverty.

The most severe and permanent damage from malnutrition—specifically, from the lack of protein—takes place in the brains of children before they reach age four. "If they don't get enough protein during that critical period," says a scientist for the U.S. Department of Agriculture, "the brain just never does develop properly." Such malnutrition-induced brain damage, many now believe, may be the perpetuator of poverty from generation to generation as well as the drag on progress in the underdeveloped nations of the world. In their Delta investigations, the doctors found that three-quarters of all the children they examined were getting less than the vital amount of protein. There exists today, in fact, a silent, half-hidden subculture—an underdeveloped nation within our nation—whose constant hunger seems so out-of-place in this "most affluent, properous [etc., etc.] period in U.S. history" that no efforts have been made even to determine its extent. Says the U.S. Surgeon General, not only does the Government not know the number of malnourished Americans—but it is not even the specific job of any Federal agency to find out.

Northern ghettos get their share of poor Negro field hands who found they were obsolete on newly mechanized Southern farms. But it is the ones left behind, the poorest of the poor, who often live forgotten lives outside every social, legal and medical advance of this century. And their reproduction rate almost makes up for the number of those who migrate to the cities. ("You sees what happens when you eat them commodity beans," laughs a large mother-to-be in Belzoni, Miss. "You sprouts!") The remnant who are unaided by Federal food programs —estimated to number from 400,000 to 4 million—lead such isolated inarticulate, single-focus lives that they are, says sociologist Gunnar Myrdal, "the world's least revolutionary proletariat." They are not riot fodder.

When mass malnutrition in the Delta came to light, the Senate rammed through a $75 million emergency measure to feed and help the undernourished in America. The senators acknowledged that the nation's commodity-distribution and food-stamp programs now reached only a fraction of those in need. Yet by the time the bill got to the House Agriculture Committee, its members were suddenly struck with "compassion fatigue." The congressmen quoted Biblically to each other: "The poor you have with you always." (Besides, if these people are really so poor that they can't eat, they won't be with us very long anyway.) At any rate, the Senate's emergency bill was shelved this fall, until the congressmen someday can study where all these strange, hungry, quiet folk came from and what kind of statistics can be made from them and whether a hopeless, empty child is a national concern to begin with.

Meanwhile, the Teresa Pilgrims— who are neither statistics nor "causes" —continue to exist on rice, grits, collards, tree bark, laundry starch, clay and almost anything else chewable. Meanwhile, their bodies suffer steady depletion of tissues, slow disintegration and the progressive, piecemeal abbreviation of life. In time, they become physical and psychological cripples. But still, there is some taste of hope. There may come a day when different and indifferent groups like the House Agriculture Committee will run dry of words and act. And it may happen, though the Pilgrims don't expect it, that something just might turn up, perhaps by dinner—some Christmas.

SUGGESTED READINGS

PUERTO RICAN YOUTH

LEWIS, OSCAR, *La Vida*. New York: Random House, 1966.

MAYERSON, CHARLOTTE LEON (ed.), *Two Blocks Apart*. New York: Holt, Rinehart and Winston, 1965.

PADILLA, ELENA, *Up From Puerto Rico*. New York: Columbia University Press, 1958.

SEXTON, PATRICIA CAYO, *Spanish Harlem*. New York: Harper and Row, 1965.

THOMAS, PIRI, *Down These Mean Streets*. New York: Alfred A. Knopf, Inc., 1967.

MIGRANT WORKERS YOUTH

COLES, ROBERT, *Uprooted Children: The Early Life of Migrant Farm Workers*. Pittsburgh: University of Pittsburgh Press, 1970.

COMPTON, H., "The Green Valley Isn't so Jolly; Migrant Labor Camp Conditions," Yakima, *New Republic*, 159: 19–20, Sept. 7, 1968.

GAGAN, J. F., "The Invisible Poor of the Garden State, Conditions of Migrant Workers in New Jersey," *Commonweal*, 86: 540–1, September 8, 1967.

KOOS, E. L., *They Follow the Sun*. Jacksonville, Fla. Fla. State Board of Health, 1957.

MOORE, TRUMAN, *The Slaves We Rent*. New York: Random House, 1965.

WRIGHT, DALE, They Harvest Despair: *The Migrant Farm Worker*. Boston: Beacon Press, 1965.

MEXICAN AMERICAN YOUTH

HELLER, CELIA S., *Mexican American Youth: Forgotten Youth at the Crossroads.* New York: Random House, 1966.

MADSEN, WILLIAM, *Mexican Americans of South Texas.* New York: Holt, Rinehart and Winston, 1964.

MANUEL, HERSCHEL T., *Spanish-Speaking Children of the Southwest.* Austin: University of Texas Press, 1965.

STEINER, STAN, *La Raza: The Mexican Americans.* New York: Harper and Row, 1970.

AMERICAN INDIAN YOUTH

A Workshop in Cross-Cultural Education. Summary Report and Project Evaluation. Prepared by Abt Associates, 1969.

BORLAND, HAL, *When the Legends Die.* Philadelphia: J. B. Lippincott Company, 1963.

CAHN, EDGAR S. (ed.), Citizen's Advocate Center. *Our Brother's Keeper: The Indian in White America.* Washington, D.C.: New Community Press, 1969.

CUSHMAN, DAN, *Stay Away Joe.* New York: The Viking Press, 1953.

DELORIA, VINE, JR., *Custer Died for Your Sins: An Indian Manifesto.* London: The Macmillan Company, 1969.

LEVINE, S. (ed.), *The American Indian Today.* Deland, Florida: Edwards, Everett Press Inc., 1969.

STEINER, STAN, *The New Indians.* New York: Harper and Row, 1968.

APPALACHIAN YOUTH

CAUDILL, HARRY, "Appalachia: The Path From Disaster;" from *Poverty in Affluence,* Robert E. Will and Harold G. Vatter, editors. New York: Harcourt, Brace and World Inc., 1965.

CAUDILL, HENRY, *Night Comes to the Cumberland.* Boston: Little, Brown and Company, 1963.

FORD, THOMAS R. (ed.), *The Southern Appalachian Region: A Survey.* Lexington: University of Kentucky Press, 1962.

SCHRAG, P., "Appalachia: Again the Forgotten Land," *Saturday Review*, 51: 14–18, January 27, 1968.

WELLER, JACK E., *Yesterday's People*. Lexington: University of Kentucky Press, 1966.

BLACK YOUTH

BROWN, CLAUDE, *Manchild In The Promised Land*. New York: The Macmillan Company, 1965.

CLEAVER, ELDRIDGE, *Soul on Ice*. A Delta Book published by Dell Publishing Co. New York: 1968.

DAVID, JAY (ed.), *Growing Up Black*. New York: William Morrow and Company Inc., 1968.

HERNDON, JAMES, *The Way It Spozed To Be*. New York: Simon and Schuster, 1965.

JEFFERS, CAMILLE, *Living Poor*. Ann Arbor: Ann Arbor Publishers, 1967.

JOSEPH, STEPHEN M. (ed.), *The Me Nobody Knows: Children's Voices From the Ghetto*. New York: Avon Books, 1969.

KOHL, HERBERT, *36 Children*. New York: A Signet Book, The American Library, 1967.

KOZOL, JONATHON, *Death At An Early Age*. Boston: Houghton Mifflin Company, 1967.

MALCOLM X, *The Autobiography of Malcolm X*. New York: with Alex Haley, Grove Press Inc., 1964.

MILLER, WARREN, *The Cool World*. Boston: Little, Brown and Company, 1959.

SCHULTZ, DAVID A., *Coming Up Black*. Englewood Cliffs, N.J.: Prentice-Hall, Inc., 1969.

GENERAL

BAGDIKIAN, BEN H., *In The Midst of Plenty*. Boston: Beacon Press, 1964.

BRODY, EUGENE B., M.D., *Minority Group Adolescents in the United States*. Baltimore: The William and Wilkins Co., 1968.

CAPLOVITZ, DAVID, *The Poor Pay More*. New York: Free Press, 1963.

COLES, R., *Still Hungry in America*. New York: World Publishers, 1969.

GOOD, P., *American Serfs*. New York: Putnam and Sons, 1968.

GOTTLIEB, DAVID, "Poor Youth: A Study in Forced Alienation," *Journal of Social Issues,* Vol. 25, No. 2, Spring 1969.

GOTTLIEB, DAVID and CHARLES E. RAMSAY, *Understanding Children of Poverty.* Science Research Associates, Inc., 1967.

HARRINGTON, MICHAEL, *The Other America: Poverty in the United States.* Baltimore: Penquin Books, 1962.

MILLER, HERMAN P., *Poverty American Style.* Belmont, Calif.: Wadsworth, 1966.

MOYNIHAN, D. P. (ed.), *On Understanding Poverty.* New York: Basic Books, 1969.

SCHON, A. L., *Poor Kids.* New York: Basic Books, 1966.

WILL, ROBERT E. and HAROLD G. VATTER, Editors, *Poverty in Affluence.* New York: Harcourt, Brace and World Inc., 1965.